# Young Investigators Workshop on Computational Approaches to Languages of the Americas 2010



**Held at NAACL HLT 2010**

## Los Angeles, California, USA
## 6 June 2010

ISBN: 978-1-61738-685-5

**Printed from e-media with permission by:**

Curran Associates, Inc.
57 Morehouse Lane
Red Hook, NY 12571

**Some format issues inherent in the e-media version may also appear in this print version.**



Printed by Curran Associates, Inc. (2010)

For permission requests, please contact the Association for Computational Linguistics
at the address below.

Association for Computational Linguistics
209 N. Eighth Street
Stroudsburg, Pennsylvania 18360

Phone: 1-570-476-8006
Fax: 1-570-476-0860

acl@aclweb.org

**Additional copies of this publication are available from:**

Curran Associates, Inc.
57 Morehouse Lane
Red Hook, NY 12571 USA
Phone: 845-758-0400
Fax: 845-758-2634
Email: curran@proceedings.com
Web: www.proceedings.com

# Introduction

Welcome to the First Young Investigators Workshop on Computational Approaches to Languages of the Americas. This workshop will be held on June 6, 2010 in Los Angeles, immediately following the 11th Annual Conference of the North American Chapter of the Association for Computational Linguistics, NAACL-HLT 2010. The goal of this workshop is to bring together researchers from all of the Americas developing human language technologies that are interested in establishing international collaborations. We believe a more interactive community within the Americas can contribute to the advancement of the field, not only with respect to the improvement of performance on specific areas of NLP but more important, with respect to motivating the growth of its community by providing a conducive collaboration infrastructure that facilitates the active involvement of researchers in the field.

We are very excited about the response to the call for papers. We received a total of 21 submissions from 8 countries. The final program brings together researchers from Argentina, Brazil, Colombia, Costa Rica, Mexico, Uruguay and the USA. The contributions in the proceedings are of three types: research papers, project overviews and opinion papers. The research papers include recent advances in topics from opinion mining, to textual entailment, to adaptation of NLP approaches to software engineering. The survey papers present an overview of larger research projects by a single university or research group. These overviews present interesting efforts in dialogue systems, text simplification, language generation, and corpus based approaches to verb subcategorization and relation extraction. The proceedings also include two opinion papers that describe the research situation of the NLP communities in Costa Rica and Brazil. All contributions describe how international collaborations can push research forward by either listing the resources and/or experience sought or what specific resources and experience can be contributed. In sum, these proceedings provide a broad coverage of research on computational linguistics south of the Rio Bravo addressing three different languages: Spanish, Brazilian Portuguese and English.

We would like to thank the program committee members for their support in spreading the call for papers and providing a conscientious and timely review. Without their support this workshop would have not been as successful. We would also like to thank the NAACL-HLT 2010 Workshop Chairs, David Traum and Richard Sproat for all their help and great overseeing of the logistics of this workshop. Lastly, we were able to offer travel support and full conference registration waivers due to the very generous support of the NAACL Executive Board, and the Information and Intelligent Systems Directorate and the Office of International Science and Engineering of the National Science Foundation (USA) award number 1008711.

As part of the one day workshop, the program will also include a panel discussion to brainstorm on ways to promote a more interactive community on this side of the globe, and the possibility of having more workshops of this kind. A summary from this panel will be available on the workshop website soon after the event: (http://groups.google.com/group/naacl-2010-yi-workshop).

We are are looking forward to a great event and hope that initiatives like these will eventually lead to a stronger and tighter computational linguistics research community on the Americas.

Thamar Solorio and Ted Pedersen

**Organizers:**

Thamar Solorio, University of Alabama at Birmingham, USA
Ted Pedersen, University of Minnesota–Duluth, USA

**Program Committee:**

Laura Alonso Alemani, Universidad Nacional de Córdoba, Argentina
John Atkinson, Universidad de Concepción, Chile
Diego Burgos, Instituto Tecnológico Metropolitano, Colombia
Vitor Carvalho, Microsoft Bing, USA
Maria das Graças Volpe Nunes, Universidade de São Paulo, Brazil
Ana Feldman, Montclair State University, USA
Caroline Gasperin, Universidade de São Paulo, Brazil
Alexander Gelbukh, CIC, IPN, Mexico
Carlos Gómez Gallo, Harvard, USA
Agustin Gravano, Universidad de Buenos Aires, Argentina
Diana Inpken, University of Ottawa, Canada
Greg Kondrak, University of Alberta, Canada
Jorge Antonio Leoni de León, Universidad de Costa Rica, Costa Rica
Aurelio López López, INAOE, Mexico
Lucia Helena Machado Rino, Universidade Federal de São Carlos, Brazil
Rada Mihalcea, University of North Texas, USA
Raymond Mooney, University of Texas at Austin, USA
Manuel Montes y Gómez, INAOE, Mexico
Thiago A. S. Pardo, Universidade de São Paulo, Brazil
Renata Vieira, Pontifícia Universidade Católica do Rio Grande do Sul, Brazil
Luis Villaseñor-Pineda, INAOE, Mexico
Dina Wonsever, Universidad de la Republica, Uruguay

# Table of Contents

# Workshop Program

**Sunday, June 6, 2010**

**Session 1**

8:45–9:00 Opening Remarks

9:00–9:30 *Computational Linguistics in Brazil: An Overview*
Thiago Pardo, Caroline Gasperin, Helena de Medeiros Caseli and Maria das Graças Nunes

9:30–10:00 *Data-driven computational linguistics at FaMAF-UNC, Argentina*
Laura Alonso Alemany and Gabriel Infante-Lopez

10:00–10:30 *Variable-Length Markov Models and Ambiguous Words in Portuguese*
Fabio Natanael Kepler and Marcelo Finger

10:30–11:00 **Break**

**Session 2**

11:00–11:30 *Using Common Sense to generate culturally contextualized Machine Translation*
Helena de Medeiros Caseli, Bruno Akio Sugiyama and Junia Coutinho Anacleto

11:30–12:30 **Poster Session**

*Human Language Technology for Text-based Analysis of Psychotherapy Sessions in the Spanish Language*
Horacio Saggion, Elena Stein-Sparvieri, David Maldavsky and Sandra Szasz

*Computational Linguistics in Costa Rica: an overview*
Jorge Antonio Leoni de León

*Fostering Digital Inclusion and Accessibility: The PorSimples project for Simplification of Portuguese Texts*
Sandra Aluisio and Caroline Gasperin

*Opinion Identification in Spanish Texts*
Aiala Rosá, Dina Wonsever and Jean-Luc Minel

**Sunday, June 6, 2010 (continued)**

| | |
|---|---|
| | *A Machine Learning Approach for Recognizing Textual Entailment in Spanish*<br>Julio Castillo |
| | *The emergence of the modern concept of introspection: a quantitative linguistic analysis*<br>Iván Raskovsky, Diego Fernández Slezak, Carlos Diuk and Guillermo A. Cecchi |
| | *Combining CBIR and NLP for Multilingual Terminology Alignment and Cross-Language Image Indexing*<br>Diego Burgos |
| | *IRASubcat, a highly parametrizable, language independent tool for the acquisition of verbal subcategorization information from corpus*<br>Ivana Romina Altamirano and Laura Alonso Alemany |
| | *The TermiNet Project: an Overview*<br>Ariani Di Felippo |
| | *Automated Detection of Language Issues Affecting Accuracy, Ambiguity and Verifiability in Software Requirements Written in Natural Language*<br>Allan Berrocal Rojas and Elena Gabriela Barrantes Sliesarieva |
| | *Recognition and extraction of definitional contexts in Spanish for sketching a lexical network*<br>Cesar Aguilar, Olga Acosta and Gerardo Sierra |
| 12:30–2:00 | **Lunch** |
| | **Session 3** |
| 2:00–2:30 | *Computational Linguistics for helping Requirements Elicitation: a dream about Automated Software Development*<br>Carlos Mario Zapata Jaramillo |
| 2:30–3:00 | *Text Generation for Brazilian Portuguese: the Surface Realization Task*<br>Eder Novais, Thiago Tadeu and Ivandre Paraboni |
| 3:00–3:30 | **Break** |

**Sunday, June 6, 2010 (continued)**

**Session 4**

3:30–4:00 *Dialogue Systems for Virtual Environments*
Luciana Benotti, Paula Estrella and Carlos Areces

**Panel Session**

4:00–5:00 Challenges and Opportunities for Conducting Research and Forming Collaborations in the Americas

5:00–5:30 Concluding Discussion

# Computational Linguistics in Brazil: An Overview

**Thiago A. S. Pardo[1], Caroline V. Gasperin[1], Helena M. Caseli[2], Maria das Graças V. Nunes[1]**

Núcleo Interinstitucional de Lingüística Computacional (NILC)

[1] Instituto de Ciências Matemáticas e de Computação, Universidade de São Paulo
Av. Trabalhador São-carlense, 400 - Centro
P.O.Box 668. 13560-970 - São Carlos/SP, Brazil

[2] Departamento de Computação, Universidade Federal de São Carlos
Rod. Washington Luís, Km 235
P.O.Box 676. 13565-905 - São Carlos/SP, Brazil

{taspardo,cgasperin}@icmc.usp.br, helenacaseli@dc.ufscar.br, gracan@icmc.usp.br

## Abstract

In this paper we give an overview of Computational Linguistics / Natural Language Processing in Brazil, describing the general research scenario, the main research groups, existing events and journals, and the perceived challenges, among other relevant information. We also identify opportunities for collaboration.

## 1 Brazilian Research Scenario

Computational Linguistics (CL) / Natural Language Processing (NLP) is an emerging and growing area in Brazil. Although there is no consensus, it is traditionally understood as a research field within Artificial Intelligence, gathering researchers mainly from Computer Science/Engineering and Linguistics. There is also modest interaction with Information Sciences area.

In general the CL/NLP area in Brazil started with researchers that finished their PhD abroad and, after coming back, initiated the first CL/NLP projects. Since then, but mainly more recently, the area has experienced some internationalization due to the fact that the number of undergraduate and graduate students that undergo internships on renowned foreign NLP research centers has increased. In Brazil, PhD students have the possibility to take their complete PhD course abroad or, alternatively, only a part of it. In both cases, students may count on Brazilian funding agencies.

The area is more strongly represented and promoted by Brazilian Computer Society (SBC)[1], particularly by its Special Interest Group on NLP (CEPLN)[2], created in 2007. It is interesting that most researchers in Brazil (independent from their background area) do not differentiate CL from NLP, using both terms interchangeably.

Research in Brazil is carried out mainly at public universities and at a few private universities and business companies. Differently from most countries, in Brazil public universities are generally considered the top ones, although exceptions do exist.

Currently, there are no undergraduate courses on CL/NLP in Brazil, therefore researchers in this field come mainly from Computer Science and Linguistics courses. However, there are a few graduate courses on CL/NLP, with both computing and language emphases, such as the MSc and PhD programs at USP/São Carlos[3], UFSCar[4], UNESP/Araraquara[5], PUC-RS[6], and UFRGS[7], among others.

---

[1] http://www.sbc.org.br
[2] http://www.sbc.org.br/cepln
[3] http://www.icmc.usp.br/~posgrad/computacao.html
[4] http://ppgcc.dc.ufscar.br and http://www.ppgl.ufscar.br
[5] http://www.fclar.unesp.br/poslinpor
[6] http://www.pucrs.br/inf/pos
[7] http://www.ufrgs.br



*Proceedings of the NAACL HLT 2010 Young Investigators Workshop on Computational Approaches to Languages of the Americas*, pages 1–7, Los Angeles, California, June 2010. 

Funding for research comes mainly from governmental agencies. Nowadays Brazil has 4 agencies that significantly support research in the country (in this order): CNPq[8] (National Council for Scientific and Technological Development), FAPESP[9] (São Paulo Research Foundation), CAPES[10] (*Coordenação de Aperfeiçoamento de Pessoal de Nível Superior*), and FINEP[11] (Research and Projects Financing). Private funding is still modest, which reflects the limited interaction between universities and companies. Some of the above agencies have tried to change this scenario by providing special joint university-industry funding programs. For instance, FAPESP and Microsoft Research recently formed a partnership to fund socially relevant projects in the state of São Paulo, e.g., the PorSimples[12] text simplification project. FAPESP also funds special university-company programs, where the research to be developed must be of interest to a company, which, in turn, has to support the research and work together with the researchers.

NLP research in Brazil is varied and deals not only with Portuguese processing, but also with English and Spanish mainly. Given that Portuguese is among the most spoken languages in the world (it is estimated that almost 250 million people speak some variant of Portuguese in the world[13]), research interests on Portuguese processing is shared with other countries, mainly Portugal. In this sense, Portugal has launched an initiative to create and maintain a unified information storage center that indexes resources and publications for/on Portuguese processing. The initiative is the Linguateca project[14], which was officially created in 2002, but initial works date back to 1998. Santos (2009) presents and evaluates the work carried out by Linguateca.

Brazil and Portugal have a history of partnership on Portuguese processing, which formally started in 1993 with the first PROPOR conference (PROPOR event series is introduced in Section 4). We maintain this partnership active by having collaborative projects and promoting joint events.

As far as we know, other Portuguese speaking countries do not have a tradition of CL/NLP research. However, curiously, there are researchers from other non-Portuguese speaking countries that develop relevant research on Portuguese language. For example, to the best of our knowledge, currently the best syntactical parsers for Portuguese were developed by researchers from Denmark and the USA. These researchers actively work with the Brazilian research community.

In what follows, we briefly present the Brazilian research profile (Section 2), the main research groups (Section 3), and the Brazilian events and journals (Section 4). We also report the main challenges for research in Brazil (Section 5) and the collaboration opportunities with other American researchers that we envision (Section 6).

## 2 Research Profile

In 2009 CEPLN proposed a survey of the status of CL/NLP research in Brazil and published the results during the 7th Brazilian Symposium in Information and Human Language Technology (Pardo et al., 2009). The survey aimed at gathering information both about researchers (such as their location, education level, number of students, etc.) and their research (main research topics, number of funded projects, main challenges, etc.).

The survey was carried out mainly on-line. A call for participation was sent to all known e-mail lists from scientific associations from varied areas. Data was also obtained from the Registry of Latin American Researchers in Natural Language Processing and Computational Linguistics[15].

148 researchers responded to the survey: 35% of these were academic staff with a PhD degree, 16% academic staff with a Master's degree, 1% academic staff with a Bachelors degree, 9% PhD students, 26% Master's students, 14% undergraduate students, and 5% others. Table 1 summarizes the main results of the survey, showing the percentage of answers for each issue. One may see that CL/NLP research is mainly carried out in the south and southeast regions of Brazil.

[8] http://www.cnpq.br
[9] http://www.fapesp.br
[10] http://www.capes.gov.br
[11] http://www.finep.gov.br
[12] http://caravelas.icmc.usp.br
[13] Besides Brazil and Portugal, Portuguese is an official language in Angola, Cape Verde, East Timor, Equatorial Guinea, Guinea-Bissau, Macau, Mozambique, and São Tomé and Príncipe.
[14] http://www.linguateca.pt
[15] http://ww.d.umn.edu/~tpederse/registry/registry.cgi

Table 1. CEPLN survey

| **Issues** | **Results** |
|---|---|
| Geographic distribution | 48% São Paulo state<br>18% Rio Grande do Sul state<br>8% Paraná state<br>7% Rio de Janeiro state<br>19% Other states |
| National collaboration | 52% Yes, 48% No |
| International Collaboration | 25% Yes, 75% No |
| Background area | 62% Computer Science<br>29% Linguistics<br>9% Other |
| Supervision of postgraduate students | 28% Yes, 72% No |
| Funded projects | 28% Yes, 72% No |
| Source of funding | 43% Federal government agencies<br>25% São Paulo state government agency<br>31% Other state government agencies |

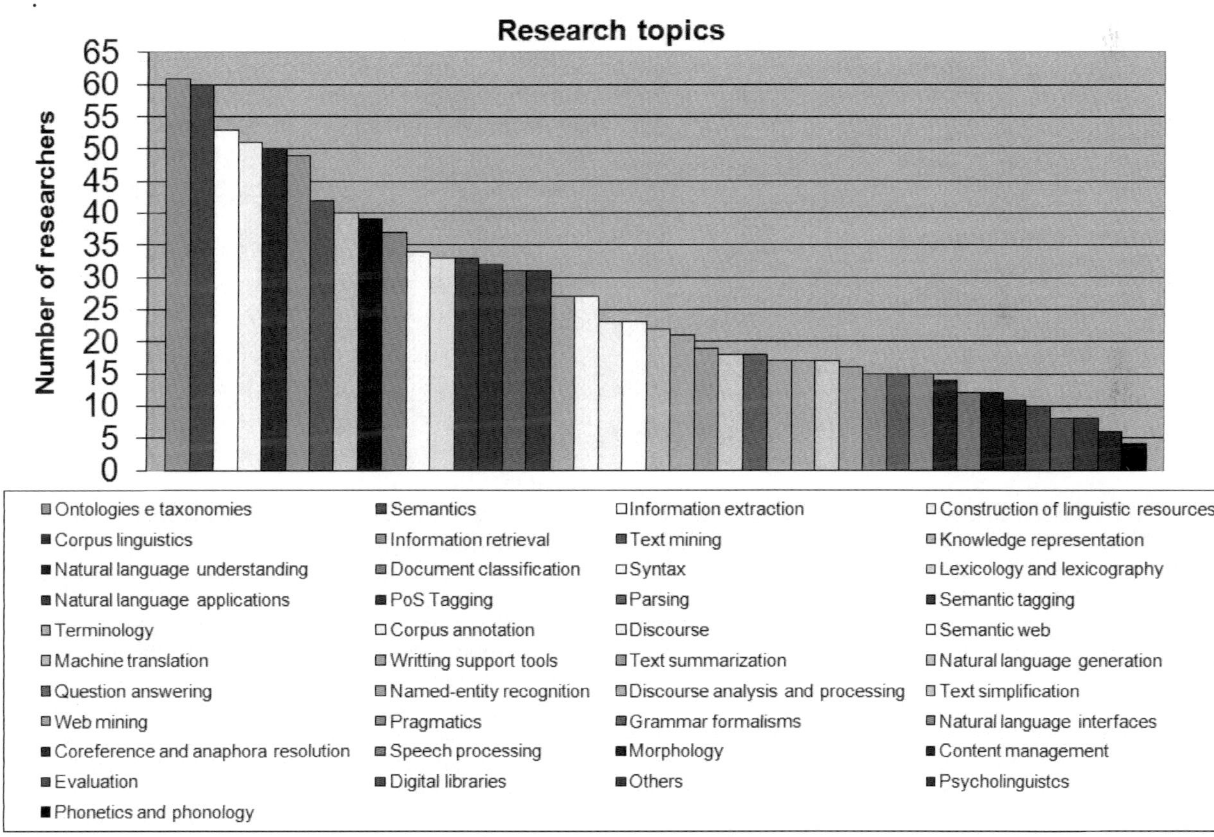

Figure 1. Research topics

The survey also inquired the participants about their research topics. Figure 1 shows the distribution of topics among researchers who responded to the survey. Researchers could mark as many research topics as they wanted. Some topics subsume others, so these were marked more often by respondents.

Ontologies and semantics were the topics marked by most respondents. We believe that there is indeed a significant number of researchers working on them, but we also believe that they are not the main topic of research of most people who listed them. For example, the statistics for "Ontologies" probably also include researchers who simply make use of ontologies in their work and not necessarily develop ontologies or ontology generation methods. Other researchers believe that we are in a changing period, moving from syntax-centered research to semantics-centered research, due to the fact that more recently the community has produced more robust semantic tools and resources, e.g., the first versions of Portuguese language wordnets, as TeP 2.0[16], Wordnet.PT[17], and MWN.PT[18], as well as named entities recognizers, e.g., REMBRANDT[19].

Interestingly, corpus linguistics is one of the hottest topics but, at the same time, it is not seen as a genuine CL/NLP topic: most researchers that indicated corpus linguistics as a research topic marked it as "other area of interest". Some researchers have advocated that CL/NLP area and corpus linguistics should be considered a unique area, while others argue that these areas have different purposes and, therefore, different scientific methods, what would avoid such unification. Text mining is another curious case: research on this theme is mostly carried out by non-CL/NLP researchers, but instead by researchers on general AI and database areas

Based on the publications on the last Brazilian scientific events and on the fact that we personally know most of the CL/NLP researchers in Brazil, we dare to indicate the following topics as the most recurrent ones (in no particular order): text summarization, machine translation, text simplification, automatic discourse analysis, coreference and anaphora resolution, information retrieval, text mining, terminology/lexicon research, ontologies and semantic tagging, and corpus linguistics.

Based on the survey, we estimate that Brazil has about 250 researchers (including students) with interest in CL/NLP area. Although only 148 researchers attended the CEPLN survey, we computed other researchers in the Registry of Latin American Researchers in Natural Language Processing and Computational Linguistics and in the CEPLN e-mail list that did not attend the survey. In general, we estimate that about 35-40 of these are active researchers, whose main topic of research is CL/NLP, and who supervise undergraduate and graduate students on the subject. We also estimate that there are 5-10 researchers on speech processing that actively collaborate with the CL/NLP community.

## 3 Main research groups

The largest CL/NLP research group in Brazil is NILC (Interinstitutional Center for Research and Development in Computational Linguistics)[20], which includes researchers mainly from University of São Paulo (USP; Computer Science and Physics departments), Federal University of São Carlos (UFSCar; Computer Science and Linguistics departments) and State University of São Paulo (UNESP; Linguistics department). The group was created at 1993.

NILC has a long history of research in CL/NLP, which has thrived since the ReGra[21] project, in which the grammar checker for Portuguese that is currently used within Microsoft Word since its 2000 version was built. In fact, ReGra project was born from a university-industry collaboration, one of the few successful ones in CL/NLP area in Brazil. At the moment most of the research at NILC is concentrated on the following topics: automatic summarization, text simplification, coreference resolution, and terminology. NILC has hosted STIL 2009 (STIL event series is introduced in the next section). NILC also currently holds the presidency of CEPLN.

The NLP group at the Computer Science department at the Catholic University of Rio Grande do Sul (PUC-RS)[22] also has a tradition of research on CL/NLP. Their current projects focus on information retrieval, ontology engineering and anaphora resolution. The group also has research on multi-agent systems applied to NLP tasks and, more recently, on text categorization. The group hosts PROPOR 2010 (PROPOR event series is also introduced in the next section). The group has held the presidency of CEPLN from its creation (2007) until 2009.

The above research group and NILC form the main CL/NLP research vein in Brazil. They have joint research projects and have strong

[16] http://www.nilc.icmc.usp.br/tep2/index.htm
[17] http://www.clul.ul.pt/clg/wordnetpt
[18] http://mwnpt.di.fc.ul.pt
[19] http://xldb.di.fc.ul.pt/Rembrandt
[20] http://www.nilc.icmc.usp.br
[21] http://www.nilc.icmc.usp.br/nilc/projects/regra.htm
[22] http://www.inf.pucrs.br/~linatural

collaboration, constantly hosting graduate students from each other in internship research periods.

There are also other very relevant NLP groups in Brazil that regularly carry out projects on the area. We may cite the Catholic University of Rio de Janeiro (PUC-Rio)[23], Federal University of Rio Grande do Sul (UFRGS), State University of Campinas (UNICAMP), University of the Sinos River Valley (Unisinos), and State University of Maringá (UEM), among others.

## 4 Events and Journals

The Brazilian Symposium on Information and Human Language Technology (STIL) is the main event on CL/NLP in South America and is in its seventh edition. It is promoted by CEPLN and is carried out since 1993. It is intended to be a forum for gathering everyone with interest in CL/NLP. It happens regularly (every one or two years) and accepts contributions in Portuguese, Spanish and English. Details about the event are available at www.nilc.icmc.usp.br/til.

The International Conference on Computational Processing of Portuguese Language (PROPOR) is an international conference jointly promoted by Brazil and Portugal and is in its ninth edition. It is the main conference with focus on Portuguese language, giving equal space to research on text and speech processing. It is carried out in Brazil and in Portugal interchangeably (every two or three years) and accepts submissions in English only. PROPOR's proceedings are published as part of Springer Lecture Notes series. Details about the event are available at www.nilc.icmc.usp.br/cgpropor.

STIL and PROPOR are the most relevant conferences for researchers in CL/NLP in Brazil. Their last editions received support from NAACL.

AI events are also recurrent forums for CL/NLP researchers. The Brazilian AI events are the Brazilian Symposium on Artificial Intelligence (SBIA)[24] and the National Meeting on Artificial Intelligence (ENIA)[25], also promoted by SBC. They are already in their twentieth and seventh editions, respectively.

Other related events in Brazil are the Corpus Linguistics Meeting (ELC)[26] and Brazilian School on Computational Linguistics (EBRALC)[27], which are in their eighth and third editions, respectively. These events are mainly organized by the Linguistics research community. EBRALC is mainly intended for new students in the area and has been held together with ELC.

Brazilian researchers count mainly on the following journals for national periodical publications:

- JBCS[28] (Journal of the Brazilian Computer Society), which is published by SBC and covers all Computer Science areas, including CL/NLP;
- RITA[29] (Journal of Theoretical and Applied Computing), also of general scope.

It is important to cite Linguamática[30], which is an European initiative to publish CL/NLP research on the Iberian languages.

CEPLN is also organizing a joint journal with other SBC AI-related special interest groups.

## 5 Challenges

At STIL 2009, the research community discussed challenging issues (raised by respondents of the CEPLN survey) that hamper research on CL/PLN in Brazil. The main issues raised were:

- Lack of large and robust language resources for Portuguese;
- Lack of formal models for linguistic description and analysis of Portuguese;
- Difficulty in attracting students and researchers to the area;
- Lack of multidisciplinary collaboration;
- CL/NLP marginalization in both Computer Science and Linguistics.
- Poor interaction between universities and industry;
- Insufficient funding.

Here we discuss some of these points. Although Portuguese has got state of the art tools (as POS taggers and syntactic parsers) and comprehensive corpora of contemporary written language, there is

---

[23] www.letras.puc-rio.br/Clic/ogrupo.htm
[24] http://www.jointconference.fei.edu.br/
[25] http://csbc2009.inf.ufrgs.br/
[26] http://www.corpuslg.org/elc/Inicial.html
[27] http://www.corpuslg.org/ebralc/Inicial.html
[28] http://www.springer.com/computer+science/journal/13173
[29] http://www.seer.ufrgs.br/index.php/rita
[30] http://linguamatica.pt

still a need for resources for particular applications or domains. Many researchers feel that Portuguese syntactic parsers (which are considered basic NLP tools) and wordnet-like resources are still too limited, not attending their demands. Brazil also lacks representative spoken corpora, what may be explained by the fact that, in Brazil, written and spoken language processing communities have modest interaction. While written language processing research is reported at SBC events, spoken language processing is mainly conducted under SBrT (Brazilian Telecommunications Society)[31]. PROPOR series have tried to bring together these two communities, fostering joint research and mutual awareness of both research lines.

The lack of formal models for Portuguese linguistic description and analysis was mainly perceived by linguists that work with CL/NLP. In fact, they acknowledge that Brazil has no tradition in carrying out events on these themes, what would eventually harm CL/NLP research. This goes along with Spärck Jones (2007) opinion paper. One first step towards overcoming this lack of formal models for Portuguese description was the Workshop on Portuguese Description[32], carried out together with the last edition of STIL.

Another point that deserves attention is the sentiment that CL/NLP research suffers from marginalization in both Computer Science and Linguistics areas, as it is usually the case for multidisciplinary subjects. We believe this might be fueled by the way research is assessed in Brazil. In Brazil, the quality of research is mainly assessed by the publications generated from it, and publication vehicles from Linguistics are usually rated worse in Computer Science, and vice versa. It is expected that different areas may have different scientific methods and perspectives, as well as it is natural that such differences are mirrored in any evaluation instrument. However, such factors lead some researchers to feel uncomfortable with the multidisciplinary nature of CL/NLP field and the way they are recognized in their own major areas. Many researchers (not only from Brazil, but also from Portugal) have supported that CL/NLP should become a new "major" area, instead of being part of Computer Science or Linguistics.

Concerning insufficient funding, we believe that the main complaints came from Brazilian regions other than south and southeast, which currently concentrate CL/NLP research. In fact, during a lengthy discussion at STIL 2009 about the raised challenges, this issue was dismissed by many participants as non-representative. We believe that the funding situation in each region of Brazil contributes to the status of research on all topics, not particularly CL/NLP, in these regions. While in most Brazilian states researchers have to compete for funding from national agencies, some states (mainly in the southeast region) can rely on strong state-based funding agencies, such as FAPESP, in the state of São Paulo.

## 6 Opportunities for Collaboration

We believe that there are many opportunities for collaboration on CL/NLP with other researchers in the Americas, mainly due to the fact that the research community in Brazil works not only with Portuguese, but also with English and Spanish.

One first step towards collaboration in Latin America was given in the event CHARLA 2008 (Grand Challenges in Computer Science Research in Latin America Workshop). Organized by several scientific societies (including SBC), the event aimed at contributing to the definition of a long-term research agenda in Latin America with the potential to significantly advance science and motivate the networking of abilities and competencies in Latin America. One of the recognized challenges was "multilinguism", which involves several CL/NLP topics. CHARLA immediate impact in Brazil was the adaptation of Brazilian CL/NLP events to receive contributions in Spanish, which has a vast number of speakers in Latin America. Contributions in English were already traditionally considered in Brazilian events.

We believe that another important source of collaboration comes from awareness of the ongoing research projects in the Americas. Workshops such as this seem to be a channel for the exchange of information. We envision that initial collaborations may arise within machine translation projects, which naturally already deal with the representative languages of the Americas.

Letting aside technical collaboration, we believe there is room for higher-level concrete actions that

[31] http://www.sbrt.org.br
[32] http://www.ppgl.ufscar.br/jdp/index.html

could foster collaboration in the Americas. These are actions that may increase the visibility of the research done in Latin America, as well as motivate new research. One first action that we envisage is the opening of evaluation challenges and shared tasks to the languages of the Americas other than English. For instance, contests/conferences such as TAC[33], Senseval/SemEval[34], and TREC[35], among others, might make Portuguese/Spanish datasets available, as CLEF[36] has done in its last editions. This has certainly an organizational cost, but it may turn out to be a valuable investment.

Another action that could stimulate the progress of CL/NLP research in Latin America consists of including the proceedings of other American CL/NLP conferences in the ACL Anthology[37], for example, the proceedings of STIL and PROPOR, to mention the Brazilian examples. This could be restricted to conferences that received ACL/NAACL endorsement and/or sponsorship.

While the first action we proposed would make it feasible for more countries to participate in the evaluation contests, the second action would allow the works carried out in these countries to be better known.

In a different strategy, we imagine that it must be possible for regional scientific associations to establish formal partnerships, granting some advantages to associated researchers from the corresponding countries, such as: registration discounts in the CL/NLP conferences from the countries (for instance, ACL/NAACL members would have discounts for registering in Brazilian events, as well as SBC members for ACL/NAACL events); and distribution of relevant publications for members of the associations (for instance, SBC traditionally distributes to its members the JBCS journal, which is considered a prestigious international publication).

Our last idea would be to create a fund (possibly through the associations' partnership) for funding visits for knowledge transfer (1-2 weeks) for researchers and mainly students. These could be an opportunity for studying/working with researchers from other countries that work on topics of interest, as well as for renowned researchers to visit research groups in order to stimulate work on a particular topic. Such opportunities would be very positive for Brazilian students.

We believe that the actions suggested above can lead to a more integrated research scenario in the Americas.

## Acknowledgments

The authors are grateful to SBC, CEPLN, FAPESP, and CAPES for supporting this work and the realization of STIL 2009, where part of the data shown in this paper was presented.

## References

Pardo, T.A.S.; Caseli, H.M.; Nunes, M.G.V. (2009). Mapeamento da Comunidade Brasileira de Processamento de Línguas Naturais. In the *Proceedings of the 7th Brazilian Symposium in Information and Human Language Technology* - STIL, pp. 1-21. September 8-10, São Carlos/SP, Brazil.

Santos, D. (2009). Caminhos percorridos no mapa da portuguesificação: A Linguateca em perspectiva. *Linguamática*, N. 1, pp. 25-58.

Spärck Jones, K. (2007). Computational Linguistics: What About the Linguistics? *Computational Linguistics*, Last Words Section, Vol. 33, N. 3, pp. 437-441.

[33] http://www.nist.gov/tac
[34] http://www.senseval.org
[35] http://trec.nist.gov
[36] http://www.clef-campaign.org
[37] http://aclweb.org/anthology-new

# Data-driven computational linguistics at FaMAF-UNC, Argentina

**Laura Alonso i Alemany** and **Gabriel Infante-Lopez**
Grupo de Procesamiento de Lenguaje Natural
Sección de Ciencias de la Computación
Facultad de Matemática, Astronomía y Física
Universidad Nacional de Córdoba
Córdoba, Argentina
{gabriel|alemany}@famaf.unc.edu.ar

### Abstract

This paper provides a survey of some ongoing research projects in computational linguistics within the group of Natural Language Processing at the University of Córdoba, Argentina. We outline our future plans and spotlight some opportunities for collaboration.

## 1 Introduction

In this paper we present our group, describe its members, research agenda, interests and possible collaboration opportunities. The research agenda of the NLP group contains diverse lines of work. As a group, we have a special interest in producing language technologies for our languages, at a level comparable in performance with the state-of-the-art technology for English. We are developing such technology by deeply understanding its underling models and either adapting them to our languages or by creating new ones.

In this paper we present only those related to Natural Language Parsing and data-driven characterisation of linguistic phenomena. For both lines we provide a small survey of our results so far, we describe our current research questions and we spotlight possible opportunities of collaboration.

The paper is organized as follows. The following Section describes the group, its composition, projects and goals. Section 3 briefly introduces the research agenda related to natural language parsing and structure finding. Section 4 sketches the work on data-driven characterisation of linguistic phenomena in three main parts: semi-structured text mining, characterisation of verbal behaviour and mining of relations in biomedical text. Finally, Section 5 presents outlines our overall vision for collaboration with other researchers in the Americas.

## 2 Description of the group

The NLP Group[1] is part of the Computer Science section at the Facultad de Matemática, Astronomía y Física, at the Universidad Nacional de Córdoba. The group was started in 2005, with two full time researchers who had just got their doctorate degree in Amsterdam and Barcelona. Then, in 2009 and 2010 three more full-time researchers joined the group, coming from the Universities of Geneva and Nancy.

As of 2010, the group has 5 faculty researchers, 4 PhD students and several undergraduate students. The computer science section has around 20 members – including the NLP group, faculty members and PhD students.

The faculty researchers are, by alphabetical order:

- Laura Alonso Alemany, working in text mining and data-driven systematization of language.
- Carlos Areces, investigating different reasoning tasks and their applications in natural language processing.
- Luciana Benotti, investigates the addition of pragmatic abilities into dialogue systems.
- Paula Estrella, working in Machine Translation.
- Gabriel Infante-Lopez, working on Natural Language Parsing and Structure Finding.

[1] http://www.cs.famaf.unc.edu.ar/~pln/



*Proceedings of the NAACL HLT 2010 Young Investigators Workshop on Computational Approaches to Languages of the Americas*, pages 8–14, Los Angeles, California, June 2010. 

One of the main aims of the group has been education, both at undergraduate and graduate levels. Computer Science is an under-developed area in Argentina, and Natural Language Processing even more so. When the group was created, there were very few NLP researchers in the country, and they worked in isolation, with little connection to other researchers from neighbouring countries. One of the strategic goals of our University and of the NLP group itself were to create a critical mass of researchers in NLP. To that aim, we worked on incorporating researchers to our group and establishing relations with other groups. Researchers were incorporated via special programmes from both the Faculty and the Argentinean Government to increase the number of doctors in Computer Science in the scientific system in Argentina.

Most of our efforts in the first years went to raise awareness about the area and provide foundational and advanced courses. This policy lead to a significant number of graduation theses[2] and to the incorporation of various PhD students to our group.

We taught several undergraduate and graduate courses on various NLP topics at our own University, at the University of Río Cuarto, at the University of Buenos Aires and at the Universidad de la República (Uruguay), as well as crash courses at the Society for Operative Investigations (SADIO) and at the Conferencia Latinoamericana de Informática (CLEI 2008). We also gave several talks at various universities in the country, and participated in local events, like JALIMI'05 (*Jornadas Argentinas de Lingüística Informática: Modelización e Ingeniería*) or the Argentinean Symposium on Artificial Intelligence.

Since the beginning of its activities, the group has received funding for two major basic research projects, funded by the Argentinean Agency for the Development of Science and Technology. A third such project is pending approval.

We have a special interest in establishing working relations and strengthening the synergies with the research community in NLP, both within South America and the rest of the world. We have had scientific and teaching exchanges with the NLP group in Montevideo, Uruguay. From that collaboration, the Microbio project emerged[3], bringing together researchers on NLP from Chile, Brazil, Uruguay, France and Argentina. This project was funded by each country's scientific institutions (MinCyT, in the case of Argentina) within STIC-AmSud[4], a scientific-technological cooperation programme aimed to promote and strengthen South America regional capacities and their cooperation with France in the area of Information Technologies and Communication. Within this project, we hosted the kick-off workshop on February 2008, with attendants representing all groups in the project.

We have also had billateral international cooperation in some smaller projects. Together with the CNR-INRIA in Rennes, France, we have worked in a project concerning the smallest grammar problem. We tackle the same problem, finding small grammars in two different domains: ADN sequences and Natural Language sentences. In collaboration with several universities in Spain (UB, UOC, UPC, EHU/UPV), we have taken part in the major basic research programme KNOW[5], aiming to aggregate meaning, knowledge and reasoning to current information technologies. This project has now received funding to carry on a continuating project[6].

Moreover, we are putting forward some proposals for further international collaboration. Following the path opened by the Microbio project, we are working on a proposal to the Ecos Sud programme for joint collaboration with research teams in France[7].

We are also working in strengthening relations within Argentinean NLP groups. To that aim, we are collaborating with the NLP group at the University of Buenos Aires in the organization of the School on Computational Linguistics ELiC[8], with several grants for students sponsored by NAACL. We are also putting forward a proposal for a workshop on

[2] http://cs.famaf.unc.edu.ar/~pln/Investigacion/tesis_grado/tesis_grado.html

[3] http://www.microbioamsud.net/

[4] http://www.sticamsud.org/

[5] KNOW project: http://ixa.si.ehu.es/know.

[6] Representation of Semantic Knowledge, TIN2009-14715-C04-03 (Plan Nacional de I+D+i 2008-2011).

[7] ECOS-SUD programme: http://www.mincyt.gov.ar/coopinter_archivos/bilateral/francia.htm.

[8] ELiC school on Computational Linguistics: http://www.glyc.dc.uba.ar/elic2010/.

NLP to be co-located with the IBERAMIA conference on Artificial Intelligence, to be held at Bahía Blanca on November 2010.

## 3 Natural Language Parsing and Structure Finding

### 3.1 Unsupervised Parsing

Unsupervised parsing of Natural Language Syntax is a key technology for the development of language technology. It is specially important for languages that have either small treebanks or none at all. Clearly, there is a big difference between producing or using a treebank for evaluation and producing or using them for training. In the former case, the size of the treebank can be significantly smaller. In our group, we have investigated different approaches to unsupervised learning of natural language. and we are currently following two different lines, one that aims at characterizing the potential of a grammar formalism to learn a given treebank structure and a second that uses only regular automata to learn syntax.

**Characterization of Structures** In (Luque and Infante-Lopez, 2009) we present a rather unusual result for language learning. We show an upper bound for the performance of a class of languages when a grammar from that class is used to parse the sentences in any given treebank. The class of languages we studied is the defined by Unambiguous Non-Terminally Separated (UNTS) grammars (Clark, 2006). UNTS grammars are interesting because, first, they have nice learnability properties like PAC learnability (Clark, 2006), and, second, they are used as the background formalism that won the Omphalos competition (Clark, 2007). Our strategy consists on characterizing all possible ways of parsing all the sentences in a treebank using UNTS grammars, then, we find the one that is closest to the treebank. We show that, in contrast to the results obtained for learning formal languages, UNTS are not capable of producing structures that score as state-of-the-art models on the treebanks we experimented with.

Our results are for a particular, very specific type of grammar. We are currently exploring how to widen our technique to provide upper bounds to a more general class of languages. Our technique does not state how to actually produce a grammar that performs as well as the upper bound, but it can be useful for determining how to transform the training material to make upper bounds go up. In particular we have defined a generalization of UNTS grammars, called $k$-$l$-UNTS grammars, that transform a word $w$ in the training material in a 3-uple $\langle \alpha, w, \beta \rangle$ where $\alpha$ contains the $k$ previous symbols to $w$ and $\beta$ contains the $l$ symbols following $w$. Intuitively, $k$-$l$-UNTS augments each word with a variable length context. It turns out that the resulting class of languages is more general than UNTS grammars: they are PAC learnable, they can be learned with the same learning algorithm as UNTS and, moreover, their upper bound for performance is much higher than for UNTS. Still, it might be the case that the existing algorithm for finding UNTS is not the right one for learning the structure of a treebank, it might be the case that strings in the PTB have not been produced by a $k$-$l$-UNTS grammar. We are currently investigating how to produce an algorithm that fits better the structure given in a treebank.

**Learning Structure Using Probabilistic Automata** DMV+CCM (Klein and Manning, 2004; Klein and Manning, 2002) is a probabilistic model for unsupervised parsing, that can be successfully trained with the EM algorithm to achieve state of the art performance. It is the combination of the Constituent-Context Model, that models unlabeled constituent parsing, and the Dependency Model with Valence, that models projective dependency parsing. On the other hand, CCM encodes the probability that a given string of POS tags is a constituent. DMV is more of our interest in this work, because it encodes a top-down generative process where the heads generate their dependents to both directions until there is a decision to stop, in a way that resembles successful supervised dependency models such as in (Collins, 1999). The generation of dependents of a head on a specific direction can be seen as an implicit probabilistic regular language generated by a probabilistic deterministic finite automaton.

Under this perspective, the DMV model is in fact an algorithm for learning several automata at the same time. All automata have in common that they have the same number of states and the same number of arcs between states, which is given by the definition of the DMV model. Automata differ in that they have different probabilities assigned to the transitions. The simple observation that DMV actually suppose a fixed structure for the automata it induces might explain its poor performance with freer order languages like Spanish. Using our own implementation (see (Luque, 2009)) we have empirically tested that DMV+CMV works well in languages with strict word order, like English, but for other languages with freer word order, like Spanish, DMV+CMV performance decreases dramatically. In order to improve DMV+CCM performance for this type of languages, the structure of the automaton might be modified, but since the DMV model has an *ad hoc* learning algorithm, a new parametric learning algorithm has to be defined. We are currently investigating different automaton structures for different languages and we are also investigating not only the induction of the parameters for fixed structure, but also inducing the structure of the automata itself.

### 3.2 Smallest Grammar and Compression for Natural Language

The smallest grammar problem has been widely studied in the literature. The aim of the problem is to find the smallest (smallest in the sense of number of symbols that occur in the grammar) context free grammar that produces only one given string. The smallest grammar can be thought as a relaxation of the definition of Kolmogorov Complexity where the complexity is given by a context free grammar instead of a Turing machine. It is believed that the smallest grammar can be used both for computing optimal compression codes and for finding meaningful patterns in strings.

Moreover, since the procedure for finding the smallest grammar is in fact a procedure that assigns a tree structure to a string, the smallest grammar problem is, in fact, a particular case of unsupervised parsing that has a very particular objective function to be optimized.

Since the search space is exponentially big, all existing algorithms are in fact heuristics that look for a small grammar. In (Carrascosa et al., 2010) we presented two algorithms that outperform all existing heuristics. We have produce and algorithm that produces 10% smaller grammars for natural language strings and 1.5% smaller grammars for DNA sequences.

Even more, we show evidence that it is possible to find grammars that share approximately the same small score but that have very little structure in common. Moreover, the structure that is found by the smallest grammar algorithm for the sentences in PTB have little in common with the structure that the PTB defines for those sentences.

Currently, we are trying to find answers to two different questions. First, is there a small piece of structure that is common to all grammars having comparable sizes? and second, can the grammars that are found by our algorithms be used for improving compression algorithms?

## 4 Data-driven characterisation of linguistic phenomena

### 4.1 Semi-structured text mining

One of our lines of research is to apply standard text mining techniques to unstructured text, mostly user generated content like that found in blogs, social networks, short messaging services or advertisements. Our main corpus of study is constituted by classified advertisements from a local newspaper, but one of our lines of work within this project is to assess the portability of methods and techniques to different genres.

The goals we pursue are:

**creating corpora** and related resources, and making them publicly available. A corpus of newspaper advertisements and a corpus of short text messages are underway.

**normalization of text** bringing ortographic variants of a word (mostly abbreviations) to a canonical form. To do that, we apply machine learning techniques to learn the parameters for edit distances, as in (Gómez-Ballester et al., 1997; Ristad and Yanilos, 1998; Bilenko and Mooney, 2003; McCallum et al., 2005; Oncina and Sebban, 2006). We build upon previous work on normalization by (Choudhury et al., 2007; Okazaki et al., 2008; Cook and Stevenson, 2009; Stevenson et al., 2009). Preliminary results show a significant improvement of learned distances over standard distances.

**syntactic analysis** applying a robust shallow parsing approach aimed to identify entities and their modifiers.

**ontology induction** from very restricted domains, to aid generalization in the step of information extraction. We will be following the approach presented in (Michelson and Knoblock, 2009).

**information extraction** inducing templates from corpus using unsupervised and semi-supervised techniques, and using induced templates to extract information to populate a relational database, as in (Michelson and Knoblock, 2006).

**data mining** applying traditional knowledge discovery techniques on a relational database populated by the information extraction techniques used in the previous item.

This line of research has been funded for three years (2009-2012) by the Argentinean Ministry for Science and Technology, within the PAE project, as a PICT project (PAE-PICT-2007-02290).

This project opens many opportunities for collaboration. The resulting corpora will be of use for linguistic studies. The results of learning edit distances to find abbreviations can also be used by linguists as an input to study the regularities found in this kind of genres, as proposed in (Alonso Alemany, 2010).

We think that some joint work on learning string edit distances would be very well integrated within this project. We are also very interested in collaborations with researchers who have some experience in NLP in similar genres, like short text messages or abbreviations in medical papers.

Finally, interactions with data mining communities, both academic and industrial, would surely be very enriching for this project.

### 4.2 Characterisation of verbal behaviour

One of our research interests is the empirical characterization of the subcategorization of lexical items, with a special interest on verbs. This line of work has been pursued mainly within the KNOW project, in collaboration with the UB-GRIAL group[9].

Besides the theoretical interest of describing the behaviour of verbs based on corpus evidence, this line has an applied aim, namely, enriching syntactic analyzers with subcategorization information, to help resolving structural ambiguities by using lexical information. We have focused on the behaviour of Spanish verbs, and implemented some of our findings as a lexicalized enhancement of the dependency grammars used by Freeling[10]. An evaluation of the impact of this information on parsing accuracy is underway.

We have applied clustering techniques to obtain a corpus-based characterization of the subcategorization behaviour of verbs (Alonso Alemany et al., 2007; Castellón et al., 2007). We explored the behaviour of the 250 most frequent verbs of Spanish on the SenSem corpus (Castellón et al., 2006), manually annotated with the analysis of verbs at various linguistic levels (sense, aspect, voice, type of construction, arguments, role, function, etc.). Applying clustering techniques to the instances of verbs in these corpus, we obtained coarse-grained classes of verbs with the same subcategorization. A classifier was learned from considering clustered instances as classes. With this classifier, verbs in unseen sentences were assigned a subcategorization behaviour.

Also with the aim of associating subcategorization information to verbs using evidence found in corpora, we developed IRASubcat (Altamirano, 2009). IRASubcat[11]. is a highly flexible system designed to gather information about the behaviour of verbs from corpora annotated at any level, and in any language. It identifies patterns of linguistic constituents that co-occur with verbs, detects optional constituents and performs hypothesis testing of the co-occurrence of verbs and patterns.

We have also been working on connecting predicates in FrameNet and SenSem, using WordNet synsets as an interlingua (Alonso Alemany et al., SEPLN). We have found many dissimilarities between FrameNet and SenSem, but have been able to connect some of their predicates and enrich these resources with information from each other.

We are currently investigating the impact of different kinds of information on the resolution of pp-attachment ambiguities in Spanish, using the ANCORA corpus (Taulé et al., 2006). We are exploring

[9] `http://grial.uab.es/`

[10] `http://www.lsi.upc.edu/~nlp/freeling/`

[11] `http://www.irasubcat.com.ar/`

the utility of various WordNet-related information, like features extracted from the Top Concept Ontology, in combination with corpus-based information, like frequencies of occurrence and co-occurrence of words in corpus.

The line of research of characterisation of verbal behaviour presents many points for collaboration. In collaboration with linguists, the tools and methods that we have explained here provide valuable information for the description and systematization of subcategorization of verbs and other lexical pieces. It would be very interesting to see whether these techniques, that have been successfully applied to Spanish, apply to other languages or with different resources. We are also interested in bringing together information from different resources or from different sources (corpora, dictionaries, task-specific lexica, etc.), in order to achieve richer resources. We also have an interest for the study of hypothesis testing as applied to corpus-based computational linguistics, to get some insight on the information that these techniques may provide to guide research and validate results.

### 4.3 Discovering relations between entitites

As a result of the Microbio project, we have developed a module to detect relations between entities in biomedical text (Bruno, 2009). This module has been trained with the GENIA corpus (Kim et al., 2008), obtaining good results (Alonso Alemany and Bruno, 2009). We have also explored different ways to overcome the data sparseness problem caused by the small amount of manually annotated examples that are available in the GENIA corpus. We have used the corpus as the initial seed of a bootstrapping procedure, generalized classes of relations via the GENIA ontology and generalized classes via clustering. Of these three procedures, only generalization via an ontology produced good results. However, we have hopes that a more insightful characterization of the examples and smarter learning techniques (semi-supervised, active learning) will improve the results for these other lines.

Since this area of NLP has ambitious goals, opportunities for collaboration are very diverse. In general, we would like to join efforts with other researchers to solve part of these complex problems, with a special focus in relations between entities and semi-supervised techniques.

## 5 Opportunities for Collaboration

We are looking for opportunities of collaboration with other groups in the Americas, producing a synergy between groups. We believe that we can articulate collaboration by identifying common interests and writing joint proposals. In Argentina there are some agreements for billateral or multi-lateral collaboration with other countries or specific institutions of research, which may provide a framework for starting collaborations.

We are looking for collaborations that promote the exchange of members of the group, specially graduate students. Our aim is to gain a level of collaboration strong enough that would consider, for example, co-supervision of PhD students. Ideally, co-supervised students would spend half of their time in each group, tackle a problem that is common for both groups and work together with two supervisors. The standard PhD scholarship in Argentina, provided by Conicet, allows such modality of doctorate studies, as long as financial support for travels and stays abroad is provided by the co-supervising programme. We believe that this kind of collaboration is one that builds very stable relations between groups, helps students learn different research idiosyncrasies and devotes specific resources to maintain the collaboration.

## References


Laura Alonso Alemany and Santiago E. Bruno. 2009. Learning to learn biological relations from a small training set. In *CiCLing*, pages 418–429.

Laura Alonso Alemany, Irene Castellón, and Nevena Tinkova Tincheva. 2007. Obtaining coarse-grained classes of subcategorization patterns for spanish. In *RANLP'07*.

Laura Alonso Alemany, Irene Castellón, Egoitz Laparra, and German Rigau. SEPLN. Evaluación de métodos semi-automáticos para la conexión entre FrameNet y SenSem. In *2009*.

Laura Alonso Alemany. 2010. Learning parameters for an edit distance can learn us tendencies in user-generated content. Invited talk at *NLP in the Social Sciences*, Instituto de Altos Estudios en Psicologia y Ciencias Sociales, Buenos Aires, Argentina, May 2010.

I. Romina Altamirano. 2009. Irasubcat: Un sistema para adquisición automática de marcos de subcategorización de piezas léxicas a partir de corpus. Master's thesis, Facultad de Matemática, Astronomía y Física, Universidad Nacional de Córdoba, Argentina.

Mikhail Bilenko and Raymond J. Mooney. 2003. Adaptive duplicate detection using learnable string similarity measures. In *Proceedings of the ninth ACM SIGKDD*.

Santiago E. Bruno. 2009. Detección de relaciones entre entidades en textos de biomedicina. Master's thesis, Facultad de Matemática, Astronomía y Física, Universidad Nacional de Córdoba, Argentina.

Rafael Carrascosa, François Coste, Matthias Gallé, and Gabriel Infante-Lopez. 2010. Choosing Word Occurrences for the Smallest Grammar Problem. In *Proceedings of LATA 2010*. Springer.

Irene Castellón, Ana Fernández-Montraveta, Glòria Vázquez, Laura Alonso, and Joanan Capilla. 2006. The SENSEM corpus: a corpus annotated at the syntactic and semantic level. In *5th International Conference on Language Resources and Evaluation (LREC 2006)*.

Irene Castellón, Laura Alonso Alemany, and Nevena Tinkova Tincheva. 2007. A procedure to automatically enrich verbal lexica with subcategorization frames. In *Proceedings of the Argentine Simposium on Artificial Intelligence, ASAI'07*.

Monojit Choudhury, Rahul Saraf, Vijit Jain, Animesh Mukherjee, Sudeshna Sarkar, and Anupam Basu. 2007. Investigation and modeling of the structure of texting language. *Int. J. Doc. Anal. Recognit.*, 10(3):157–174.

Alexander Clark. 2006. Pac-learning unambiguous nts languages. In *International Colloquium on Grammatical Inference*, pages 59–71.

Alexander Clark. 2007. Learning deterministic context free grammars: the omphalos competition. *Machine Learning*, 66(1):93–110.

M. Collins. 1999. *Head-Driven Statistical Models for Natural Language Parsing*. Ph.D. thesis, University of Pennsylvania, PA.

Paul Cook and Suzanne Stevenson. 2009. An unsupervised model for text message normalization. In *Workshop on Computational Approaches to Linguistic Creativity*. NAACL HLT 2009.

E. Gómez-Ballester, M. L. Micó-Andrés, J. Oncina, and M. L. Forcada-Zubizarreta. 1997. An empirical method to improve edit-distance parameters for a nearest-neighbor-based classification task. In *VII Spanish Symposium on Pattern Recognition and Image Analysis*, Barcelona, Spain.

Jin D. Kim, Tomoko Ohta, and Jun'ichi Tsujii. 2008. Corpus annotation for mining biomedical events from literature. *BMC Bioinformatics*, 9(1).

Dan Klein and Christopher D. Manning. 2002. A generative constituent-context model for improved grammar induction. In *ACL*, pages 128–135.

Dan Klein and Christopher D. Manning. 2004. Corpus-based induction of syntactic structure: Models of dependency and constituency. In *Proc. of ACL 42*.

Franco Luque and Gabriel Infante-Lopez. 2009. Upper bounds for unsupervised parsing with unambiguous non-terminally. In *International Workshop Computational Linguistic Aspects of Grammatical Inference. EACL*, Greece.

Franco M. Luque. 2009. Implementation of the DMV+CCM parser. `http://www.cs.famaf.unc.edu.ar/~francolq/en/proyectos/dmvccm`.

Andrew McCallum, Kedar Bellare, and Fernando Pereira. 2005. A conditional random field for discriminatively-trained finite-state string edit distance. In *Proceedings of the Proceedings of the Twenty-First Conference Annual Conference on Uncertainty in Artificial Intelligence (UAI-05)*, pages 388–395, Arlington, Virginia. AUAI Press.

Matthew Michelson and Craig A. Knoblock. 2006. Phoebus: a system for extracting and integrating data from unstructured and ungrammatical sources. In *AAAI'06: proceedings of the 21st national conference on Artificial intelligence*, pages 1947–1948. AAAI Press.

Matthew Michelson and Craig A. Knoblock. 2009. Exploiting background knowledge to build reference sets for information extraction. In *Proceedings of the 21st International Joint Conference on Artific ial Intelligence (IJCAI-2009)*, Pasadena, CA.

Naoaki Okazaki, Sophia Ananiadou, and Jun'ichi Tsujii. 2008. A discriminative alignment model for abbreviation recognition. In *COLING '08: Proceedings of the 22nd International Conference on Computational Linguistics*, pages 657–664, Morristown, NJ, USA. Association for Computational Linguistics.

José Oncina and Marc Sebban. 2006. Learning stochastic edit distance: Application in handwritten character recognition. *Pattern Recognition*, 39(9):1575–1587.

E. S. Ristad and P. N. Yanilos. 1998. Learning string edit distance. *IEEE Transactions on Pattern Analysis and Machine Intelligence*, 20:522–532.

Mark Stevenson, Yikun Guo, Abdulaziz Al Amri, and Robert Gaizauskas. 2009. Disambiguation of biomedical abbreviations. In *BioNLP '09: Proceedings of the Workshop on BioNLP*, pages 71–79, Morristown, NJ, USA. Association for Computational Linguistics.

M. Taulé, M.A. Martí, and M. Recasens. 2006. Ancora: Multilevel annotated corpora for catalan and spanish. In *LREC'06*.

# Variable-Length Markov Models and Ambiguous Words in Portuguese*

**Fabio Natanael Kepler**
Institute of Mathematics and Statistics
University of Sao Paulo
Sao Paulo, SP, Brazil
kepler@ime.usp.br

**Marcelo Finger**
Institute of Mathematics and Statistics
University of Sao Paulo
Sao Paulo, SP, Brazil
mfinger@ime.usp.br

## Abstract

Variable-Length Markov Chains (VLMCs) offer a way of modeling contexts longer than trigrams without suffering from data sparsity and state space complexity. However, in Historical Portuguese, two words show a high degree of ambiguity: *que* and *a*. The number of errors tagging these words corresponds to a quarter of the total errors made by a VLMC-based tagger. Moreover, these words seem to show two different types of ambiguity: one depending on non-local context and another on right context. We searched ways of expanding the VLMC-based tagger with a number of different models and methods in order to tackle these issues. The methods showed variable degrees of success, with one particular method solving much of the ambiguity of *a*. We explore reasons why this happened, and how everything we tried fails to improve the precision of *que*.

## 1 Introduction

In the Computational Linguistics area, the task of *part-of-speech tagging* (POS tagging) consists in assigning to words in a text the grammatical class they belong. Since the same word may belong to more than one class, models for POS tagging have to look at the context where each word occurs to try to solve the ambiguity.

Previous and current work have developed a wide range of models and methods for tagging. The vast majority uses supervised learning methods, which need an already tagged corpus as input in order to train the model, calculating relations, weights, probabilities etc.

Among the various models for tagging, there are Maximum Entropy models (dos Santos et al., 2008; de Almeida Filho, 2002; Ratnaparkhi, 1996), Hidden Markov Models (HMMs) (Brants, 2000), Transformation Based Learning (Brill, 1993), and other succesful approaches (Toutanova et al., 2003; Tsuruoka and Tsujii, 2005; Shen et al., 2007).

Current state-of-the-art precision in tagging is achieved by supervised methods. Although precision is pretty high – less than $3\%$ error rate for English – the disavantage is exactly the need of a tagged corpus, usually built manually. This is a very restrictive issue for languages with lack of resources such as linguistic especialists, corpora projects etc.

The Portuguese language falls in between resourceful languages, such as English, and languages with restricted resources. There have been initiatives both in Brazil and in Portugal, which include modern Brazilian Portuguese corpora (ICMC-USP, 2010), European Portuguese corpora (Flo, 2008), and historical Portuguese corpora (IEL-UNICAMP and IME-USP, 2010). Also, some supervised POS taggers have already been developed for Portuguese (dos Santos et al., 2008; Kepler and Finger, 2006; Aires, 2000) with a good degree of success. And finally, there has also been increasing effort and interest in Portuguese annotation tools, such as E-Dictor[1] (de Sousa et al., 2009).

Despite these advances, there is still lack of material and resources for Portuguese, as well as research

*During the course of this work Fabio received support from Brazilian funding agencies CAPES and CNPq.

[1]See http://purl.org/edictor.



*Proceedings of the NAACL HLT 2010 Young Investigators Workshop on Computational Approaches to Languages of the Americas*, pages 15–23, Los Angeles, California, June 2010. 

in unsupervised methods to bootstrap text annotation.

Our work focuses on further improvement of the current state-of-the-art in Portuguese tagging. For this, we focus on the *Tycho Brahe* (IEL-UNICAMP and IME-USP, 2010) corpus for testing and benchmarking, because of its great collaboration potential: it is easily accessible[2]; is under continuous development; and has recently started using E-Dictor, which also offers a great collaboration potential.

### 1.1 Previous Works

One popular approach to tagging is to use HMMs of order 2. Order 2, or *trigram*, means the tagger considers the previous two words/tags when tagging a word. This adds context to help disambiguation. The drawback is that this context may not be sufficient. Increasing the order does not help, since this incurs in too many model parameters and suffers from the data sparsity problem.

In (Kepler and Finger, 2006), we developed a tagger for Portuguese that uses Markov chains of variable length, that is, orders greater than 2 can be used conditioned on certain tags and sequences of tags. This approach is better at avoiding the sparsity and complexity problems, while being able to model longer contexts. However, one interesting conclusion from that work is that, even using longer contexts, some words stay extremely hard to disambiguate. Apparently, those words rely on flexible contexts not captured by pure VLMCs.

Motivated by this problem, we improve over the previous work, and developed a set of tagger models based on Variable-Length Markov Chains (VLMCs) extended with various other approaches in order to try to tackle the problem.

In the next section we describe the VLMC theory, the results it achieves, and the problems with two common words. Then, in Section 3, we explain in summary the set of models and approaches we tried to mix with VLMCs, and the different types of results they give. Conclusions are drawn in Section 4. Finally, Section 5 describes how this work can be incorporated in other projects, and Section 6 presents ideas for future work.

[2]More information at `http://www.tycho.iel.unicamp.br/~tycho/corpus/en/index.html`.

## 2 Variable-Length Markov Chains

The idea is to allow the memory of a Markov chain to have variable length, depending on the observed past values. (Bühlmann and Wyner, 1999) give a formal description of VLMCs, while here we will explain them in terms of the POS-tagging task.

Consider a Markov chain with a finite, large order $k$. Let $t_i$ be a tag, and $t_{i-k,i-1}$ be the $k$ tags preceding $t_i$. Variable length memory can be seen as a cut of irrelevant states from the $t_{i-k,i-1}$ history. We call the set of these states the *context* of $t_i$. Given a tag $t_i$, its context $t_{i-h,i-1}$, $h \leq k$, is given by the *context function* $c(t_{i-k,i-1})$.

A *context tree* is a tree in which each internal node has at most $|\mathcal{T}|$ children, where $\mathcal{T}$ is the tagset. Each value of a context function $c(\cdot)$ is represented as a branch of such tree. For example, the context given by $c(t_{i-k,i-1})$ is represented as a branch whose sub-branch at the top is determined by $t_{i-1}$, the next sub-branch by $t_{i-2}$, and so on, until the leaf, determined by $t_{i-h}$.

The parameters of a VLMC are the underlying functions $c(\cdot)$ and their probabilities. To obtain these parameters we use a version of the context algorithm of (Rissanen, 1983). First, it builds a big context tree, using a training corpus. For a tag $t_i$, its maximal history $t_{i-k,i-1}$ is placed as a branch in the tree. Then, the algorithm uses a pruning function considering a local decision criterion. This pruning cuts off the irrelevant states from the tags' histories. For each leaf $u$ in the context tree, and branch $v$ that goes from the root to the parent node of $u$, $u$ is pruned from the tree if

$$\Delta_{vu} = \sum_{t \in \mathcal{L}} P(t|vu) \log \left( \frac{P(t|vu)}{P(l|v)} \right) C(vu) < K,$$

where $C(vu)$ is the number of occurrences of the sequence $vu$ in the training corpus, and $K$ is a threshold value, called the *cut value* of the context tree,

If the probability of a tag does not change much between considering the entire branch together with the leaf (all past history) and considering only the branch (the history without the furthest tag), then the leaf does not need to be considered, and can be removed from the tree.

We want to find the best sequence of tags $t_1 \ldots t_n$ for a given sequence of words $w_1 \ldots w_n$ of size $n$, that is,

$$\arg\max_{t_1 \ldots t_n} \left[ \prod_{i=1}^{n} P(t_i | c(t_{i-k,i-1})) P(w_i | t_i) \right].$$

Probabilities are computed from a tagged training corpus using maximum likelihood estimation from the relative frequencies of words and sequences of tags. The context tree is built with sequences of tags of maximum length $k$ and then pruned, thus defining the context functions. For decoding, the Viterbi Algorithm is used (Viterbi, 1967).

### 2.1 Initial Results

We used the tagged texts available by the Tycho Brahe Corpus of Historical Portuguese (IEL-UNICAMP and IME-USP, 2010). The Tycho Brahe project uses 377 POS and inflectional tags, and contains annotated texts written by authors born between 1380 and 1845. We have selected 19 texts for composing our corpus, which contains 1035593 tagged words and has 262 different tags. This corpus was then randomly divided into 75% of the sentences for generating a training corpus and 25% for a testing corpus. The training corpus has 775602 tagged words, while the testing corpus has 259991 tagged words. The Tycho Brahe project is undergoing rapid development, so as for today there are more texts available which are not present in the corpus we used[3].

Because of some of the approaches explained below, we also created a new training corpus and a new testing corpus by segmenting contracted words from the original corpus. Contracted words are words like *da*, which has the tag `P+D-F` and is a contraction of the preposition *de* (`P`) with the feminine determiner *a* (`D-F`).

Using the original corpus, our VLMC implementation, which we will call VLMM TAGGER[4] (from *Variable Length Markov Model*), and which better implements under- and overflow control, achieves 96.29% of precision[5], while the VLMC TAGGER from (Kepler and Finger, 2006) achieves 95.51%. Table 1 shows the numbers for both taggers, where P and E means Precision and Error, respectively. The difference in precision is mainly due to a 21.64% error reduction in known words tagging[6]. That, combined with 6.82% error reduction in unknown words, results in 17.50% total error reduction. With the segmented corpus the VLMM TAGGER achieved 96.54% of precision.

| TAGGER | WORDS | P (%) | ERR. / OCURR. |
|---|---|---|---|
| VLMC | Unknown | 69.53 | 2713 / 8904 |
| | Known | 96.39 | 9065 / 251087 |
| | Total | 95.51 | 11674 / 259991 |
| VLMM | Unknown | 71.60 | 2528 / 8904 |
| | Known | 97.17 | 7102 / 251087 |
| | Total | 96.29 | 9630 / 259991 |

Table 1: Precision of VLMC-based taggers.

Table 2 shows numbers for the two words that present the most number of errors made by the VLMM TAGGER. Note that they are not necessarily the words with the highest error percentage, since there are known words that appear only a couple of times in the testing corpus and may get wrong tags half of this times, for example.

| WORDS | P (%) | E (%) | ERR. / OCURR. |
|---|---|---|---|
| *que* | 84.7413 | 15.2586 | 1687 / 11056 |
| *a* | 90.9452 | 9.0547 | 661 / 7300 |

Table 2: Results for words with the most number of errors using the VLMM TAGGER with the normal corpus.

These two words draw attention because together they correspond to almost 25% of the errors made by the tagger, where most confusion for each of these words is between two different tags:

- The word *que* is, most of the times, either a relative pronoun – denoted by the tag `WPRO` and

[3]We can provide the training and testing corpus if requested by email.

[4]A package containing the VLMM TAGGER will be available at `http://www.ime.usp.br/~kepler/vlmmtagger/`, but requests for the raw source code can be made by email. Currently, there is only an automake bundle ready for download containing the VLMC TAGGER.

[5]Precision is given by the number of correctly assigned tags to the words in the testing corpus over the total number of words in the testing corpus.

[6]Known words are words that appear both in the training and the testing corpus.

equivalent to the word *which* in English –, or a subordinating conjunction – denoted by the tag `C` and equivalent, in English, to the words *that* or *than*;

- The word *a* is, usually, either a feminine determiner (tag `D-F`), or a preposition (tag `P`).

As a baseline, assigning the most common tag to *que* yields a precision of 55.64%, while *a* gets a precision of 58.09%. Also, these words seem to show two different types of ambiguity: one that needs context to the right, and one that needs non-local context. The VLMM model does not have parameters for these contexts, since it tags from left to right using context immediately to the left.

### 2.2 Objectives

It seems that *a* could be better disambiguated by looking at words or tags following it: for example, if followed by a verb, *a* is much more likely to be a preposition. For *que*, it seems that words occuring not immediately before may add important information. For example, if *que* follows *mais* (*more than*, in English), it is more likely that *que* has tag `C`. However, like in the English expression, it is possible to have various different words in between *mais* and *que*, as for example: "*mais provável que*" ("*more likely than*"); "*mais caro e complexo que*" ("*more expensive and complex than*"); and so on. Thus, it may yield better results if non-local context could be efficiently modeled.

In order to develop these ideas about *que* and *a* and prove them right or wrong, we searched ways of expanding the VLMM tagger with a number of different models and methods that could help solving these two issues. Those models are described next.

## 3 Auxiliary Approaches

### 3.1 Syntactic Structure

The first idea we had was to generalize nodes in the VLMM's context tree, that is, to model a way of abstracting different sequences of tags into the same node. This could make it possible to have branches in the context tree like `ADV * C`, that could be used for *mais * que*.

One way of doing this is to use sequences of tags that form phrases, like noun phrases (`NP`), prepositional phrases (`PP`), and verbal phrases (`VP`), and use them in the context tree in place of the sequences of tags they cover. The context tree will then have branches like, say, `P VP N`.

In order to train this mixed model we need a treebank, preferably from the texts in the Tycho Brahe corpus. However, it does not have a sufficiently large set of parsed texts to allow efficient supervised learning. Moreover there is not much Portuguese treebanks available, so we were motivated to implement an unsupervised parsed for Portuguese.

Based on the work of (Klein, 2005), we implemented his CCM model, and used it over the Tycho Brahe corpus. The CCM model tries to learn constituents based on the contexts they have in common. We achieved 60% of f-measure over a set of texts from the Tycho Brahe project that were already parsed.

Using the CCM constituents learned, we extended the VLMM TAGGER to use this extra information. It yielded worse results, so we restricted the use of constituents to *que* (the VLMM+SPANS-QUE TAGGER). This yielded a precision of 96.56%, with a *que* precision increase of 3.73% and an *a* precision reduction of 0.67%. A comparison with the plain VLMM TAGGER over the segmented corpus can be seen in Table 3. We use the segmented corpus for comparison because the constituents only use segmented tags. Even after many tries and variations in the way the VLMM TAGGER could use constituents, the result did not improve. This led us to a new approach, shown in the next section.

| WORDS | P (%) | ERR. / OCURR. |
|---|---|---|
| *que* | *84.50* | *1715 / 11063* |
| | 85.18 | 1651 / 11063 |
| *a* | *94.52* | *745 / 13597* |
| | 94.49 | 750 / 13597 |
| Total | *96.5433* | *9559 / 276541* |
| | 96.5636 | 9503 / 276541 |

Table 3: Comparison of precision using the VLMM TAGGER (in italics) and the VLMM+SPANS-QUE TAGGER (upcase) with the segmented corpus.

### 3.2 Chunks

Since induced syntactic structure did not help, a new idea was to, this time, begin with the already parsed and revised texts from the Tycho Brahe, even with they summing only a little more than 300 thousand words. To ease the problem of sparsity, the trees were flattened and merged in such a way that only NPs, PPs and VPs remained. Then the bracketed notation was converted to the IOB notation, now forming a chunked corpus.

*Chunking*, or *shallow parsing*, divides a sentence into non-overlapping phrases (Manning and Schütze, 1999). It is used in information extraction and in applications where full parsing is not necessary, offering the advantage of being simpler and faster.

We made a small experiment with the chunked corpus: divided the sentences randomly into 90% and 10% sets, the former for training and the later for testing. Then we ran the VLMM TAGGER with these chunked sets, and got a precision in chunking of 79%.

A model for chunks processing was mixed into the VLMM model, similar but not equal to the mixed model with CCM. The chunked corpus uses segmented words, because the parsed texts available in Tycho Brahe only use segmented words. Thus, we ran the VLMM TAGGER with the segmented training corpus and the chunked corpus, testing over the segmented test corpus. The precision yielded with this VLMM+CHUNKS TAGGER was 96.55%.

Table 4 shows the results for the segmented corpus with the VLMM TAGGER and the VLMM+CHUNKS TAGGER. Interestingly, results did not change much, in spite of the VLMM+CHUNKS TAGGER achieving a higher precision. Interestingly, the word *a* error rate is reduced by around 13% with the help of chunks, while the *que* error rate increases almost 3%.

| WORDS | P (%) | ERR. / OCURR. |
|---|---|---|
| *que* | *84.50* | *1715 / 11063* |
| | 84.05 | 1764 / 11063 |
| *a* | *94.52* | *745 / 13597* |
| | 95.26 | 644 / 13597 |
| Total | *96.5433* | *9559 / 276541* |
| | 96.5506 | 9539 / 276541 |

Table 4: Comparison of precision using the VLMM TAGGER (in italics) and the VLMM+CHUNKS TAGGER (upcase) with the segmented corpus.

### 3.3 Bidirectional

Another approach was to follow the intuition about *a*: that the right context should help solving some ambiguities. The problem that makes this approach non trivial is that a right tag context is not yet available when tagging a word, due to the natural left-to-right order the tagger follows when tagging a sentence. A right context that is available is the context of words to the right, but this presents the problem of sparsity and will probably not yield good results.

Our approach was then to model a right context of tags when the words to the right were not ambiguous, that is, if they could be assigned only one specific tag. During training, a new context tree is built for the right context, where, for each word in a sentence, a continuous but variable-length sequence of tags from unambiguous words to the right is added as a branch to the right context tree. That is, if $k$ words to right of a given word are not ambiguous, then the sequence of the $k$ tags these words will have is added to the right tree. The right context tree is also prunned like the left context tree and the Viterbi algorithm for tagging is adapted to consider these new parameters.

| WORDS | P (%) | ERR. / OCURR. |
|---|---|---|
| *que* | *84.74* | *1687 / 11056* |
| | 84.80 | 1680 / 11056 |
| *a* | *90.94* | *661 / 7300* |
| | 92.15 | 573 / 7300 |
| Total | *96.29* | *9630 / 259991* |
| | 96.33 | 9544 / 259991 |

Table 5: Comparison of precision using the VLMM TAGGER (in italics) and the VLMM+A-RIGHT TAGGER (upcase) with the normal corpus.

After various tests with different options for the right context tree, the result over the original VLMM tagger did not improve. We then experimented building the right context tree only for the word *a*, resulting in the VLMM+RIGHT-A TAGGER. Table 5 shows what happens with the normal corpus.The error rate of *a* is decreased almost 5% with this bidirectional approach.

### 3.4 Perceptron

The Perceptron algorithm was first applied to POS-tagging by (Collins, 2002). It is an algorithm for supervised learning that resembles Reinforcement Learning, but is simpler and easier to implement.

(Collins, 2002) describes the algorithm for trigram HMM taggers. Here, we will describe it for the VLMM tagger, adapting the notation and explanation.

Instead of using maximum-likelihood estimation for the model parameters, the perceptron algorithm works as follows. First, the model parameters are initialized to zero. Then, the algorithm iterates a given number of times over the sentences of the training corpus. For each sentence $s$, formed by a sequence of words $w^s$ paired with a sequence of tags $t^s$, the Viterbi decoding is ran over $w^s$, returning $z^s$, the predicted sequence of tags. Then, for each sequence of tags $o$ of length at most $k$, $k$ the maximum order of the VLMC, seen $c_1$ times in $t^s$ and $c_2$ times in $z^s$, we make $\alpha_{c(o)} = \alpha_{c(o)} + c_1 - c_2$. $c(o)$ is the context function defined in Section 2 applied to the tag sequence $o$, which returns the maximum subsequence of $o$ found in the context tree. $\alpha_{c(o)}$ represents the parameters of the model associated to $c(o)$, that is, the branch of the context tree that contains $c(o)$.

The above procedure effectively means that parameters which contributed to errors in $z^s$ are penalized, while parameters that were not used to predict $z^s$ are promoted. If $t^s = z^s$ then no parameter is modified. See (Collins, 2002) for the proof of convergence.

Implementing the perceptron algorithm into the VLMM tagger resulted in the VLMM+PERCEPTRON TAGGER. Table 6 shows the results obtained. Note that no prunning is made to the context tree, because doing so led to worse results. Training and predicting with a full context tree of height 10 achieved better precision. The numbers reported were obtained after 25 iterations of perceptron training. The total precision is lower than the VLMM TAGGER's precision, but it is interesting to note that the precision for *que* and *a* actually increased.

| WORDS | P (%) | ERR. / OCURR. |
|---|---|---|
| *que* | *84.74* | *1687 / 11056* |
| | 85.15 | 1641 / 11056 |
| *a* | *90.94* | *661 / 7300* |
| | 92.41 | 554 / 7300 |
| Total | *96.29* | *9630 / 259991* |
| | 95.98 | 10464 / 259991 |

Table 6: Comparison of precision using the VLMM TAGGER (in italics) and the VLMM+PERCEPTRON TAGGER (upcase) with the normal corpus.

### 3.5 Guided Learning

(Shen et al., 2007) developed new algorithms based on the easiest-first strategy (Tsuruoka and Tsujii, 2005) and the perceptron algorithm. The strategy is to first tag words that show less ambiguity, and then use the tags already available as context for the more difficult words. That means the order of tagging is not necessarily from left to right.

The inference algorithm works by maintaining hypotheses of tags for spans over a sequence of words, and two queues, one for accepted spans and one for candidate spans. Beam search is used for keeping only a fixed number of candidate hypotheses for each accepted span. New words from the queue of candidates are tagged based on their scores, computed by considering every possible tag for the word combined with all the available hypotheses on the left context and on the right context. The highest scoring word is selected, the top hypotheses are kept, and the two queues are updated. At each step one word from the queue of candidates is selected and inserted in the queue of accepted spans.

The core idea of Guided Learning (GL) training is to model, besides word, tag, and context parameters, also the order of inference. This is done by defining scores for hypotheses and for actions of tagging (actions of assigning a hypothesis). The score of a tagging action if computed by a linear combination of a weight vector and a feature vector of the action, which also dependes on the context hypotheses. The score of a given span's hypothesis is the sum of the scores of the top hypothesis of the left and right contexts (if available) plus the score of the action that led to this hypothesis.

The GL algorithm estimates the values of the weight vector. The procedure is similar to the inference algorithm. The top scoring span is selected from the queue of candidate spans and, if its top hipothesis matches the gold standard (the tags from the training corpus), the queues of accepted and candidate spans are updated as in the inference algorithm. Otherwise, the weight vector is updated in a perceptron style by promoting the features of the gold standard action and demoting the features of the top hypothesis' action. Then the queue of candidate spans is regenerated based on the accepted spans.

This model uses trigrams for the left and right contexts, and so it could be potentially extended by the use of VLMCs. It is our aim to develop a tagger combining the VLMM and the GL models. But as for today, we have not yet finished a succesful implementation of the GL model in C++, in order to combine it with the VLMM TAGGER's code (current code is crashing during training). Original GL's code is written in Java, which we had access and were able to run over our training and testing corpora.

Table 7 shows the result over the normal corpus. The first thing to note is that the GL model does a pretty good job at tagging. The precision means a 10% error reduction. However, the most interesting thing happens with our two words, *que* and *a*. The precision of *que* is not significantly higher. However, the error rate of *a* is reduced by half. Such performance shows that the thought about needing the right context to correctly tag *a* seems correct. Table 8 shows the confusion matrix of the most common tags for *a*.

| WORDS | P (%) | ERR. / OCURR. |
|---|---|---|
| *que* | *84.74* | *1687 / 11056* |
| | 84.90 | 1670 / 11056 |
| *a* | *90.94* | *661 / 7300* |
| | 95.49 | 329 / 7300 |
| Total | *96.29* | *9630 / 259991* |
| | 96.67 | 8650 / 259991 |

Table 7: Comparison of precision using the VLMM TAGGER (in italics) and the GUIDED LEARNING TAGGER (upcase) with the normal corpus.

| | D-F | P | CL |
|---|---|---|---|
| D-F | <4144> | 92 | 5 |
| P | 189 | <2528> | 2 |
| CL | 26 | 9 | <294> |

Table 8: Confusion matrix for *a* with the most common tags in the normal corpus (line: reference; column: predicted).

## 4 Conclusions

In almost all extended versions of the VLMM TAGGER, *que* and *a* did not suffer a great increase in precision. With the approaches that tried to generalize context – by using syntactic structure – and capture longer dependencies for *que*, the results did not change much. We could see, however, that the right context does not help disambiguating *que* at all. Training the VLMM model with a long context (order 10) helped a little with *a*, but showed overall worse results. Modeling a right context for *a* in a simple manner did also help a little, but not significantly. The model that gave good results for *a* was the one we still have not finished extending with VLMM. It looks promising, but a way of better disambiguating *que* was not found. A better approach to generalize contexts and to try to capture non-local dependencies is needed. Some further ideas for future work or work in progress are presented in Section 6.

## 5 Oportunities for Collaboration

Tycho Brahe is a corpus project undergoing continuous development. Since there is already a good amount of resource for supervised tagging, our tagger can be used for boosting new texts annotation. Furthermore, the project has started using E-Dictor, an integrated annotation tool. E-Dictor offers a range of easy to use tools for corpora creators: from transcription, philological edition, and text normatization, to morphosyntactic annotation. This last tool needs an integrated POS-tagger to further ease the human task of annotation. Besides, an increasing number of projects is starting and willing to start using E-Dictor, so the need for an automatic tagger is getting urgent. We have already been contacted by the E-Dictor developers for further collaboration, and should integrate effors during this year.

Another project that can benefit from a good POS-tagger is the *Brasiliana Digital Library*, from the University of Sao Paulo[7]. It started last year digitalizing books (and other pieces of literature) about Brazil from the 16th to the 19th century, making them available online. Many books have been OCRed, and a side project is already studying ways of improving the results. Since the library is an evolving project, the texts will soon be of reasonable size, and will be able to form another corpus of historical Portuguese A POS-tagger will be of great help in making it a new resource for Computational Linguistics research. We are already negotiating a project for this with the Brasiliana directors.

There is a tagger for Portuguese embedded in the CoGrOO[8] gramatical corrector for Open Office. They seem to implement some interesting rules for common use Portuguese that maybe would help some of our disambigation problems. Besides inspecting the available open source code, we have contacted the current maintainer for further conversation. A possibility that has appeared is to integrate the VLMM TAGGER with CoGrOO.

Using different data would be interesting in order to check if the exactly same problems arise, or if other languages show the same kind of problems. We will try to get in contact with other projects having annotated resources available, and seek for further collaboration. Currently, we got in touch with people working on another corpus of Portuguese[9]. Both sides are hoping to form a partnership, with us providing a POS tagger and them the annotated corpora.

## 6 Future Work

Short term future work includes implementing Guided Learning in C++ and mixing it with VLMCs. This looks promising since the current GL implementation uses a fixed trigram for contexts to the left and to the right. Also, there is a need for fast execution in case our tagger is really integrated into E-Dictor, so converting GL to C++ seems more natural than implementing the VLMM TAGGER in Java.

To try to tackle the difficulty in tagging *que* there are some ideas about using context trees of non-local tags. It seems a potentialy good model could be achieved by mixing such context trees with the Guided Learning approach, making a hypothesis consider non adjacent accepted spans. This is still a fresh idea, so further investigation on maybe other approaches should be done first.

Further investigation involves analyzing errors made by POS taggers over modern Portuguese and other romance languages like Spanish in order to verify if *que* and *a* continue to have the same degree of ambiguity or, in case of Spanish, if there are similar words which show similar issues. This also involves testing other taggers with our training and testing sets, to check if they get the same errors over *que* and *a* as we did.

[7] `http://www.brasiliana.usp.br/bbd`

[8] `http://cogroo.sf.net/`.

[9] *History of Portuguese spoken in São Paulo (caipira Project).*

## References

Rachel Virgínia Xavier Aires. 2000. Implementação, adaptação, combinação e avaliação de etiquetadores para o português do brasil. mathesis, Instituto de Ciências Matemáticas e Computação, Universidade de São Paulo - Campus São Carlos, Oct.

Thorsten Brants. 2000. Tnt – a statistical part-of-speech tagger. In *Proceedings of the Sixth Applied Natural Language Processing Conference (ANLP-2000)*, Seattle, WA.

Eric Brill. 1993. Automatic grammar induction and parsing free text: A transformation-based approach. In *Proceedings of the 21st Annual Meeting of the Association for Computational Linguistics*.

Peter Bühlmann and Abraham J. Wyner. 1999. Variable length markov chains. *Annals of Statistics*, 27(2):480–513.

Michael Collins. 2002. Discriminative training methods for hidden markov models: theory and experiments with perceptron algorithms. In *EMNLP '02: Proceedings of the ACL-02 conference on Empirical methods in natural language processing*, pages 1–8, Morristown, NJ, USA. Association for Computational Linguistics.

Archias Alves de Almeida Filho. 2002. Maximização de entropia em lingüística computacional para a língua portuguesa, 12.

Maria Clara Paixão de Sousa, Fábio Natanael Kepler, and Pablo Picasso Feliciano de Faria. 2009. E-Dictor: Novas perspectivas na codificação e edição de corpora de textos históricos. In *Linguística de Corpus: Sínteses e Avanços. Anais do VIII Encontro de Linguística de Corpus*, UERJ, Rio de Janeiro, RJ, Brasil, 11. Shepherd, T. and Berber Sardinha, T. and Veirano Pinto, M. To be published.

Cícero Nogueira dos Santos, Ruy L. Milidiú, and Raúl P. Rentería. 2008. Portuguese part-of-speech tagging using entropy guided transformation learning. In *PROPOR - 8th Workshop on Computational Processing of Written and Spoken Portuguese*, volume 5190 of *Lecture Notes in Artificial Intelligence*, pages 143–152, Vitória, ES, Brazil. Springer-Verlag Berlin Heidelberg.

Linguateca.pt, 2008. *The Floresta Sintá(c)tica project.*

ICMC-USP, 2010. *NILC's Corpora.* ICMC-USP.

IEL-UNICAMP and IME-USP, 2010. *Córpus Histórico do Português Anotado Tycho Brahe.* IEL-UNICAMP and IME-USP.

Fábio Natanael Kepler and Marcelo Finger. 2006. Comparing two markov methods for part-of-speech tagging of portuguese. In Jaime Simão Sichman, Helder Coelho, and Solange Oliveira Rezende, editors, *IBERAMIA-SBIA*, volume 4140 of *Lecture Notes in Artificial Intelligence*, pages 482–491, Ribeirão Preto, Brazil, 10. Springer Berlin / Heidelberg.

Dan Klein. 2005. *The Unsupervised Learning of Natural Language Structure.* phdthesis, Stanford University.

Christopher D. Manning and Hinrich Schütze. 1999. *Foundations Of Statistical Natural Language Processing.* MIT Press, Cambridge, MA, USA.

Adwait Ratnaparkhi. 1996. A maximum entropy model for part-of-speech tagging. In *Conference on Empirical Methods in Natural Language Processing*, University of Pennsylvania, 5.

Jorma Rissanen. 1983. A universal data compression system. *IEEE Trans. Inform. Theory*, IT-29:656 – 664.

Libin Shen, Giorgio Satta, and Aravind Joshi. 2007. Guided learning for bidirectional sequence classification. In *Proceedings of the 45th Annual Meeting of the Association of Computational Linguistics*, pages 760–767, Prague, Czech Republic, 6. Association for Computational Linguistics.

Kristina Toutanova, Dan Klein, Christopher D. Manning, and Yoram Singer. 2003. Feature-rich part-of-speech tagging with a cyclic dependency network. In *NAACL '03: Proceedings of the 2003 Conference of the North American Chapter of the Association for Computational Linguistics on Human Language Technology*, pages 173–180, Morristown, NJ, USA. Association for Computational Linguistics.

Yoshimasa Tsuruoka and Jun'ichi Tsujii. 2005. Bidirectional inference with the easiest-first strategy for tagging sequence data. In *HLT '05: Proceedings of the conference on Human Language Technology and Empirical Methods in Natural Language Processing*, pages 467–474, Morristown, NJ, USA. Association for Computational Linguistics.

Andrew James Viterbi. 1967. Error bounds for convolutional codes and an asymptotically optimal deconding algorithm. *IEEE Transactions on Information Theory*, pages 260 – 269, 4.

# Using Common Sense to generate culturally contextualized Machine Translation

**Helena de Medeiros Caseli** **Bruno Akio Sugiyama** **Junia Coutinho Anacleto**
Department of Computer Science (DC)
Federal University of São Carlos (UFSCar)
Rod. Washington Luís, km 235 – CP 676
CEP 13565-905, São Carlos, SP, Brazil
{helenacaseli,bruno_sugiyama,junia}@dc.ufscar.br

## Abstract

This paper reports an ongoing work in applying Common Sense knowledge to Machine Translation aiming at generating more culturally contextualized translations. Common Sense can be defined as the knowledge shared by a group of people in a given time, space and culture; and this knowledge, here, is represented by a semantic network called ConceptNet. Machine Translation, in turn, is the automatic process of generating an equivalent translated version of a source sentence. In this work we intend to use the knowledge represented in two ConceptNets, one in Brazilian Portuguese and another in English, to fix/filter translations built automatically. So, this paper presents the initial ideas of our work, the steps taken so far as well as some opportunities for collaboration.

## 1 Introduction

In this paper we describe an ongoing work concerning the studies in gathering and using Common Sense knowledge and building Machine Translation applications. Common Sense (CS) can be defined as the knowledge shared by a group of people in a given time, space and culture.[1] Machine Translation (MT), in turn, is the application of computer programs to generate a translated equivalent version of a source text, in a target language.

MT is one of the oldest and most important areas of Natural Language Processing (NLP) / Computational Linguistics (CL).[2] From its beginnings we have witnessed some changes in the proposed MT paradigms ranging from the basic level —in which MT is performed by just replacing words in a source language by words in a target language— to more sophisticated ones —which rely on manually created translation rules (Rule-based Machine Translation) or automatically generated statistical models (Statistical Machine Translation, SMT). Nowadays, the majority of the researches has being centered around the phrase-based statistical MT (PB-SMT) approach —such as (Koehn et al., 2003) and (Och and Ney, 2004). PB-SMT is considered the state-of-the-art according to the automatic evaluation measures BLEU (Papineni et al., 2002) and NIST (Doddington, 2002)[3].

Although PB-SMT models have achieved the state-of-the-art translation quality, there are strong evidences that these models will not be able to go further without more linguistically motivated features, as stated by Tinsley and Way (2009). This is already being illustrated by the recent shift of researches towards linguistically enriched models as (Koehn and Hoang, 2007) and (Tinsley and Way, 2009) among others.

Following the same idea of these most recent researches, here we are also interested in seeing

[1]This definition of Common Sense is adopted by *Open Mind Common Sense* (OMCS) and *Brazilian Open Mind Common Sense* (OMCS-Br) projects and is only one of the several possible definitions.

[2]In this paper we will use the terms NLP and CL interchangeably since this is the assumption adopted in Brazil.

[3]BLEU and NIST are two automatic measures widely applied to evaluate the target MT output sentence regarding one our more reference sentences.



*Proceedings of the NAACL HLT 2010 Young Investigators Workshop on Computational Approaches to Languages of the Americas*, pages 24–31, Los Angeles, California, June 2010. ©2010 Association for Computational Linguistics

how it is possible to improve MT performance based on more linguistically motivated features. In our case, we intend to investigate how to apply Common Sense knowledge to generate more culturally contextualized automatic translations.

For example, considering the translation of slangs[4] as in the English sentence "*Jump, you chicken!*"[5]. In this case, the word "*chicken*" do not mean "*a kind of bird*" but "*a coward*" or "*a person who is not brave*". However, its translation to Portuguese ("*galinha*") can also be applied as a slang with a completely different meaning. In the Portuguese language, the slang "*galinha*" means a men with a lot of girlfriends. Although the problem stated in the given example could also be fixed by some dictionary entries, CS knowledge is the kind of information that varies a lot and frequently can not be found in traditional dictionaries. Thus, we believe that the CS knowledge derived from the OMCS projects is an alternative way to cope with these translation problems.

Before presenting our ideas, section 2 describes some related work on SMT and more recent linguistically motivated empirical MT. Common sense and the Open Mind Common Sense project are the subjects of sections 3. Section 4 brings some of our ideas on how to apply the common sense knowledge in the automatic translation from/to Brazilian Portuguese and to/from English. After presenting the current scenario of our ongoing work, we point out some opportunities for collaboration in section 5. Finally, section 6 finishes this paper with insights about the next steps of our research.

## 2 Machine Translation

Machine Translation (MT) has about 70 years of history and lot of its recent achievements are directly related to the advances in computer science, which enable almost everyone to have access and use MT tools. Some of these tools were traditionally developed following the rule-based approach (e.g., Systran[6] and Apertium[7]) but the statistical approach is now being widely applied at least in part (e.g., Google[8]) (Cancedda et al., 2009).

The SMT was born in the late 1980s as an effort of researchers from IBM (Brown et al., 1990). In those days, SMT was performed based on two models: a word-based translation model and a language model. While the first model is concerned with the production of target equivalent versions of the source sentences, the second one guarantees that the output sentence is a possible one (it is grammatical and fluent) in the target language. In the current PB-SMT systems, the word-based models were replaced by the phrase-based ones built based on sequences of words (the *phrases*).[9]

The translation and language models used in SMT are built from a training parallel corpora (a set of source sentences and their translations into the target language) by means of IBM models (Brown et al., 1993) which calculate the probability of a given source word (or sequences of words) be translated to a target word (or sequence of words). The availability of some open-source toolkits (such as Moses (Koehn et al., 2007)[10]) to train, test and evaluate SMT models has helping the widely employment of this MT approach to perhaps almost any language pair and corpus type. In fact, SMT is an inexpensive, easy and language independent way for detecting recurrent phrases that form the language and translation models.

However, while PB-SMT models have achieved the state-of-the-art translation quality, its performance seams to be stagnated. Consequently, there is a recent common trend towards enriching the current models with some extra knowledge as the new approaches of factored translation models (Koehn and Hoang, 2007) or syntax-based (or syntax-augmented) MT systems (Tiedemann and Kotzé, 2009; Tinsley and Way, 2009; Zollmann et al., 2008).

More related to our work are the proposals of Musa et al. (2003) and Chung et al. (2005). Both

[4] Slangs are typically cultural because they characterize the mode of a group's speech in a given space and time.

[5] Sentence extracted from Cambridge Advanced Learner's Dictionary: `http://dictionary.cambridge.org/define.asp?key=13018&dict=CALD`.

[6] `http://www.systransoft.com/`

[7] `http://www.apertium.org/`

[8] `http://www.google.com/language_tools`

[9] In SMT, a *phrase* is a sequence of two or more words even though they do not form a syntactic phrase.

[10] `http://www.statmt.org/moses/`

of them are CS-based translation tools which take the topics of a bilingual conversation guessed by a topic spotting mechanism, and use them to generate phrases that can be chosen by the end-user to follow the conversation. Since they are interactive tools, the phrases are first displayed on the screen in the end-user's native language and, then, he/she selects a phrase to be translated (by a text-to-speech engine) in the language in which the conversation is taking place.

In our work, the main goal is also investigating new ways to improve MT performance, but instead of greater BLEU or NIST values we are interested in producing more culturally contextualized translations. Similarly to (Musa et al., 2003) and (Chung et al., 2005), we intend to help two bilingual users to develop a communication. However, in our case we are not only concerned with the language differences, but also the cultural divergences. To achieve this ambitious goal we rely on common sense knowledge collected from Brazilian and North-American individuals as explained in the next section.

## 3 Common Sense

Common sense (CS) plays an important role in the communication between two people as the interchanged messages carries their prior beliefs, attitudes, and values (Anacleto et al., 2006b). When this communication involves more than one language, translation tools can help to deal with the language barrier but they are not able to cope with the cultural one. In this case, the CS knowledge is a powerful mean to guarantee that the understanding will overcomes the cultural differences.

The CS knowledge applied in our research was collaboratively collected from volunteers through web sites and reflects the culture of their communities (Anacleto et al., 2006a; Anacleto et al., 2006b). More specifically, our research relies on CS collected as an effort of the Open Mind Common Sense projects in Brazil (OMCS-Br[11]) and in the USA (OMCS[12]).

The OMCS started in 1999, at the MIT Media Lab, to collect common sense from volunteers on the Internet. More than ten years later, this project encompass many different areas, languages, and problems. Nowadays, there are over a million sentences in the English site collected from over 15,000 contributors.[13]

OMCS-Br is a younger project that has being developed by LIA-DC/UFSCar (Advanced Interaction Laboratory of the Federal University of São Carlos) since August 2005. Figure 1 illustrates the OMCS-Br architecture to collect and manipulate CS knowledge in five work fronts: (1) common sense knowledge collection, (2) knowledge representation, (3) knowledge manipulation, (4) access and (5) use. A detailed explanation of each work front can be found in (Anacleto et al., 2008a).[14]

As can be seen in Figure 1, the CS knowledge is collected in the OMCS-Br site (bottom-left) by means of templates[15]. Then, the collected fact is stored in a knowledge base (up-left) from which it is converted into graphs that form a semantic network. These semantic networks, called ConceptNets, are composed of nodes and arcs (to connect nodes) as shown in the bottom-right part of Figure 1. The nodes represent the knowledge derived from the CS base while the arcs represent relations between two nodes based on studies on the theory of (Minsky, 1986). Examples of Minsky relations extracted from the ConceptNet, in English, related to the term *"book"* are: IsA (*"book" IsA "literary work"*), UsedFor (*"book" UsedFor "learn"*), CapableOf (*"book" CapableOf "store useful knowledge"*), PartOf (*"book" PartOf "library"*) and DefinedAs (*"book" DefinedAs "foundation knowledge"*).

Figure 2 brings an extract of our Brazilian ConceptNet (Anacleto et al., 2008b) and Figure 3, a parallel extract obtained from the North-American ConceptNet (Singh, 2002). As it is possible to notice from these figures, there is a straight relationship between these ConceptNets. It is possible to find many cases in which relations in English have

[11]http://www.sensocomum.ufscar.br

[12]http://commons.media.mit.edu/en/

[13]http://csc.media.mit.edu/

[14]Examples of successful applications using the CS knowledge derived from OMCS-Br can be fount at http://lia.dc.ufscar.br/

[15]The templates are semi-structured statements in natural language with some gaps that should be filled out with the contributors' knowledge so that the final statement corresponds to a common sense fact (Anacleto et al., 2008a).

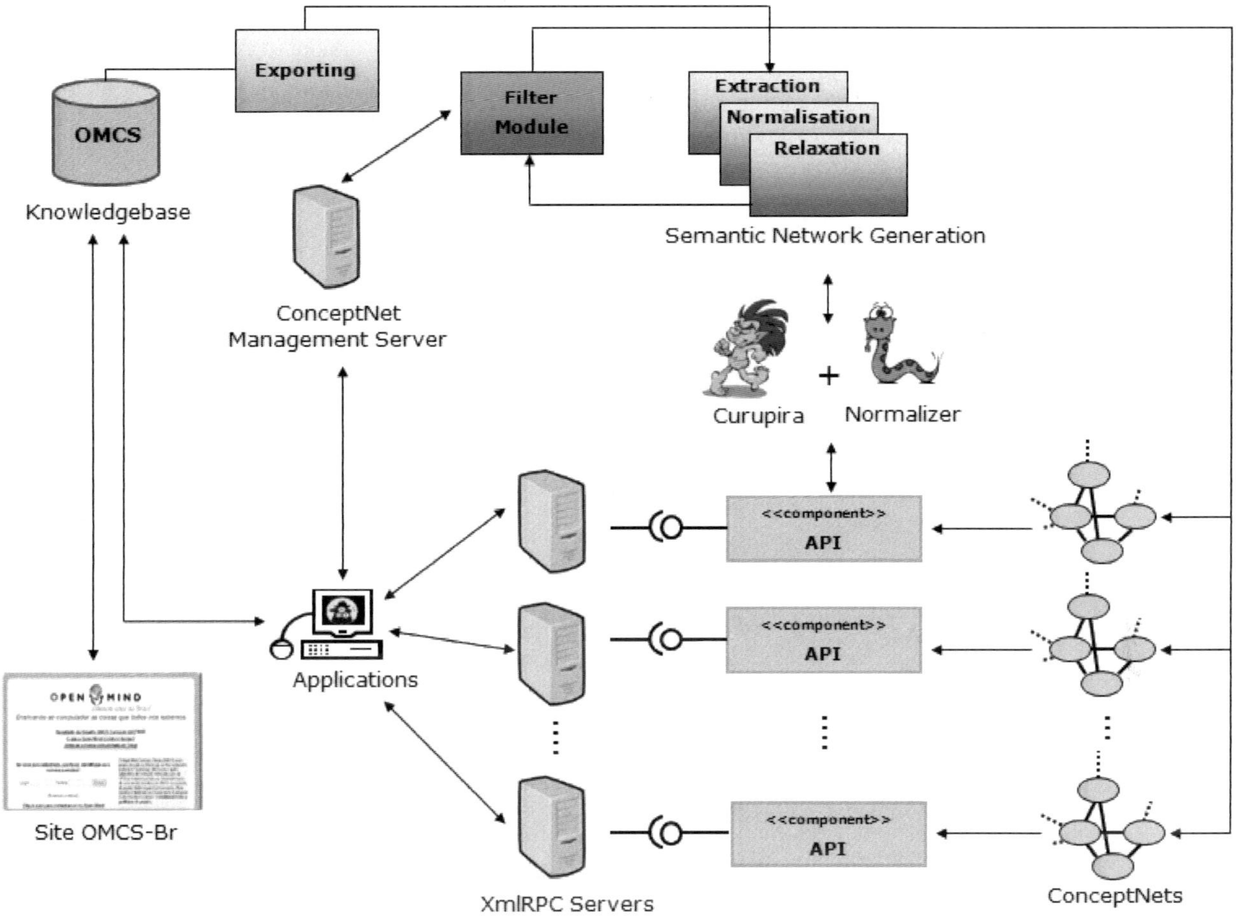


Figure 1: OMCS-Br Project architecture (Anacleto et al., 2008a)

their counterpart in Portuguese as in the example given in which *"book"* is connected with *"learn"* by the relation *UsedFor* and the *book*'s translation to Portuguese, *"livro"*, is also linked with the translation of *learn* (*"aprender"*) by a relation of the same type.

Different from other researches using semantic networks, such as MindNet[16] (Vanderwende et al., 2005), WordNet[17] (Fellbaum, 1998) and FrameNet[18] (Baker et al., 1998), here we propose the application of source and target ConceptNets together in the same application.

[16] http://research.microsoft.com/en-us/projects/mindnet/

[17] http://wordnet.princeton.edu/

[18] http://framenet.icsi.berkeley.edu/

## 4 Culturally Contextualized Machine Translation

As presented in the previous sections, the main goal of our research is to investigate how CS knowledge can help MT systems to generate more culturally contextualized translations. To do so, we are working with two ConceptNets derived from OMCS and OMCS-Br projects, that represent the CS knowledge in English and Brazilian Portuguese, respectively, as presented in section 3.

In this context, we intend to investigate the application of CS knowledge in the MT process in three different moments:

1. Before the automatic translation – In this case the source sentence input is enriched with some CS knowledge (for example, context information) that can help the MT tool to choose the best translation;

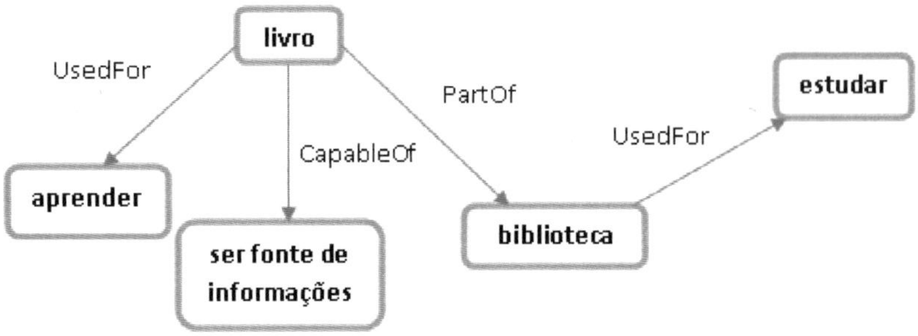


Figure 2: Graphical representation of the Brazilian ConceptNet (Meuchi et al., 2009)

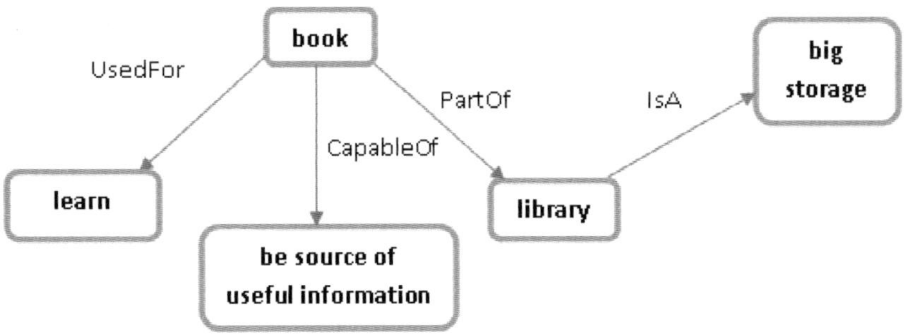


Figure 3: Graphical representation of the North-American ConceptNet (Meuchi et al., 2009)

2. During the automatic translation – In this case the CS knowledge is used as a new feature in the machine learning process of translation;

3. After the automatic translation – In this case some target words in the output sentence can be enriched with CS knowledge (for example, the knowledge derived from the "DefinedAs" or "IsA" Minsky relations) to better explain their meanings.

Currently, we are dealing with the last moment and planing some ways to fix/filter the target sentences produced by a SMT system. This part of the work is being carried out in the scope of a master's project which aims at building a bilingual culturally contextualized chat. By using a SMT tool (SMTT) and a CS knowledge tool (CSKT), this chat will help the communication between two users with different languages and cultures.

The SMTT is a phrase-based one trained using Moses and a corpus of 17,397 pairs of Portuguese–English parallel sentences with 1,026,512 tokens (494,391 in Portuguese and 532,121 in English). The training corpus contains articles from the online version of the Brazilian scientific magazine *Pesquisa FAPESP*[19] written in Brazilian Portuguese (original) and English (version) and, thus, a vocabulary that do not fit exactly the one found in chats. The SMTT trained based on this training corpus had a performance of 0.39 BLEU and 8.30 NIST for Portuguese–English translation and 0.36 BLEU and 7.83 NIST for English–Portuguese, in a test corpus composed of 649 new parallel sentences from the same domain of the training corpus (Caseli and Nunes, 2009).[20] For our experiments with culturally-contextualized MT, the option of using SMT models trained on general language in spite of building specific ones for the chat domain was taken aiming at measuring the impact that the CSKT has on the final translation.

The CSKT, in turn, will help one user to write his/her messages taking into account the

[19] `http://revistapesquisa.fapesp.br`

[20] In previous experiments carried out on the same corpora, the best online MT system was Google with 0.33 BLEU and 7.61 NIST for Portuguse–English and 0.31 BLEU and 6.87 NIST for English–Portuguese translation (Caseli et al., 2006).

cultural differences between he/she and the other user. A culturally contextualized translation will be generated by applying the knowledge derived from the two ConceptNets (see section 3) to fix/filter the automatically generated translations in a semi-automatic process assisted by both chat users.

To illustrate the use of both tools in the production of a culturally contextualized translation, lets work with slangs in the following example. Imagine a Brazilian and an American communicating through our bilingual chat supported by the SMTT and the CSKT. The American user writes the sentence:

American says: *"Hey **dude**, I will borrow a **C-note** from someone tomorrow!"*.

Supposing that our SMTT is not able to provide a translation for the words *"dude"* and *"C-note"* —what is, indeed, a true possibility— outputting an incomplete translation in which these words remain untranslated. Consequently, the Brazilian user would not understand the American's sentence incompletely translated to Portuguese. So, since the SMTT do not know the translation of these slangs, the CSKT will be started to look for possible definitions in the CS knowledge bases. At this moment, the CSKT could provide some basic information about the untranslated words, for example that *"dude is a slang"* and *"dude (is) defined as guy"* or that *"C-note (is) defined as 100 dollars"*, etc. Being aware of the untranslated words and their cultural meanings displayed by the CSKT, the American user could change or edit his/her original message by writing:

American says: *"Hey **guy**, I will borrow **100 dollars** from someone tomorrow!"*.

The final edited sentence has a higher probability to occur in the target language than the original one and, so, to be corrected translated by the SMTT.

In addition to this master's project, we are also developing two undergraduate researches aiming at discovering useful knowledge from the "parallel" ConceptNets. The first ongoing undergraduate research (Barchi et al., 2009) aims at aligning the parallel concepts found in Brazilian and English ConceptNets. This alignment can be performed, for example, based on lexical alignments automatically generated by GIZA++[21] (Och and Ney, 2000) or the hierarchical structure of the nodes and arcs in the ConceptNets. The second ongoing undergraduate research (Meuchi et al., 2009), in turn, is involved with the enrichment of one ConceptNet based on the relations found in the other (parallel) ConceptNet and also in lexically aligned parallel texts.

## 5 Opportunities for Collaboration

The work described in this paper presents the first steps towards applying semantic knowledge to generate more culturally contextualized translations between Brazilian Portuguese and English texts. In this sense, we see some opportunities for collaboration regarding the roles that are played by: (1) our research work, (2) the semantic resources available to be used and (3) the resources and results that will be produced by our work.

First of all, this work is a joint effort of two research areas: NLP/CL (machine translation) and human-computer interaction (HCI) (common sense knowledge gathering and usage). From this fact, we see a great opportunity to bring a new "vision" to the NLP/CL applications in which we are concerned with not only to produce a correct answer to the proposed problem, but also an answer that sounds more natural and user-friendly. So, regarding our work's role, we see the opportunity to improve the collaboration between researchers from NLP/CL and HCI.

The second possibility of collaboration envisioned by us is related to other sources of semantic knowledge that could be applied to our work. Although we are using common sense knowledge to support the generation of more culturally contextualized translations, other semantic information bases could also be applied. In this case, we believe that this workshop is a great opportunity to be aware of other research projects that apply semantic knowledge to MT or are engaged with the construction of semantic resources that could be used in our work.

Finally, we also see a future source of collaboration regarding the use of the bilingual resources obtained as the product of this research.

[21] `http://code.google.com/p/giza-pp/`

The parallel-aligned (in Brazilian Portuguese and English) common sense base, the translation knowledge inferred from this aligned base or even the bilingual culturally contextualized chat would be useful in other research projects in MT or other bilingual applications such as information retrieval or summarization. We also believe that the methodology applied to develop these resources and the results obtained from this work could be applied to other language pairs to derive new bilingual similar resources.

## 6 Conclusions and Future Work

In this paper we have described the first ideas and steps towards the culturally contextualized machine translation, a new approach to generate automatic translations using a phrase-based SMT tool and a common sense knowledge tool.

It is important to say that this proposal involves researchers from NLP/CL an HCI and it brings an opportunity for collaboration between these related areas. Furthermore, this work aims at stimulating researchers from other countries to work with the Brazilian Portuguese and presenting its ideas in this workshop is a great opportunity to achieve this goal.

Future steps of this ongoing work are concerned with the implementation of the proposed prototypes designed for the bilingual culturally contextualized chat, the alignment and the enrichment of the ConceptNets. After the implementation of these prototypes they will be tested and refined to encompass the needed improvements.

## Acknowledgments

We thank the support of Brazilian agencies CAPES, CNPq and FAPESP and also the workshop organizers by making possible the presentation of this work.

## References

Junia Coutinho Anacleto, Henry Lieberman, Aparecido Augusto de Carvalho, Vânia Paula de Almeida Néris, Muriel de Souza Godoi, Marie Tsutsumi, José H. Espinosa, Américo Talarico Neto, and Silvia Zem-Mascarenhas. 2006a. Using common sense to recognize cultural differences. In *IBERAMIA-SBIA*, pages 370–379.

Junia Coutinho Anacleto, Henry Lieberman, Marie Tsutsumi, Vnia Neris, Aparecido Carvalho, Jose Espinosa, and Silvia Zem-mascarenhas. 2006b. Can common sense uncover cultural differences in computer applications. In *Proceedings of IFIP WCC2006, Spring-Verlag*, pages 1–10.

Junia Coutinho Anacleto, Aparecido Fabiano P. de Carvalho, Alexandre M. Ferreira, Eliane N. Pereira, and Alessandro J. F. Carlos. 2008a. Common sense-based applications to advance personalized learning. In *Proceedings of the IEEE International Conference on Systems, Man and Cybernetics (SMC 2008)*, pages 3244–3249, Singapore.

Junia Coutinho Anacleto, Aparecido Fabiano P. de Carvalho, Eliane N. Pereira, Alexandre M. Ferreira, and Alessandro J. F. Carlos. 2008b. Machines with good sense: How can computers become capable of sensible reasoning? In *IFIP AI*, pages 195–204.

Collin F. Baker, Charles J. Fillmore, and John B. Lowe. 1998. The Berkeley FrameNet Project. In *Proceedings of the COLING-ACL*, Montreal, Canada.

Paulo Henrique Barchi, Helena de Medeiros Caseli, and Junia Coutinho Anacleto. 2009. Alinhamento de Grafos: Investigação do Alinhamento de ConceptNets para a Tradução Automática. In *Anais do I Workshop de Iniciação Científica em Tecnologia da Informação e da Linguagem Humana (TILic)*, pages 1–4.

Peter F. Brown, John Cocke, Stephen A. Della Pietra, Vincent J. Della Pietra, Fredrick Jelinek, John D. Lafferty, Robert L. Mercer, and Paul S. Roossin. 1990. A statistical approach to machine translation. *Computational Linguistics*, 16(2):79–85.

Peter F. Brown, Vincent J.Della Pietra, Stephen A. Della Pietra, and Robert. L. Mercer. 1993. The Mathematics of Statistical Machine Translation: Parameter Estimation. *Computational Linguistics*, 19:263–311.

Nicola Cancedda, Marc Dymetman, George Foster, and Cyril Goutte, 2009. *A Statistical Machine Translation Primer*, chapter 1, pages 1–36. The MIT Press.

Helena de Medeiros Caseli and Israel Aono Nunes. 2009. Statistical machine translation: little changes big impacts. In *Proceedings of the 7th Brazilian Symposium in Information and Human Language Technology*, pages 1–9.

Helena de Medeiros Caseli, Maria das Graças Volpe Nunes, and Mikel L. Forcada. 2006. Automatic induction of bilingual resources from aligned parallel corpora: application to shallow-transfer machine translation. *Machine Translation*, 20:227–245.

Jae-woo Chung, Rachel Kern, and Henry Lieberman. 2005. Topic Spotting Common Sense Translation Assistant. In Gerrit C. van der Veer and Carolyn Gale, editors, *Extended Abstracts Proceedings of the 2005*

*Conference on Human Factors in Computing Systems (CHI 2005)*, Portland, Oregon, USA, April 2-7. ACM.

G. Doddington. 2002. Automatic evaluation of machine translation quality using n-gram cooccurrence statistics. In *Proceedings of the Human Language Technology Conference (HLT 2002)*, pages 128–132.

Christiane Fellbaum, editor. 1998. *WordNet: An Electronic Lexical Database*. MIT Press, Cambridge, MA.

Philipp Koehn and Hieu Hoang. 2007. Factored Translation Models. In *Proceedings of the 2007 Joint Conference on Empirical Methods in Natural Language Processing and Computational Natural Language Learning*, pages 868–876, Prague, June. Association for Computational Linguistics.

Philipp Koehn, Franz Josef Och, and Daniel Marcu. 2003. Statistical phrase-based translation. In *Proceedings of the Human Language Technology (HLT/NAACL 2003)*, pages 127–133.

Philipp Koehn, Hieu Hoang, Alexandra Birch, Chris Callison-Burch, Marcello Federico, Nicola Bertoldi, Brooke Cowan, Wade Shen, Christine Moran, Richard Zens, Chris Dyer, Ondřej Bojar, Alexandra Constantin, and Evan Herbst. 2007. Moses: Open Source Toolkit for Statistical Machine Translation. In *Proceedings of the 45th Annual Meeting of the Association for Computational Linguistics (ACL 2007)*, pages 177–180, Prague, Czech Republic, June. Association for Computational Linguistics.

Laís Augusta Silva Meuchi, Helena de Medeiros Caseli, and Junia Coutinho Anacleto. 2009. Inferência de relações em ConceptNets com base em corpus paralelo alinhado. In *Anais do VI WorkShop de Trabalhos de Iniciação Científica (WTIC) - evento integrante do WebMedia 2009*, pages 1–3.

M. Minsky. 1986. *The Society of Mind*. Simon and Schuster, New York.

Rami Musa, Madleina Scheidegger, Andrea Kulas, and Yoan Anguilet. 2003. Globuddy, a dynamic broad context phrase book. In *CONTEXT*, pages 467–474.

Franz Josef Och and Hermann Ney. 2000. Improved statistical alignment models. In *Proceedings of the 38th Annual Meeting of the ACL (ACL 2000)*, pages 440–447, Hong Kong, China.

Franz Josef Och and Hermann Ney. 2004. The Alignment Template Approach to Statistical Machine Translation. *Computational Linguistics*, 30(4):417–449.

K. Papineni, S. Roukos, T. Ward, and W. J. Zhu. 2002. BLEU: a method for automatic evaluation of machine translation. In *Proceedings of the 40th Annual meeting of the Association for Computational Linguistics (ACL 2002)*, pages 311–318.

P. Singh. 2002. The OpenMind Commonsense project. KurzweilAI.net. Available at: <http://web.media.mit.edu/~push/OMCSProject.pdf>.

Jörg Tiedemann and Gideon Kotzé. 2009. Building a large machine–aligned parallel treebank. In Marco Passarotti, Adam Przepirkowski, Savina Raynaud, and Frank Van Eynde, editors, *Proceedings of the 8th International Workshop on Treebanks and Linguistic Theories (TLT'08)*, pages 197–208. EDUCatt, Milano/Italy.

John Tinsley and Andy Way. 2009. Automatically generated parallel treebanks and their exploitability in machine translation. *Machine Translation*, 23:1–22.

Lucy Vanderwende, Gary Kacmarcik, Hisami Suzuki, and Arul Menezes. 2005. Mindnet: an automatically-created lexical resource. In *Proceedings of HLT/EMNLP on Interactive Demonstrations*, pages 8–9, Morristown, NJ, USA. Association for Computational Linguistics.

Andreas Zollmann, Ashish Venugopal, Franz Och, and Jay Ponte. 2008. A systematic comparison of phrase–based, hierarchical and syntax–augmented statistical mt. In *COLING '08: Proceedings of the 22nd International Conference on Computational Linguistics*, pages 1145–1152, Morristown, NJ, USA. Association for Computational Linguistics.

# Human Language Technology for Text-based Analysis of Psychotherapy Sessions in the Spanish Language

**Horacio Saggion**[α], **Elena Stein-Sparvieri**[β], **David Maldavsky**[β], **Sandra Szasz**[γ]
[α]DTIC - Universitat Pompeu Fabra
Calle Tanger 122-140, Poble Nou
Barcelona - Spain
H.Saggion@dcs.shef.ac.uk
[β]IAEPCS - Universidad de Ciencias Sociales y Empresariales
Paraguay 1401, PB, Bs. As. Argentina
estein@solutiion.com.ar;dmaldavsky@elsitio.net
[γ]University of Sheffield - Department of Computer Sciences
211 Portobello Street - Sheffield - UK
S.Szasz@sheffield.ac.uk

## Abstract

We present work in progress in the application of Natural Language Processing (NLP) technology to the analysis of textual transcriptions of psychotherapy sessions in the Spanish Language. We are developing a set of NLP tools as well as adapting an existing dictionary for the analysis of interviews framed on a psychoanalytic theory. We investigate the application of NLP techniques, including dictionary-based interpretation, and speech act identification and classification for the (semi) automatic identification in text of a set of psychoanalytical variables. The objective of the work is to provide a set of tools and resources to assist therapist during discourse analysis.

## 1 Introduction

Computer-based textual analysis in psychology is not new; in psychotherapy, electronic dictionaries and other lexical resources are widely used to analyse both therapist's and patient's discourses produced during psychotherapy sessions. In this paper we present work in progress in the application of Natural Language Processing (NLP) technology to the analysis of psychotherapy sessions in the Spanish Language. Based on a psychoanalytic theory, we are developing a set of NLP tools as well as adapting an existing dictionary for the analysis of interviews. We investigate the application of NLP techniques, including dictionary-based interpretation, and speech act identification and classification for the automatic analysis of spoken transcriptions in Spanish of psychoanalysis sessions between therapists and patients. In Figure 1 we show a fragment of a manually transcribed interview in Spanish (and its translation to English) from our development corpus.

The automatic analysis of the sessions, which is used as a tool for assessment and interpretation of the transcribed psychotherapy sessions is based on a theory developed by Liberman and extended by Maldavsky (Liberman and Maldavsky, 1975) and framed on Freudian theory (Freud, 1925). The automatic tools to be presented here aim at recognizing a subset of *Freudian drives* manifested in both patient's and therapist's discourse.

The objective of the analysis is not to provide a full automated solution to discourse interpretation in this area, but a set of tools and resources to assist therapists during discourse analysis. Although work in text-based interpretation in psychology is not new, researchers in our project have identified limitations in current practices due to the fact that current text-based systems do not tackle ambiguity problems at lexical, syntactic, or semantic levels: for example systems that consider out-of-context superficial forms would are unable to distinguish between different used of the same lexical item ("para" as a preposition vs. "para" as a form of the verb "parar" (to stop); "rio" as a common noun vs. "rio" as a contextual clue for the identification of a geographical name; etc.). The use of advanced natural language processing techniques could help produce



*Proceedings of the NAACL HLT 2010 Young Investigators Workshop on Computational Approaches to Languages of the Americas*, pages 32–39, Los Angeles, California, June 2010. 

| Transcribed Session (Spanish/English Version) |
|---|
| T: ¿con que te cortaste? (T: What did you cut yourself with?) |
| L: con un vidrio que encontré en el patio (L: With a glass I found in the patio.) |
| T: ¿donde lo tenías? (T: Where did you have it?) |
| L: en el locker, en la puertita del locker, y después lo puse en la jabonera cuando baje a bañarme (L: In the locker, in the locker's small door, and then I put it in the soap box when I went down to have a bath.) |
| T: o sea, ya tenías un vidrio escondido (T: so, you already had the glass hidden.) |
| L: síı, ayer lo encontré (L: Yes, I found it yesterday.) |
| T: ¿ayer a la tarde? (T: Yesterday afternoon?) |
| L: sí, sí, de ayer a la tarde (L: Yes, yes, yesterday afternoon.) |

Figure 1: Transcription of a small fragment of a therapy session in Spanish and its translation to English. **T** indicates therapist and **L** indicates patient.

better analysis of the input material and therefore be used for a better diagnosis and follow-up. It is worth mentioning that full interpretation of therapy sessions is not only based on textual analysis, but also in other elements of the session such as the actual speech (e.g. pitch), para-verbal elements such as patient movement, etc. This work addresses only text interpretation issues.

The rest of the paper is organized as follows: Section 2 describes related work in the area of computational tools for text analysis in psychology. In Section 3, the theoretical framework for our work is briefly introduced. Section 4 describes the implementation of NLP tools for the analysis of the interviews and Section 5 closes the paper describing current and future work.

## 2 Related Work

There are a number of well-established computational tools for the analysis and extraction of meaning from text in the social sciences (See (Alexa and Zuell, 2000) for an overview of tools and resources). Some tools are bound to particular theoretical principles, for example the LWIC dictionary (Pennebaker et al., 2001) encodes specific categories to be identified in text while others follow a theory-free approach (Iker and Klein, 1974) where the theory emerges from the analysis of the data.

There has been substantial research in the development of methods to analyze linguistic input in the field of psychotherapy in order to measure a number of psychological variables such as emotion, abstraction, referential activity, etc. among them Bucci's Referential Activity (RA) non-weighted (Bucci, 2002) and weighted dictionaries (Bucci and Maskit, 2006) for the English language, or Höltzer and others' affective dictionary (Hölzer et al., 1997) for the German language. The LIWC tool has been used to detect different types of personalities in written self-descriptions (Chung and Pennebaker, 2008). This program counts meaningful words that express emotion, abstraction, verbal behavior, demographic variables, traditional personality measures, formal and informal settings, deception and honesty, emotional upheavals, social interaction, use of cognitive and emotion words, word analysis in psychotherapy, references to self and others. For Spanish (Roussos and O'Connell, 2005) have developed a dictionary in the area of psychotherapy to measure referential activity.

Early work on dictionaries in the area of psychology include the General Inquirer psycho-sociological dictionary (Stone and Hunt, 1963) which can be used in various applications; current work on lexical resources for identifying particular text variables – such as measuring strong/weak opinions, sentiments, subjective/objective language, etc. – include the SentiWordnet resource (Esuli and Sebastiani, 2006) derived from WordNet which has been used in various opinion mining works (Devitt and Ahmad, 2007); other lines of research include the derivation of word-lists (semi) automatically for opinion classification (Turney, 2002). To the best of our knowledge, little research has been carried out on natural language processing for discourse interpretation in psychology.

## 3 Theoretical Framework Overview

Liberman's theory identifies 7 drives (i.e., a subset of Freud's drives) which are introduced in Table 1 we may associate these drives with emotional or affective states such as: strong emotions associated with IL; ecstasy or trance with O1; sadness with O2; anger with A1; concrete language with A2; warnings, suspense, and premonition with UPH ; and congratulation, adulation, and promises with GPH. In diagnosis these variables are associated to pathologies such as addiction, schizophrenia, depression, paranoia, obsession, phobia, and hysteria; so their manifestation in text is of paramount importance for diagnosis.

| Abbreviation | Drive Name |
|---|---|
| IL | Intra-somatic libido |
| O1 | Primary oral |
| O2 | Secondary oral sadistic |
| A1 | Primary anal sadistic |
| A2 | Secondary anal sadistic |
| UPH | Urethrae phallic |
| GPH | Genital phallic |

Table 1: Drives in Liberman and Maldavsky theory

The theory also associates lexicalizations to each of the drives (Maldavsky, 2003), thus creating a semantic dictionary with 7 categories, the main working hypothesis is that drives manifest through linguistic style, present at word level, phrase, and narrative. Lexicalisations for each drive have been carefully selected following a variety of methods including manual derivation of words from concepts, study of texts where a scene is clearly present (e.g., everyday activities), use of thesaurus, etc. Ambiguity is preserved and a lexicalisation can signal more than one drive. We show some lexicalisations in Table 2.

| Drive | Lexicalisation |
|---|---|
| IL | **verbs**: to throw up, to break; **nouns**: hospital, throat; **adjectives**: sick, fat; **adverbs**: fatally, greedily |
| O1 | **verbs**: to sip, to suck; **nouns**: enigma, research; **adjectives**: mystical, enlightening; **adverbs**: elliptically, enigmatically |
| O2 | **verbs**: to feel, to feel like; **nouns**: feeling, victim; **adjectives**: sensitive, happy, sad; **adverbs**: fondly, obediently |
| A1 | **verbs**: to bother, to kick; **nouns**: violence, transgression; **adjectives**: angry, locked; **adverbs**: angrily,boldly, crossly |
| A2 | **verbs**: must, to know; **nouns**: vice, doubt; **adjectives**: good, bad; **adverbs**: but, although, however |
| UPH | **verbs**: to be able, to dare; **nouns**: scar, precipice, wound; **adjectives**: coward, scared; **adverbs**: almost, a bit |
| GPH | **verbs**: to promise, to give; **nouns**: beauty, ugliness; **adjectives**: wavy, pretty; **adverbs**: more, even |

Table 2: Sample of drives and associated lexicalisation

In addition to word-level analysis, the theory provides methods for analysis at narrative and speech act level.

Speech acts are actions performed when making an utterance (Searle, 1969) and they include (Searle, 1976) illocutionary (e.g. assert, suggest), perlocutionary (e.g. convince, insult), and propositional (e.g. making a reference) types. There has been substantial work on speech act segmentation and classification. Different authors adopt different classifications or theories of speech acts in order to restrict the categories to those relevant for the purpose of analysis. For example, in dialogue systems (Allen et

| Drive | Speech Acts |
|---|---|
| IL | references to the state of things; reference to body and body processes; etc. |
| O1 | abstract deduction; negation; reference to physical disomfort; etc. |
| O2 | lamentation; complain; beg; etc. |
| A1 | verbally abuse; provoke; confront; etc. |
| A2 | judge; clarify; confirm; etc. |
| UPH | forewarning; warning; inquest; counsel; etc. |
| GPH | congratulate; thank; promise; exaggerate; etc. |

Table 3: Drives and Speech Acts

al., 1996; Henry Prakken, 2000), the list of speech acts may vary from 4 to 10 categories and it may include acts such as assertion, WH-question, directives, greeting, direct/indicrect request, etc.
The pychoanalytic framework we are following has its own inventory of speech acts. The objective is also to link scenes in narratives and speech acts to the 7 drives (in Table 1). There is a variety of speech acts in the adopted framework, in Table 3 we present a sample of speech acts associated to each of the drives. The objective of the semi-automatic analysis is to help their identification to facilitate the work of the psychotherapist.

## 4 Text Analysis of Interviews

We have implemented a series of programs, lexical resources, and grammars to process interviews and other types of textual data in Spanish. We are using the GATE system (Maynard et al., 2002) as an infrastructure or development framework; most developments are new, not included in the GATE system, and they are packaged in a plug-in which can be accessed through the GATE system or used standalone. We have developed various programs to automatically annotate the interviews including segmentation of the transcription, word-based thematic segmentation, tagging, and dictionary-based interpretation and analysis.

### 4.1 Dictionary

One of the main components of the system is a dictionary which is taken as the basis for text interpretation. This is being implemented as a language resource in GATE. It is based on lists of word forms which have been created for each of the drives. The lists are organized according to their parts of speech. The available dictionary (Maldavsky, 2003) contains all inflected forms of verbs, nouns, adjectives, and adverbs which we are transforming into a dictionary which will contain only roots. An instance of the dictionary is created from the set of lists and kept on-line for processing. The current version of the dictionary (inflected forms) contains over 298 thousand verb forms, over 22 thousand noun forms, over 137 thousand adjectives, and over 9 thousand adverbs. An annotation tool has been implemented based on a schema for our dictionary, we use the graphical user interface functionalities provided by the GATE infrastructure allowing a researcher annotate words she may want to included in the dictionary or segment the text in units for further analysis.

### 4.2 Programs for Interviews' Interpretation

The following programs used for the automatic analysis of the interviews.

- A wrapper to the TreeTagger parts of speech package (Schmid, 1995) (See `http://www.clarin.eu/tools/treetagger`) has been implemented in order to call it from the GATE system and an alignment program has been developed to associate the output of the tagger to the actual text of the interview, therefore creating word annotations containing features from the TreeTagger and additional features computed by our programs. Note that the TreeTagger distributed with GATE was innapropriate for our purposes because it does require tokenisation of the input performed before invoking the tagger, this is the reason why we had to create our own wrapper.
- A segmentation program is used to identify patient and therapist interventions.
- Text chuncking and named entity recognition is being developed using Support Vector Machines and training data from the CoNLL

evaluation program. We have created a trainable system using machine learning resources provided by the GATE framework. The CoNLL 2002 Spanish dataset which provides information on named entities such as *Location*, *Organization*, *Person*, and *Miscellaneous* was analyzed using parts-of-speech tagging, morphological analysis, and gazetteer lookup in order to derive a set of features for learning. A supports vector machine was trained that uses gazetteer information, word level information, orthography, parts-of-speech, and lemmatization. We have collected a number of lists to assist the identification of names of organization, persons, locations, time expressions, etc. The performance of the current system is at 68% F-score. Note that named entity recognition is particularly important to track names in longitudinal analysis of interviews, but also to disambiguate names which in Spanish are ambiguous (e.g. "amado" can be a person name in addition to a form of the verb "amar"; "quito" can be the name of a place in addition to a form of the verb "quitar", etc.)

- A program uses the dictionary and interprets each word or complex term according to the drives in the dictionary taking into account parts of speech information and named entity recognition.

- A topic segmentation program has been implemented to break the interview in fragments which can be selected for fine-grained interpretation. This module is based on tf*idf similarity between candidate segments. A second module we are implementing aims at the recognition of segments referring to prototypical scenes a patient may refer to: family, work, love, health, money, etc. Further gazetteer list information has been collected from Spanish sources to create lexicons for assisting the automatic identification of the above categories. We are in the process of manually annotating a set of transcriptions as the basis for training a classification system for this task. Conceptual information will be used for this purpose.

- A processing resource has been implemented to generate an interpretation of the different languages or drives' variables for different segments chosen by the human analyst (therapist or patient or any other segment of interest) and statistics are computed for each of the segments; these can be exported for the therapist to carry out additional analysis and interpretation. Note that the current tool considerably improves the previous practises in dictionary-based interpretation, since the implemented tool takes into account syntactic and semantic information as a filter for interpretation.

### 4.3 Rule-based Speech Acts' Detection

We are carrying out induction sessions with psychotherapits in order to capture ways in which speech acts in the adopted framework are expressed. The induction sessions provided valuable material to start implementation of a rule-based speech act detection program (with regular expressions and a dictionary) based on use use of syntactic and lexical information. These procedures allow us to collect a set of expressions and lexical/syntactic patterns for objective identification of a subset of speech acts. We are also annotating the development corpus of interviews (a total of 30 will be annotated with a minimum of 2 annotators per interview) with speech acts categories. Each speech segment is annotated with one main speech act and a number (possibly zero) subordinate speech acts. We are using the GATE environment to provide appropriate support for the annotation process. In Figure 2 we show a fragment of interview in the annotation tool annotated according to the interpretation of one of our judges (the annotation window shows a "complaint" speech act associated to the fragment "no me estaba tratando de entender como él siempre hace" ("he did not understand as he always does")). We expect the annotated corpus to be a valuable resource for the development of a trainable speech act recognition program based on lexical clues and syntactic information. This trainable system will extend the rule-based approach or incorporate the rule-based analysis into it.

A sample of expressions we have identified and implemented for a subset of speech acts is presented in Table 4. The analysis of speech acts will provide an additional level for drive's identification.

## 5 Perspectives and Current Work

We have described our initial work on a set of tools being developed for the analysis of psychotherapy interviews in the Spanish language. The tools extend work on dictionary-based text interpretation by incorporating NLP tools such as tagging, topic/scene segmentation, speech act detection, and named entity recognition. One main contribution of our research is the implementation of a dictionary for the Spanish language which can be used not only for the identification of Freudian variables but also for work on affective language and sentiment analysis. We are currently working on the development of a full module for speech-act recognition and on the creation of a corpus of annotated interviews which will serve for further training and evaluation purposes. The set of resources developed in the project will be made available to the computational linguistics community for research purposes. We think that although this is work in progress it is worth mentioning evaluation. Where evaluation of the tools is concerned, we are carrying out intrinsic evaluation comparing annotated categories against predicted categories currently for named entity recognition and discourse segmentation and in the future for speech act recognition and classification. Where more extrinsic evaluation is concerned, we will evaluate how the tools presented here can help theraphist in better interpretation of clinical data. The implemented tools will also be used to compare word-level based interpretation produced by the dictionary to interpretation produced by the analysis at speech act level.

## Acknowledgements

We thank the reviewers for their very useful comments. This work was partially supported by a grant from the Royal Society (JP090069), UK. The first author is grateful to Programa Ramón y Cajal 2009 from the Ministerio de Ciencia e Innovación, Spain.

## References

M. Alexa and C. Zuell. 2000. Text analysis software: Commonalities, differences and limitations: The results of a review. *Quality & Quantity*, 34:299–231.

J. F. Allen, B. W. Miller, E. K. Ringger, and T. Sikorski. 1996. A robust system for natural spoken dialogue. In *Proceedings of the 34th annual meeting on Association for Computational Linguistics*, pages 62–70, Morristown, NJ, USA. Association for Computational Linguistics.

W. Bucci and B. Maskit. 2006. A Weighted Referential Activity Dictionary. In *Computing Attitude and Affect in Text: Theory and Applications*, volume 20 of *The Information Retrieval Series*, pages 49–60. Springer Verlag.

W. Bucci. 2002. Referential Activity (RA): Scales and computer procedures. In *An Open Door Review of Outcome Studies in Psychoanalysis*. International Psychoanalytical Association.

C.K. Chung and J.W. Pennebaker. 2008. Revealing dimensions of thinking in open-ended self-descriptions: An automated meaning extraction method for natural language. *Journal of Research in Personality*, 42:96–132.

Ann Devitt and Khurshid Ahmad. 2007. Sentiment polarity identification in financial news: A cohesion-based approach. In *Proceedings of the 45th Annual Meeting of the Association of Computational Linguistics*, pages 984–991, Prague, Czech Republic, June. Association for Computational Linguistics.

Andrea Esuli and Fabrizio Sebastiani. 2006. SENTIWORDNET: A publicly available lexical resource for opinion mining. In *Proceedings of LREC-06, 5th Conference on Language Resources and Evaluation*, pages 417–422, Genova, IT.

S. Freud. 1925. *Obras Completas*. Amorrortu (Eds.), Madrid, Spain.

H. Henry Prakken. 2000. On dialogue systems with speech acts, arguments, and counterarguments. In *Logics in Artificial Intelligence*, pages 224–238. Springer Verlag.

M. Hölzer, D. Pokorny, H. Kächele, and L. Luborsky. 1997. The Verbalization of Emotions in the Therapeutic Dialogue-A Correlate of Therapeutic Outcome? *Psychotherapy Research*, 7(3):261–273.

H.P. Iker and R. Klein. 1974. WORDS: A computer system for the analysis of content. *Behavior Research Methods and Instrumentation*, 6:430–438.

D. Liberman and D. Maldavsky. 1975. *Psicoanlisis y semitica*. Paidos, Buenos Aires, Argentina.

D. Maldavsky. 2003. *La investigacin psicoanaltica del lenguaje: algoritmo David Liberman*. Editorial Lugar, Buenos Aires, Argentina.

| Speech Act | Pattern or Expression |
|---|---|
| beg | PPX + *rogar* \| *implorar* \| *suplicar* |
| demand | PPX + *exhortar* \| *exigir* \| *demandar* \| *perdir* |
| demand recognition | *decir* que esta bien \| correcto \| perfecto \| bueno; está bien, no? |
| demand forgiveness | PPX + *perdonar* |
| justify | por que; por eso; debido a que; por esa razón |
| permission | con *PPO* permiso; *pedir*; PPX + *dejar* |
| interrupt | para... para; espera...; ah me olvide... |
| cite | como dijo NP \| PPX ; según NP \| PPX ; de acuerdo con NP \| PPX |
| sinthesis | en resumen; para concluir; en síntesis |
| doubt | no PPX *quedar* \| *ser* \| *estar* claro; quien sabe |
| trust/distrust | no *confiar* \| *desconfiar*; *confiar* \| *desconfiar* |
| submission | *tener* razón; no + PPX + *enojar* |
| appeal | decime que me querés; ... |
| compassion/self-compassion | me da pena; pobre; pobrecito;... |
| sacrifice | yo que hice todo esto; yo que te di todo; si no fuera por mi; ... |

Table 4: Speech Acts and Lexical/Syntactic Patterns (PPX = pronouns; NP = proper nouns; PPO = possessive)


D. Maynard, V. Tablan, H. Cunningham, C. Ursu, H. Saggion, K. Bontcheva, and Y. Wilks. 2002. Architectural Elements of Language Engineering Robustness. *Journal of Natural Language Engineering – Special Issue on Robust Methods in Analysis of Natural Language Data*, 8(2/3):257–274.

J.W. Pennebaker, M.E. Francis, and R.j. Both. 2001. *Linguistic Inquiry and Word Count (LIWC)*. Erlbaum Publishers.

A. Roussos and M. O'Connell. 2005. Construcción de un diccionario ponderado en español para medir la Actividad Referencial. *Revista del Instituto de Investigaciones de la Facultad de Psicología - UBA*, 10(2):99–119.

H. Schmid. 1995. Improvements in part-of-speech tagging with an application to german. In *In Proceedings of the ACL SIGDAT-Workshop*, pages 47–50.

J. Searle. 1969. *Speech acts: An essay in the philosophy of language*. Cambridge University Press.

John R. Searle. 1976. A classification of illocutionary acts. *Language in Society*, 5(1):1–23.

P. J. Stone and E. B. Hunt. 1963. A Computer Approach to Content Analysis: Studies using the General Inquirer System. In *Proceedings of the Spring Joint Computer Conference*, pages 241–256, New York, NY, USA. ACM.

P. D. Turney. 2002. Thumbs up or thumbs down?: semantic orientation applied to unsupervised classification of reviews. In *Proceedings of the 40th Annual Meeting on Association for Computational Linguistics (ACL '02)*, pages 417–424, Morristown, NJ, USA, July. Association for Computational Linguistics.

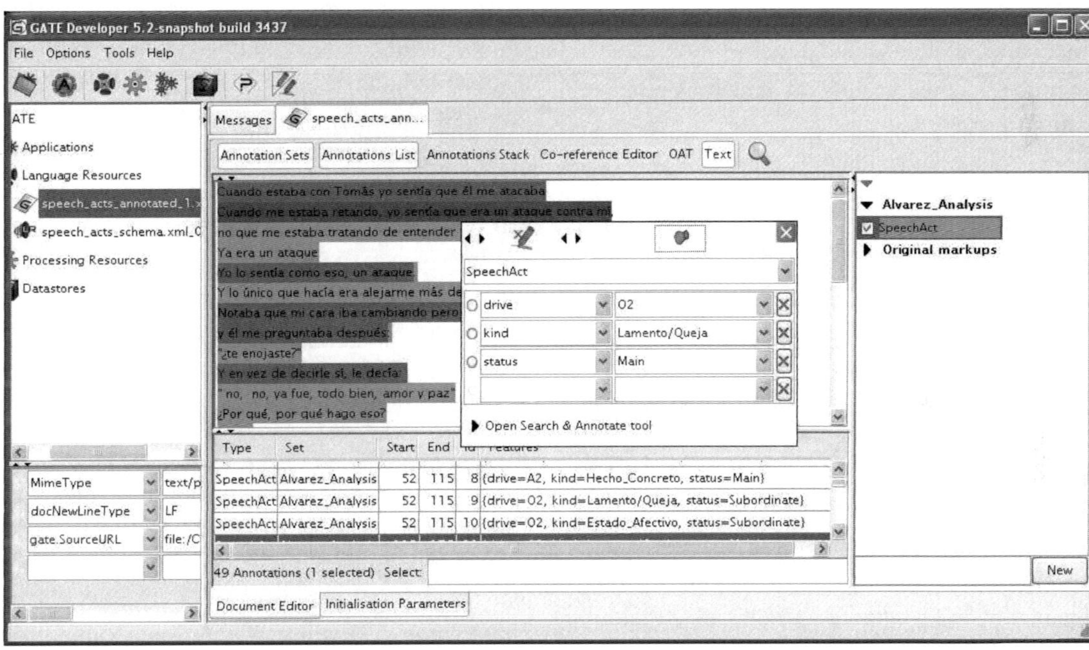


Figure 2: Speech Acts Segmentation and Interpretation

# Computational Linguistics in Costa Rica: an overview*

**Jorge Antonio Leoni de León**
Escuela de Filología, Lingüística y Literatura
Universidad de Costa Rica
Ciudad Universitaria Rodrigo Facio, San Pedro Montes de Oca
San José, Costa Rica
antonio.leoni@ucr.ac.cr

## Abstract

This paper aims to bring a general overview on the situation of Computational Linguistics in Costa Rica, particularly in the academic world.

## 1 Introduction

Costa Rica is a Central American country, well known for the abolition of its army in 1949 and for its policies in favor of the conservation of ecologically important areas. Investments in Education brought a good development of several higher educational institutions, most of them public and open to new students through an academic selection system. As a consequence, one of the main products of exportation is software (outsourcing, for example). The growing importance of Computational Linguistics (CL) in the last years has made developers to start using CL technologies at work, but unfortunately, often, they are on their own for the lack of academic structures supporting development. In the Table 1 and in the Figure 1 we provide comparative data on *Information and Communication Technologies* (ICT) for Costa Rica, Brazil, Mexico and the United States both taken from the World Economic Report for 2010 (Dutta and Mia, 2010), in order to help the reader to get a better picture of the context on which CL is growing up in Costa Rica.

This paper aims to bring a general account of CL in Costa Rica. This article is divided into three parts. The section 2 starts with some early CL articles in Costa Rica before covering academic and research infrastructure in the country. The section 4 briefly acknowledges the presence of CL industries in the country. Finally, the section 5 presents some of the current tendencies in research and teaching. The claims in this paper are not exhaustive and they only represent the Author's opinion, who aims to be as objective as possible, but who does not have a complete knowledge on the structures, institutions and companies involved in computational issues in Costa Rica. Therefore, all the topics are raised from personal interviews and experiences .

## 2 Academic infrastructure

Since the 90's, CL raised interest in main academic institutions in Costa Rica, particularly in the field of Artificial Intelligence, but this interest was not continued and well structured in time. Some researchers moved to other academic areas in computation or even to industrial research. So, in the *Instituto Tecnológico de Costa Rica*[1] (TEC) we found the first citations related to CL, mainly on number recognition (Helo and Sell, 1995), knowledge representation (Araya, 1992), connectionism (Vargas, 1991) and unification grammars (Vargas, 1992), these last from a philosophical perspective.

In Costa Rica, we found more than 40 universities and research institutes. But, computational research in the country is principally done in the TEC and in the University of Costa Rica.[2] At this moment, CL

*Thanks to Sharid Loáiciga, Natalia Bermúdez, Prof. Gabriela Barrantes, Prof. Hugo Mora Poltronieri and Prof. Álvaro de la Osa for their suggestions and comments. All the gaps and mistakes in this paper are entirely mine.

[1]Web site: http://www.tec.cr/. Visited: 03/28/2010.

[2]These institutions are public universities; in Costa Rica the best standards in higher education are found in the public insti-



*Proceedings of the NAACL HLT 2010 Young Investigators Workshop on Computational Approaches to Languages of the Americas*, pages 40–45, Los Angeles, California, June 2010. ©2010 Association for Computational Linguistics

| Variable | Costa Rica | Brazil | Mexico | United States |
|---|---|---|---|---|
| *Market Environment* | | | | |
| Venture capital availability | 2.68 | 2.73 | 2.39 | 4.17 |
| Availability of latest technologies | 4.66 | 5.29 | 4.58 | 6.58 |
| State of cluster development | 3.58 | 4.25 | 3.76 | 5.45 |
| *Political and Regulatory Environment* | | | | |
| Laws relating to ICT | 4.06 | 4.43 | 3.90 | 5.54 |
| Intellectual property protection | 3.54 | 3.04 | 3.19 | 5.44 |
| *Infrastructure Environment* | | | | |
| Secure Internet servers (hard data) | 98.75 | 23.67 | 15.67 | 1173.66 |
| Electricity production (hard data) | 1997.70 | 2259.80 | 2380.84 | 14309.62 |
| Availability of scientists and engineers | 4.74 | 4.24 | 3.64 | 5.60 |
| Quality of scientific research institutions | 4.63 | 4.22 | 3.71 | 6.18 |
| Tertiary education enrollment (hard data) | 25.34 | 29.99 | 26.93 | 81.68 |
| Education expenditure (hard data) | 4.06 | 4.44 | 5.47 | 4.79 |
| Accessibility of digital content | 4.56 | 4.85 | 4.53 | 6.33 |
| Internet bandwidth (hard data) | 8.55 | 20.83 | 2.81 | 111.22 |
| *Individual Readiness* | | | | |
| Quality of math and science education | 4.34 | 2.71 | 2.58 | 4.47 |
| Quality of the educational system | 4.69 | 3.01 | 2.80 | 4.85 |
| *Business Readiness* | | | | |
| Company spending on R&D | 3.75 | 3.79 | 2.90 | 5.63 |
| University-industry collaboration in R&D | 4.25 | 4.06 | 3.48 | 5.90 |
| *Government Readiness* | | | | |
| Government prioritization of ICT | 4.93 | 4.44 | 4.25 | 5.62 |
| Government procurement of advanced technology products | 4.00 | 3.68 | 3.28 | 4.77 |
| Importance of ICT to government vision of the future | 4.44 | 4.15 | 3.98 | 4.91 |
| *Individual Usage* | | | | |
| Personal computers (hard data) | 23.10 | 16.12 | 14.10 | 78.67 |
| *Business Usage* | | | | |
| Capacity for innovation | 3.45 | 3.90 | 2.78 | 5.49 |
| *Government Usage* | | | | |
| High-tech exports (hard data) | 25.88 | 5.79 | 12.25 | 19.84 |
| Government success in ICT promotion | 4.37 | 4.40 | 3.83 | 5.19 |
| ICT use and government efficiency | 4.49 | 4.64 | 4.37 | 5.26 |
| Presence of ICT in government agencies | 3.88 | 5.06 | 4.44 | 5.81 |
| *World rank 2009–2010 (over 133 economies)* | 49 | 61 | 73 | 5 |

Table 1: *Comparative data on Information and Communication Technologies (ICT) (Dutta and Mia, 2010)*

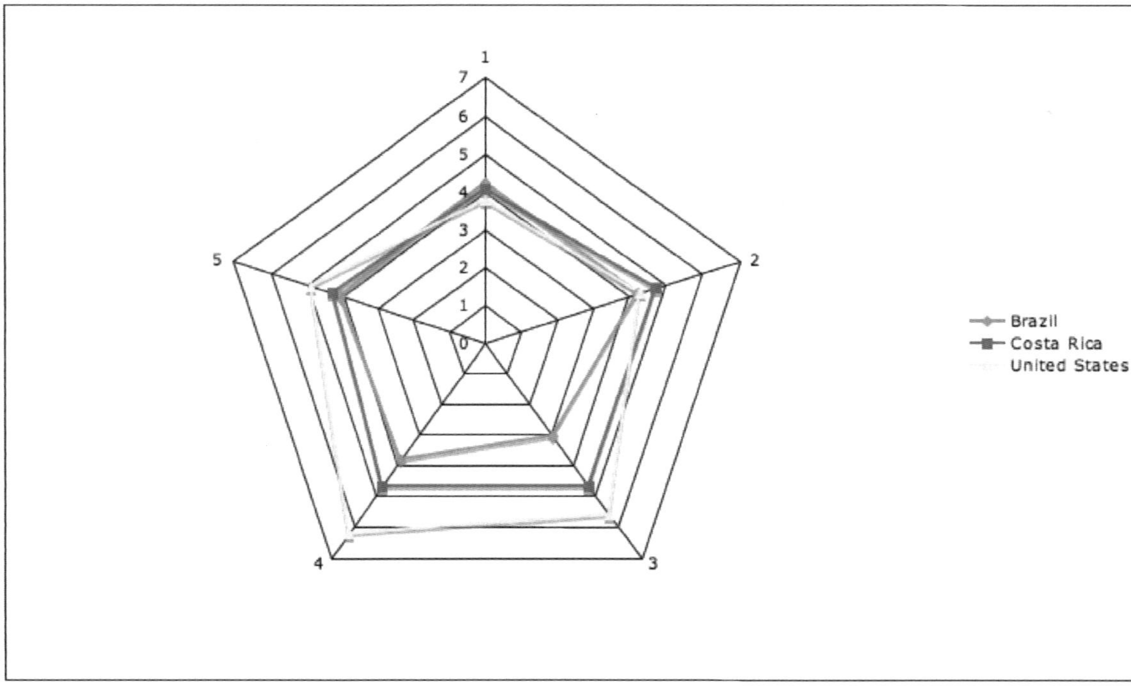


Figure 1: *Benchmarking on chosen ICT data for Costa Rica, Brazil and the United States (Dutta and Mia, 2010)*

is mainly found in the University of Costa Rica as part of the academic structure. This institution, as far as we are concerned, has two structures covering research: schools and research institutions. The former are mainly oriented towards teaching; the latter are exclusively devoted to research. CL teaching is carried out in the *School of Philology, Linguistics and Literature*[3] and in its associated postgraduate program on Linguistics[4]. Research is concentrated in the Instituto de Investigaciones Lingüísticas (INIL)[5] at the Facultad de Letras[6]. INIL is under the administrative supervision of the *Vicerrectoría de Investigación*[7], which approves project financing. All the scientific responsability falls on the members and commissions of the research institutions. At this moment, CL is attached to INIL's program ELEXHICÓS. Where a two year project is under development, with the part time assistance of a researcher. This project aims to create the bases for a hybrid parser.

In the Instituto de Investigaciones en Ingeniería (INII), we found a program on cognition and language[8]. In spite of the name, their research addresses mostly behavioral issues.

There exists the possibility of getting funding from governmental institutions, like CONARE[9], but they are meager. Nevertheless, it seems there are good options within inter-university collaboration, but this would require a long term coordination and planification.

In Costa Rica, research funding can be improved if real applications are proposed, for example educational and developmental tools. Other areas of interest are indigenous and minority languages, like Bribri and Chinese. In this sense, there are no computational projects officially inscribed in INIL at this moment, but ideas to start projects on this areas are waiting for the next inauguration of the Natural Language Processing Laboratory in the University of Costa Rica, so there are no papers to cite for the moment. Nevertheless, any inquiry on indigenous lan-

tutions.

[3]Escuela de Filología, Lingüística y Literatura.

[4]Web site: http://www.linguistica.ucr.ac.cr. Visited: 03/28/2010.

[5]Site: http://inil.ucr.ac.cr/. Visited: 02/15/2010.

[6]Roughly "Faculty of Humanities".

[7]In English, the University's Bureau for Research.

[8]Site: http://iniiserver.inii.ucr.ac.cr/picl/. Visited: 02/15/2010.

[9]Site: http://www.conare.ac.cr/. Visited: 02/15/2010.

guages can be addressed to Prof. Carla Jara Murillo, director of the Linguistic Department.

## 3 Growing needs, growing interest

In the 90's the project *Estudios de Lexicografía Hispano-Costarricense*[10] (ELEXHICÓS)[11] at the *School of Philology, Linguistics and Literature* of the University of Costa Rica was born as an initiative to do lexicographical research on contemporary Costarican Spanish and to publish dictionaries based on modern scientific methods and oriented towards different publics and usages.

Lexicographical studies appeal to large corpora in order to document accurate word values and guarantee their usefulness. The need of computational resources was felt from the beginning of ELEXHICÓS. The Murillo and Sánchez (1993) on lexical and syntactic maturity (language acquisition) is a good example of a research where this need of language computational tools is present. However, statistical dictionaries (Morales, 2009) can only be done by electronic means because of the huge calculations involved. For a long time, ELEXHICÓS counted on the limited, but important, support of the Centro de Informática (Center of Informatics) of the University of Costa Rica, but the need of developing its own resources and technologies imposed itself.

In 2002 the *School of Philology, Linguistics and Literature* of the University of Costa Rica opened the course *Tecnología y Producción Textual*[12], where text processing technologies like LaTeX, XML, HTML, CSS and Perl are taught for applications in the Humanities field. Some interesting proof-of-concept projects have been proposed as part of the course activities (Arroyo Molina, 2009; Enciso Bahler, 2008; Fuentes Vargas, 2008). As an initiative of ELEXHICÓS and the *School of Philology, Linguistics and Literature* in order to develop CL, the University of Costa Rica approved a grant for a Ph.D. on Computational Linguistics, which was fulfilled at the *Laboratoire d'Analyse et de Technologie du Langage*[13] of the University of Geneva. As part of this initiative a full time Professorship on CL was opened for 2010 and since 2009 CL is taught as postgraduate facultative course for the Master on Linguistics. Other courses on Formal Linguistics and Natural Language Processing (NLP) were accepted and will be part of the offer in 2010. Additionally, the *School of Philology, Linguistics and Literature* approved the creation of a NLP laboratory (project number 021-A9-734 of the *Vicerrectoría de Investigación*, main rcsarcher, Prof. Jorge Antonio Leoni de León, assistant researcher, Prof. Carla Jara Murillo), which is expected for 2010, and should support research and teaching, especially because a course on data processing for undergraduate students on Linguistics and Philology is under consideration.

Computational graduate students have showed their interest on CL courses at the *Postgraduate Program in Linguistics*[14]. Some of them come to the course looking for knowledge on CL, since because of their jobs they need a good understanding of NLP technologies. Although we lack of details about the job they do with NLP, the works of Berrocal Rojas (2009) and Cedeño Baltodano (2009) for the postgraduate program on Computational Sciences illustrate the growing interest in the field. At the moment, only one student started, this year, her Master's thesis on CL at the Postgraduate Program on Linguistics at the University of Costa Rica.

Off universities' campus, it's important to mention the *Centro Nacional de Alta Tecnología*[15] (CENAT), which has projects sharing similarities with CL, but with totally different aims. For example, we can cite the projects on human memory modelisation (in collaboration with the *Programa de Investigaciones en Fundamentos de la Educación a Distancia*, PROIFED, UNED) and an adaptation of computational learning methods to a parallel and distributed processing platform. CENAT has contacts with several organizations at international level. CENAT is a state inter-university research institution on super computation.

[10]In Spanish *Studies on Hispanic-Costarican Lexicography*.

[11]Site: http://www.lexicografia.ucr.ac.cr. Visited: 02/15/2010.

[12]Technology and text production.

[13]Language Technology Laboratory (Site: http://www.latl.unige.ch). Visited: 02/10/2010.

[14]Site: http://www.linguistica.ucr.ac.cr/. Visited: 02/15/2010.

[15]National Center of High Technology.

## 4 Commercial application of Language Technologies

We are aware of postgraduate students working in related areas in another countries, but we do not have details about their plans for the future. Nevertheless, national industry has not waited to have graduated specialists in order to start the commercialization of NLP related software. For example, Wordmagic Software[16] developed symbolic machine translation software Spanish–English and Tecapro presented an orthographic correction software[17]. Because of secrecy in the industry, it is difficult to know how many companies appeal to NLP technologies. Enterprise are also make themselves present in the field by scientific grants, in 2007 Juan Rodríguez won a prize proposing a glove allowing translation between sign language and Natural Langue.[18]

## 5 Research interests and collaboration issues

Presently, the idea is that Computational Linguistics would play a role, at different levels, in Lexicography and Spanish as a second language (L2). This leads to the creation of parsing systems and large corpora, where collaboration is desired. Another interesting area for CL is dialectology, where the tradition, as in Lexicography, of large collaborative initiatives exists. The new NLP laboratory will have workstations exclusively dedicated to research and the creation and storage of large copora as an intensive international initiative could be possible.

The signing of specific collaborative agreements between academic institutions is the preferred way to accomplish international research projects. This facilitates the approval of fundings.

## 6 Conclusions

In Costa Rica, CL is finding its path. At this moment it is mainly an academic interest, but, as we saw, there already are industrial products, where, eventualy, graduated students could find professional employment.

In the University of Costa Rica, where CL is rapidly growing up, collaborative initiatives are possible in a specifc and well defined frame. Additionally, many students are coming to CL, with the new academic offer. And this tendecy can increase in the next years.

In this moment, there is no CL community in Costa Rica. Before we are able to build it, we need to create a solid ground where a CL community could firmly stand up. This is starting to happen at the University of Costa Rica, where individual initiatives begin to gather around the recent course on CL taught by Prof. Jorge Antonio Leoni de León. We hope this movement will continue with the next opening of the NLP Laboratory at the *School of Philology, Linguistics and Literature* in the University of Costa Rica. This laboratory will fill the lack of equipment to make research on CL. Nevertheless, the need of a permanent research group will be there. This is an understandable situation in the sense that CL is a very new branch in the University and especially in *liberal arts*. This allows us to think that students will incorporate to CL studies and projects once the equipment and the offer on courses will be normal. It is expected that this year (2010), *School of Philology, Linguistics and Literature* will have a full time professor on CL, who will dedicate at least $\frac{1}{4}$ of his time to research.

## Acknowledgments

Thanks to *Vicerrectoría de Investigación* (http://vra.ucr.ac.cr/vra.nsf), the *Instituto de Investigaciones Lingüísticas* (INIL) and the *Escuela de Filología, Lingüística y Literatura*, for their continued support in the structured research and teaching on Computational Linguistics.

## References

C. Araya 1992. "Representación de conocimiento con una lógica modal". Tiempo Compartido 3(5):21-24.

Amparo Morales. 1986. Léxico básico del español de Puerto Rico. Academia Puertorriqueña de la Lengua Española.

[16]Site: http://www.wordmagicsoft.com. Visited: 02/15/2010.

[17]Sites: http://www.tecapro.com/ContentTeQuita.html and http://www.tecapro.com/TecApro_Historia.pdf. Visited: 02/15/2010.

[18]Read in http://www.intel.com/CostaRica/prensa/Mayo23_07.htm and http://www.nacion.com/ln_ee/2007/mayo/18/ultima-sr1101870.html. Visited: 03/28/2010.

Allan Berrocal Rojas. 2009. Automatización parcial de la revisión de aspectos de precisión, no-ambigüedad y verificabilidad en requerimientos de software escritos en lenguaje natural. Tesis de Maestría. Programa de postrado en Computación e Informática, Universidad de Costa Rica.

Allan Cedeño Baltodano 2009. Comparación del rendimiento de las aplicaciones Toscanaj y Concept Explorer para la construcción de retículas de conceptos. Tesis de Maestría. Programa de postrado en Computación e Informática, Universidad de Costa Rica.

Constanza Enciso Bahler. 2008. "Diccionario Maya–Español" Escuela de Filología, Lingüística y Literatura. Trabajo presentado en el curso FL–1036 Tecnología y Producción Textual. Universidad de Costa Rica.

J. Helo and C. Sell 1995. "Reconocimiento de dígitos mediante redes neurales y lógica difusa". Tecnología en Marcha 12, número especial sobre lógica difusa.

Marielos Murillo Rojas and Víctor Manuel Sánchez Corrales. 1993. Campos semáticos y disponibilidad léxica en preescolares. Revista de Educación. Number 2. Volume 17. Pages 15–25.

Orietta Fuentes Vargas. 2008. Propuesta de formato electrónico del Diccionario Biográfico de Escritores Costarricenses. Trabajo presentado en el curso FL–1036 Tecnología y Producción Textual". Escuela de Filología, Lingüística y Literatura. Universidad de Costa Rica.

Sergio Arroyo Molina. 2008. "Diccionario de Topónimos". Trabajo presentado en el curso FL–1036 Tecnología y Producción Textual". Escuela de Filología, Lingüística y Literatura. Universidad de Costa Rica.

Soumitra Dutta and Irene Mia (Eds.). 2010. *The Global Information Technology Report 2009–2010: ICT for Sustainability*. INSEAD / World Economic Forum. Retrieved March 27, 2010 from http://www.networkedreadiness.com/gitr/main/fullreport/index.html.

Celso, Vargas 1991. "Conexionismo: una alternativa en inteligencia artificial". Mundo de la computación. Vol. 5, No. 28.

Celso, Vargas 1992. "La utilización de formalismos basados en unificación para el análisis de las lenguas naturales". Revista de filología y lingüística de la Universidad de Costa Rica. Vol.18, No.2., p. 71-83.

# Fostering Digital Inclusion and Accessibility: The PorSimples project for Simplification of Portuguese Texts

**Sandra Maria Aluísio and Caroline Gasperin**
Department of Computer Sciences, University of São Paulo
Av. Trabalhador São-Carlense, 400. 13560-970 - São Carlos/SP, Brazil
{sandra,cgasperin}@icmc.usp.br

## Abstract

In this paper we present the PorSimples project, whose aim is to develop text adaptations tools for Brazilian Portuguese. The tools developed cater for both people at poor literacy levels and authors that want to produce texts for this audience. Here we describe the tools and resources developed over two years of this project and point directions for future work and collaboration. Since Portuguese and Spanish have many aspects in common, we believe our main point for collaboration lies in transferring our knowledge and experience to researches willing to developed simplification and elaboration tools for Spanish.

## 1 Introduction

In Brazil, according to the index used to measure the literacy level of the population (INAF - National Indicator of Functional Literacy) (INAF, 2007), only 28% of the population is classified as literate at the advanced level, while 65% of the population face difficulties in activities involving reading and comprehension depending on text length and complexity; therefore, their access to textual media is limited. The latter ones belong to the so-called *rudimentary* and *basic* literacy levels. These people are only able to find explicit information in short texts (rudimentary level) and also process slightly longer texts and make simple inferences (basic level).

The production of texts with different lengths and complexities can be addressed by the task of Text Adaptation (TA), a very well known practice in educational settings. Young (1999) and Burstein (2009) mention two different techniques for TA: *Text Simplification* and *Text Elaboration*.

The first can be defined as any task that reduces the lexical or syntactic complexity of a text, while trying to preserve meaning and information. Text Simplification can be subdivided into Syntactic Simplification, Lexical Simplification, Automatic Summarization, and other techniques.

As to Text Elaboration, it aims at clarifying and explaining information and making connections explicit in a text, for example, providing short definitions or synonyms for words known to only a few speakers of a language.

The PorSimples project[1] (Simplification of Portuguese Text for Digital Inclusion and Accessibility) (Aluisio et al, 2008a) started in November 2007 and will finish in April 2010. It aims at developing technologies to make access to information easier for low-literacy individuals, and possibly for people with other kinds of reading disabilities, by means of Automatic Summarization, Lexical Simplification, Syntactic Simplification, and Text Elaboration. More specifically, the goal is to help these readers to process documents available on the web. Additionally, it could help children learning to read texts of different genres, adults being alphabetized, hearing-impaired people who communicate to each other using sign languages and people undertaking Distance Education, in which text intelligibility is of great importance.

The focus is on texts published in government sites or by relevant news agencies, both of impor-

[1] http://caravelas.icmc.usp.br/wiki/index.php/Principal



*Proceedings of the NAACL HLT 2010 Young Investigators Workshop on Computational Approaches to Languages of the Americas*, pages 46–53, Los Angeles, California, June 2010. 

tance to a large audience with various literacy levels. The language of the texts is Brazilian Portuguese, for which there are no text simplification systems to the best of our knowledge.

In the project we have developed resources in Portuguese for research on text simplification, text simplification technology for Portuguese, and currently we are developing and adapting resources and technologies for text elaboration. We have also built applications that make the developed technology available to the public. In the Sections 2 to 4 we describe all these outcomes of the project.

We intend to foster a new interdisciplinary research area to study written text comprehension problems via the research on readability assessment, text simplification and elaboration once PorSimples ends. In Section 5 we describe future work, and in Section 6 we outline potential points for collaboration with researchers from Brazil and the rest of the Americas.

## 2 Resources

In order to understand the task of text simplification in Portuguese and to build training and evaluation data for the systems developed in the project, we have created a set of resources that formed the basis of PorSimples. Moreover, we are currently working on building resources for text elaboration. Below we describe these resources.

### 2.1 Manual for Syntactic Simplification in Portuguese

We have created a Manual for Syntactic Simplification for Portuguese (Specia et al., 2008). This manual recommends how particular syntactic phenomena should be simplified. It is based on a careful study of the Brazilian Portuguese grammar, of simplification systems developed for English (for example, (Siddharthan, 2003)), and on the Plain Language initiative[2] (Aluisio et al., 2008b).

The manual was the basis for the development of our rule-based system for syntactic simplification described in Section 3.2.

### 2.2 Corpora of Simple and Simplified Texts

We have built 9 corpora within 2 different genres (general news and popular science articles). Our first corpus is composed of general news articles from the Brazilian newspaper Zero Hora (ZH original). We had these articles manually simplified by a linguist, specialized in text simplification, according to the two levels of simplification proposed in PorSimples, natural (ZH natural) and strong (ZH strong). The Zero Hora newspaper also provides along its articles a simple version of them targeting children from 7 to 11 years old; this section is called *Para seu Filho Ler* (ZH PFSL) and our corpus from this section contains simple articles corresponding to the articles in the ZH original corpus plus additional ones.

Popular science articles compose our next set of corpora. We compiled a corpus of these articles from the *Caderno Ciência* issue of the Brazilian newspaper Folha de São Paulo, a leading newspaper in Brazil (CC original). We also had this corpus manually simplified according to the natural (CC natural) and strong (CC strong) levels. We also collected texts from a popular science magazine called *Ciência Hoje* (CH) and from its version aimed at children from 12-15, called *Ciência Hoje Crianca* (CHC). Table 1 shows a few statistics from these corpora.

### 2.3 Dictionary of Simple Words

While for English some lexical resources that help to identify difficult words using psycholinguistic measures are available, such as the MRC Psycholinguistic Database[3], no such resources exist for Portuguese. In PorSimples, we have compiled a dictionary of simple words composed by words that are common to youngsters (from Biderman (2005)), a list of frequent words from news texts for children and nationwide newspapers and a list of concrete words (from Janczura et. al (2007)).

| Corpus | Art. | Sent. | Words | Avg. words per text (std. deviation) | Avg. words p. sentence |
|---|---|---|---|---|---|
| ZH original | 104 | 2184 | 46190 | 444.1 (133.7) | 21.1 |
| ZH natural | 104 | 3234 | 47296 | 454.7 (134.2) | 14.6 |
| ZH strong | 104 | 3668 | 47938 | 460.9 (137.5) | 13.0 |
| ZH PSFL | 166 | 1224 | 22148 | 133.4 (48.6) | 18.0 |
| CC original | 50 | 882 | 20263 | 405.2 (175.6) | 22.9 |
| CC natural | 50 | 975 | 19603 | 392.0 (176.0) | 20.1 |
| CC strong | 50 | 1454 | 20518 | 410.3 (169.6) | 14.1 |
| CH | 130 | 3624 | 95866 | 737.4 (226.1) | 26.4 |
| CHC | 127 | 3282 | 65124 | 512.7 (185.3) | 19.8 |

Table 1. Corpus statistics.

[2] http://www.plainlanguage.gov/

[3] http://www.psych.rl.ac.uk/

This dictionary is being used in applications described in Section 4, such as SIMPLIFICA and the Simplification Annotation Editor.

## 3 Simplification & Elaboration technology

### 3.1 Lexical Simplification

Lexical simplification consists on replacing complex words by simpler words.

The first step of lexical simplification consists of tokenizing the original text and selecting the words that are considered complex. In order to judge a word as complex or not, we use the dictionaries of simple words described in Section 2.3.

The lexical simplification system also uses the Unitex-PB dictionary[4] for finding the lemma of the words in the text, so that it is possible to look for it in the simple words dictionaries. The problem of looking for a lemma directly in a dictionary is that there are ambiguous words and we are not able to deal with different word senses. For dealing with part-of-speech (POS) ambiguity, we use the MXPOST POS tagger[5] trained over NILC tagset[6].

Among the words that were selected as complex, the ones that are not proper nouns, prepositions and numerals are processed: their POS tags are used to look for their lemmas in the dictionaries. As the tagger has not a 100% precision and some words may not be in the dictionary, we look for the lemma only (without the tag) when we are not able to find the lemma-tag combination in the dictionary. Still, if we are not able to find the word, the lexical simplification module assumes that the word is complex and marks it for simplification.

The last step of the process consists in providing simpler synonyms for the complex words. For this task, we use the thesauri for Portuguese TeP 2.0[7] and the lexical ontology for Portuguese PAPEL[8]. This task is carried out when the user clicks on a marked word, which triggers a search in the thesauri for synonyms that are also present in the common words dictionary. If simpler words are found, they are sorted from the simpler to the more complex. To determine this order, we used Google API to search each word in the web: we assume that the higher a word frequency, the simpler it is. Automatic word sense disambiguation is left for future work. In PorSimples, we aim to use Textual Entailment (Dagan et al., 2005) as a method for gathering resources for lexical simplification.

### 3.2 Syntactic Simplification

Syntactic simplification is accomplished by a rule-based system, which comprises seven operations that are applied sentence-by-sentence to a text in order to make its syntactic structure simpler.

Our rule-based text simplification system is based on the manual for Brazilian Portuguese syntactic simplification described in Section 2.1. According to this manual, simplification operations should be applied when any of the 22 linguistic phenomena covered by our system (see Candido et al. (2009) for details) is detected. Our system treats appositive, relative, coordinate and subordinate clauses, which have already been addressed by previous work on text simplification (Siddharthan, 2003). Additionally, we treat passive voice, sentences in an order other than Subject-Verb-Object (SVO), and long adverbial phrases. The simplification operations to treat these phenomena are: split sentence, change particular discourse markers by simpler ones, change passive to active voice, invert the order of clauses, convert to subject-verb-object ordering, and move long adverbial phrases.

Each sentence is parsed in order to identify syntactic phenomena for simplification and to segment the sentence into portions that will be handled by the operations. We use the parser PALAVRAS (Bick, 2000) for Portuguese. Gasperin et al. (2010) present the evaluation of the performance of our syntactic simplification system.

Since our syntactic simplifications are conservative, the simplified texts become longer than the original due to sentence splitting. We acknowledge that low-literacy readers prefer short texts; this is why we use summarization before applying simplification in FACILITA (see (Watanabe et al., 2009)). In the future we aim to provide summarization also within SIMPLIFICA. These two applications are described in Section 4.

### 3.3 Natural and Strong Simplification

To attend the needs of people with different levels of literacy, PorSimples propose two types of sim-

[4] http://www.nilc.icmc.usp.br/nilc/projects/unitex-pb/web/dicionarios.html
[5] http://sites.google.com/site/adwaitratnaparkhi/home
[6] www.nilc.icmc.usp.br/nilc/TagSet/ManualEtiquetagem.htm
[7] http://www.nilc.icmc.usp.br/tep2/
[8] http://www.linguateca.pt/PAPEL/

plification: natural and strong. The first is aimed at people with a basic literacy level and the second, rudimentary level. The difference between these two is the degree of application of simplification operations to the sentences. For strong simplification we apply the syntactic simplification process to all complex phenomena found in the sentence in order to make the sentence as simple as possible, while for natural simplification the simplification operations are applied only when the resulting text remains "natural", considering the overall complexity of the sentence. This naturalness is based on a group of factors which are difficult to define using hand-crafted rules, and we intend to learn them from examples of natural simplifications.

We developed a corpus-based approach for selecting sentences that require simplification. Based on parallel corpora of original and natural simplified texts (ZH original, ZH natural, CC original, CC natural), we apply a binary classifier to decide in which circumstances a sentence should be split or not so that the resulting simplified text is natural and not over simplified. Sentence splitting is the most important and most frequent syntactic simplification operation, and it can be seen as a key distinctive feature between natural and strong simplification. We described this system in detail in (Gasperin et al., 2009).

Our feature set contains 209 features, including superficial, morphological, syntactic and discourse-related features. We did several feature selection experiments to determine the optimal set of features. As classification algorithm we use Weka's[9] SMO implementation of Support Vector Machines (SVM). The ZH corpus contains 728 examples of the splitting operation and 1328 examples of non-split sentences, and the CC corpus contains 59 positive and 510 negatives examples. The classifier's average performance scores (optimal feature set, both corpora as training data, and cross-validation) are 80.5% precision and 80.7% recall.

### 3.4 Readability Assessment

We developed a readability assessment system that can predict the complexity level of a text, which corresponds to the literacy level expected from the target reader: *rudimentary, basic* or *advanced.*

We have adopted a machine-learning classifier to identify the level of the input text; we use the Support Vector Machines implementation from Weka toolkit (SMO). We have used 7 of our corpora presented in Section 2.2 (all but the ones with texts written for children) to train the classifier.

Our feature set is composed by cognitively-motivated features derived from the Coh-Metrix-PORT tool[10], which is an adaptation for Brazilian Portuguese of Coh-Metrix 2.0 (free version of Coh-Metrix (Graesser et al, 2004)) also developed in the context of the PorSimples project. Coh-Metrix-PORT implements the metrics in Table 2.

We also included seven new metrics to Coh-Metrix-PORT: average verb, noun, adjective and adverb ambiguity, incidence of high-level constituents, content words and functional words.

| **Categories** | Subcategories | Metrics |
|---|---|---|
| **Shallow Readability metric** | - | Flesch Reading Ease index for Portuguese. |
| **Words and textual information** | Basic counts | Number of words, sentences, paragraphs, words per sentence, sentences per paragraph, syllables per word, incidence of verbs, nouns, adjectives and adverbs. |
| | Frequencies | Raw frequencies of content words and minimum frequency of content words. |
| | Hyperonymy | Average number of hypernyms of verbs. |
| **Syntactic information** | Constituents | Incidence of nominal phrases, modifiers per noun phrase and words preceding main verbs. |
| | Pronouns, Types and Tokens | Incidence of personal pronouns, number of pronouns per noun phrase, types and tokens. |
| | Connectives | Number of connectives, number of positive and negative additive connectives, causal / temporal / logical positive and negative connectives. |
| **Logical operators** | - | Incidence of the particles "e" (and), "ou" (or), "se" (if), incidence of negation and logical operators. |

Table 2. Metrics of Coh-Metrix-PORT.

We measured the performance of the classifier on identifying the levels of the input texts by a

[9] http://www.cs.waikato.ac.nz/ml/weka/

[10] http://caravelas.icmc.usp.br:3000/

cross-validation experiment. We trained the classifier on our 7 corpora and reached 90% F-measure on identifying texts at advanced level, 48% at basic level, and 73% at rudimentary level.

### 3.5 Semantic Role Labeling: Understanding Sense Relations between Verb and Arguments

To attend the goal of eliciting sense relations between verbs and their arguments through the exhibition of question words such as *who, what, which, when, where, why, how, how much, how many, how long, how often* and *what for*, we are specifying a new annotation task that assigns these wh-question labels to verbal arguments in a corpus of simplified texts in Portuguese. The aim is to provide a training corpus for machine learning, aiming at automatic assignment of wh-questions (Duran et al., 2010a; Duran et al., 2010b).

The annotation task involves recognizing segments that constitute answers to questions made to the verbs. Each segment should suitably answer the wh-question label. For example, in the sentence "João acordou às 6 horas da manhã." (John woke up at 6 in the morning.), two questions come up naturally in relation to the verb "acordar" (wake up): 1) *Who woke up?* and 2) *When?*.

Linking the verb and its arguments through wh-questions is a process that requires text understanding. This is a skill that the target audience of this project is weak at. In Figure 1 we show the link between the verb and its arguments (which can be subject, direct object, indirect object, time or location adverbial phrases, and also named entities).

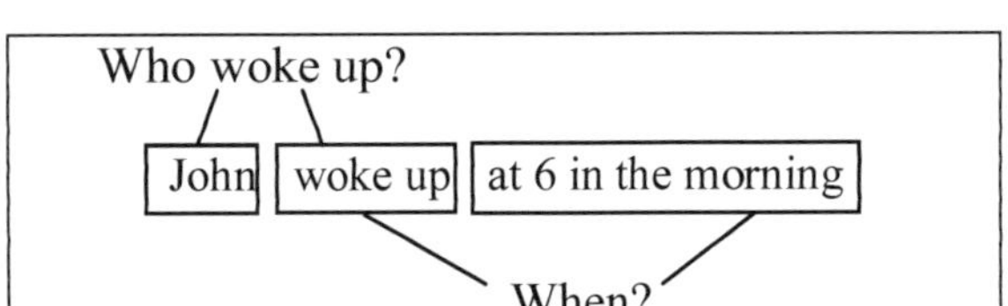

Figure 1. Assigning wh-question labels to arguments.

The corpus chosen for this work consists of the strong simplified version of 154 texts extracted from general news and popular science articles (ZH strong and CC strong) which were described in Section 2.2.

Results of such a semantic layer of annotation may be used, in addition, to identify adjunct semantic roles and multi-word expressions with specific adverbial syntactic roles. This training corpus, as well as the automatic labeling tool, an "answer-questioning" system, will be made publicly available at PorSimples site. Besides helping poor-literacy readers, the assignment of wh-questions will be used in the near future to map adjunct semantic roles (ArgMs of Propbank (Palmer et al., 2005)) in a project to build the PropBank.Br for Portuguese language. One may also take profit of this automatic tool and its training corpus to improve its opposite, question-answering systems.

## 4 Applications

The text simplification and elaboration technologies developed in the context of the project are available by means of three systems aimed to distinct users:

- An authoring system, called SIMPLIFICA[11], to help authors to produce simplified texts targeting people with low literacy levels,
- An assistive technology system, called FACILITA[12], which explores the tasks of summarization and simplification to allow poor literate people to read Web content, and
- A web content adaptation tool, named Educational FACILITA, for assisting low-literacy readers to perform detailed reading. It exhibits questions that clarify the semantic relations linking verbs to their arguments, highlighting the associations amongst the main ideas of the texts, named entities, and perform lexical elaboration.

In the following subsections we detail these and other systems developed in the project.

### 4.1 SIMPLIFICA Authoring Tool

SIMLIFICA is a web-based WYSIWYG editor, based on TinyMCE web editor[13]. The user inputs a text in the editor and customizes the simplification settings, where he/she can choose: (i) strong simplification, where all the complex syntactic phenomena (see details in Section 3.2) are treated for each sentence, or customized simplification, where the user chooses one or more syntactic simplification phenomena to be treated for each sentence, and (ii) one or more thesauri to be used in the syntactic and lexical simplification processes. Then

[11] http://www.nilc.icmc.usp.br/porsimples/simplifica/
[12] http://vinho.intermidia.icmc.usp.br:3001/facilita/
[13] http://tinymce.moxiecode.com/

the user activates the readability assessment module to predict the complexity level of a text. This module maps the text to one of the three levels of literacy defined by INAF: *rudimentary, basic* or *advanced.* According to the resulting readability level the user can trigger the lexical and/or syntactic simplifications modules, revise the automatic simplification and restart the cycle by checking the readability level of the current version of the text.

### 4.2 FACILITA

FACILITA is a browser plug-in that aims to facilitate the reading of online content by poor literate people. It includes separate modules for text summarization and text simplification. The user can select a text on any website and call FACILITA to summarize and simplify this text. The system is described in details in Watanabe et al. (2009).

The text summarization module aims to extract only the most important information from a text. It relies on the EPC-P technique (extraction of keywords per pattern), which checks the presence of keywords in the sentences: sentences that contain keywords are retained for the final summary. The summarization system is reported in Margarido et al. (2008).

The text simplification module follows the syntactic simplification framework described in Section 3.2. We have chosen to run the summarization process first and then proceed to the simplification of the summarized text since simplification increases text length.

### 4.3 Educational FACILITA

Educational FACILITA[14] is a Web application aimed at assisting users in understanding textual content available on the Web. Currently, it explores the NLP tasks of lexical elaboration and named entity labeling to assist poor literacy readers having access to web content. It is described in Watanabe et al. (2010).

Lexical Elaboration consists of mechanisms that present users with synonymous or short definitions for words, which are classified as unusual or difficult to be understood by the users. This process relies on the framework developed for lexical simplification described in Section 3.1.

[14] http://vinho.intermidia.icmc.usp.br/watinha/Educational-Facilita/

Named-entity labeling consists of displaying additional and complementary semantic and descriptive information about named entities that are contained on the Web sites text. The descriptions are extracted from Wikipedia.

It is expected that these additional information presented in the text by the proposed approach would help users better understand websites' textual content and allow users to learn the meaning of new or unusual words/expressions.

### 4.4 Simplification Annotation Editor

This editor[15] was created to support the manual simplification of texts for the creation of our corpus of simplified texts. It records and labels all the operations made by the annotator and encode texts using a new XCES[16]-based schema for linking the original-simplified information. XCES has been used in projects involving both only one language, e.g. American National Corpus (ANC)[17] (English) and PLN-BR[18] (Brazilian Portuguese); and multiple languages as parallel data, e.g.: CroCo[19] (English-German). However, to our knowledge, PorSimples is the first project to use XCES to encode original-simplified parallel texts and also the simplification operations. Two annotation layers have been added to the traditional stand-off annotation layers in order to store the information related to simplification (Caseli et al., 2009).

### 4.5 Portal of Parallel Corpora

The portal[20] allows for online querying and download of our corpora of simplified texts. The queries can include information about syntactic constructions, simplification operations, etc.

## 5 Future Work

Our main area for future work lies on the evaluation of the simplified texts resulting from our systems with the end user, that is, people at low literacy levels. We are carrying out a large-scale study with readers who fit in the rudimentary and basic literacy levels to verify whether syntactic and lexi-

[15] http://caravelas.icmc.usp.br/anotador
[16] http://www.w3.org/XML/
[17] http://americannationalcorpus.org
[18] http://www.nilc.icmc.usp.br/plnbr
[19] http://fr46.uni-saarland.de/croco/index_en.html
[20] http://caravelas.icmc.usp.br/portal/index.php

cal simplification indeed contribute to the understanding of Portuguese texts. We are applying reading comprehension tests with original texts (control group) and manually simplified texts at strong level. However we still need to assess the impact of automatic lexical and syntactic simplification and text elaboration on the understanding of a text by the target user of our applications.

We also intend to investigate how to balance simplification/elaboration and text length. We have shown that in our syntactic simplification approach it is usual to divide long sentences, which reduce sentence length but increase text length due to the repetition of the subject in the new sentences. On the other hand, in summarization-based Text Simplification, such as FACILITA's approach, text length is reduced, but relevant information can be lost, which may hinder text comprehensibility. Text Elaboration enhances text comprehensibility, but it always increases text length, since it inserts information and repetition to reinforce understanding and make explicit the connections between the parts of a text. Therefore, since we cannot achieve all the requisites at once there is a need to evaluate each aspect of our systems with the target users.

We also intend to improve the performance of our syntactic simplification approach by experimenting with different Portuguese syntactic parsers. Moreover, several methods of text elaboration are still under development and will be implemented and evaluated in this current year.

As future research, we aim to explore the impact of simplification on text entailment recognition systems. We believe simplification can facilitate the alignment of entailment pairs. In the opposite direction, text entailment or paraphrase identification may help us find word pairs for enriching the lexical resources used for lexical simplification.

## 6 Opportunities for Collaboration

Enhancing the accessibility of Portuguese and Spanish Web texts is of foremost importance to improve insertion of Latin America (LA) into the information society and to preserve the diverse cultures in LA. We believe several countries in LA present similar statistics to Brazil in relation to the number of people at low literacy levels. We see our experience in developing text simplification and elaboration tools for Portuguese as the major contribution that we can offer to other research groups in LA. We are interested in actively taking part in joint research projects that aim to create text simplification and elaboration tools for Spanish.

Since all resources that we have developed are language-dependent, they cannot be used directly for Spanish, but we foresee that due to similarities between Portuguese and Spanish a straightforward adaptation of solutions at the lexical and syntactical levels can be achieved with reasonable effort. We are willing to share the lessons learned during the PorSimples project and offer our expertise on selecting and creating the appropriate resources (e.g. corpora, dictionaries) and technology for text simplification and elaboration in order to create similar ones for Spanish.

The advances in text simplification and elaboration methods strongly depend on the availability of annotated corpora for several tasks: text simplification, text entailment, semantic role labeling, to name only a few. English has the major number of data resources in Natural Language Processing (NLP); Portuguese and Spanish are low-density languages. To solve this problem, we believe that there is a need for: (i) the development of a new area recently coined as Annotation Science; (ii) a centralized resource center to create, collect and distribute linguistic resources in LA.

We would appreciate collaboration with researchers in the USA in relation to readability assessment measures, such as those of Coh-Metrix (see Section 3.4), whose researchers already developed up to 500 measures. Only 60 of them are open to public access. Besides, the know-how needed to develop a proposition bank of Portuguese would be welcome since this involves lexical resources, such as a Verbnet[21], which do not exist for Portuguese. Other lexical resources such as the MRC Psycholinguistic Database, which help to identify difficult words using psycholinguistic measures, are also urgent for Portuguese since we have sparse projects dealing with several aspects of this database but no common project to unite them.

Brazilian research funding agencies, mainly CAPES[22], CNPq[23] and FAPESP[24], often release calls for projects with international collaboration; these could be a path to start the collaborative research suggested above.

[21] http://verbs.colorado.edu/~mpalmer/projects/verbnet.html
[22] http://www.capes.gov.br/
[23] http://www.cnpq.br/
[24] http://www.fapesp.br/

## Acknowledgments

We thank FAPESP and Microsoft Research for supporting the PorSimples project.

## References

Sandra Aluísio, Lucia Specia, Thiago Pardo, Erick Maziero and Renata Fortes. 2008a. Towards Brazilian Portuguese Automatic Text Simplification Systems. In: *Proceedings of The Eight ACM Symposium on Document Engineering (DocEng 2008)*, 240-248, São Paulo, Brazil.

Sandra Aluísio, Lucia Specia, Thiago Pardo, Erick Maziero, Helena de M. Caseli, Renata Fortes. 2008b. A Corpus Analysis of Simple Account Texts and the Proposal of Simplification Strategies: First Steps towards Text Simplification Systems In: *Proceedings of The 26th ACM Symposium on Design of Communication (SIGDOC 2008),* pp. 15-22.

Eckhard Bick. 2000. The Parsing System "Palavras": Automatic Grammatical Analysis of Portuguese in a Constraint Grammar Framework. PhD Thesis. Aarhus University.

Maria Teresa Biderman. 2005. DICIONÁRIO ILUSTRADO DE PORTUGUÊS. São Paulo, Editora Ática. 1ª. ed. São Paulo: Ática. (2005)

Jill Burstein. 2009. Opportunities for Natural Language Processing Research in Education. In the *Proceedings of CICLing*, 6-27.

Arnaldo Candido Junior, Erick Maziero, Caroline Gasperin, Thiago Pardo, Lucia Specia and Sandra M. Aluisio. 2009. Supporting the Adaptation of Texts for Poor Literacy Readers: a Text Simplification Editor for Brazilian Portuguese. In the *Proceedings of the NAACL HLT Workshop on Innovative Use of NLP for Building Educational Applications*, pages 34–42, Boulder, Colorado, June 2009.

Helena Caseli, Tiago Pereira, Lucia Specia, Thiago Pardo, Caroline Gasperin and Sandra Aluísio. 2009. Building a Brazilian Portuguese parallel corpus of original and simplified texts. In Alexander Gelbukh (ed), *Advances in Computational Linguistics, Research in Computer Science*, vol 41, pp. 59-70. 10th Conference on Intelligent Text Processing and Computational Linguistics (CICLing-2009).

Ido Dagan, Oren Glickman and Bernado Magnini. 2005. The PASCAL Recognising Textual Entailment Challenge. In: *Proceedings of The First PASCAL Recognising Textual Entailment Challenge* (RTE 1), [S.l.]: Springer, 2005. p. 1–8.

Magali Duran, Marcelo Amâncio and Sandra Aluísio. 2010a. Assigning wh-questions to verbal arguments in a corpus of simplified texts. Accepted for publication at *Propor* 2010 (http://www.inf.pucrs.br/~propor2010).

Magali Duran, Marcelo Amâncio and Sandra Aluísio. 2010b. Assigning Wh-Questions to Verbal Arguments: Annotation Tools Evaluation and Corpus Building. Accepted for publication in LREC 2010.

Caroline Gasperin, Lucia Specia, Tiago Pereira and Sandra Aluísio. 2009. Learning When to Simplify Sentences for Natural Text Simplification. In: *Proceedings of ENIA* 2009, 809-818.

Caroline Gasperin, Erick Masiero and Sandra M. Aluisio. 2010. Challenging choices for text simplification. Accepted for publication at *Propor* 2010 (http://www.inf.pucrs.br/~propor2010).

Arthur Graesser, Danielle McNamara, Max Louwerse and Zhiqiang Cai. 2004. Coh-Metrix: Analysis of text on cohesion and language. In: *Behavioral Research Methods, Instruments, and Computers*, 36, páginas 193-202.

INAF. 2007. Indicador de Alfabetismo Funcional INAF/Brasil - 2007. Available at http://www.acaoeducativa.org.br/portal/images/stories/pdfs/inaf2007.pdf

Gerson A Janczura, Goiara M Castilho, Nelson O Rocha, Terezinha de Jesus C. van Erven and Tin Po Huang. 2007. Normas de concretude para 909 palavras da língua portuguesa. *Psicologia: Teoria e Pesquisa* Abr-Jun 2007, Vol. 23 n. 2, pp. 195-204.

Martha Palmer, Daniel Gildea and Paul Kingsbury. 2005. The Proposition Bank: A Corpus Annotated with Semantic Roles, *Computational Linguistics Journal*, 31:1.

Advaith Siddharthan. 2003. Syntactic Simplification and Text Cohesion. PhD Thesis. University of Cambridge.

Lucia Specia, Sandra Aluisio and Tiago Pardo. 2008. Manual de Simplificação Sintática para o Português. Technical Report NILC-TR-08-06, 27 p. Junho 2008, São Carlos-SP.

Willian Watanabe, Arnaldo Candido Junior, Vinícius Uzêda, Renata Fortes, Tiago Pardo and Sandra Aluísio. 2009. Facilita: reading assistance for low-literacy readers. In: *Proceedings of the 27th ACM International Conference on Design of Communication. SIGDOC '09*. ACM, New York, NY, 29-36.

Willian Watanabe, Arnaldo Candido Junior, Marcelo Amancio, Matheus de Oliveira, Renata Fortes, Tiago Pardo, Renata Fortes, Sandra Aluísio. 2010. Adapting web content for low-literacy readers by using lexical elaboration and named entities labeling. Accepted for publication at W4A 2010 (http://www.w4a.info/).

Dolly J. Young. Linguistic simplification of SL reading material: effective instructional practice. *The Modern Language Journal*, 83(3):350–366, 1999.

# Opinion Identification in Spanish Texts

**Aiala Rosá**
Grupo de Procesamiento de Lenguaje Natural,
Facultad de Ingeniería, UDELAR
J. Herrera y Reissig 565
Montevideo, 11300, Uruguay
Modyco, UMR 7114,
Université Paris Ouest Nanterre La Défense,
CNRS France
200, avenue de la République, Batiment A,
Bureau 420, 92 001 Nanterre Cedex
aialar@fing.edu.uy

**Dina Wonsever**
Grupo de Procesamiento de Lenguaje Natural,
Facultad de Ingeniería, UDELAR
J. Herrera y Reissig 565
Montevideo, 11300, Uruguay
wonsever@fing.edu.uy

**Jean-Luc Minel**
Modyco, UMR 7114,
Université Paris Ouest Nanterre La Défense, CNRS France
200, avenue de la République, Batiment A,
Bureau 420, 92 001 Nanterre Cedex
jean-luc.minel@u-paris10.fr

## Abstract

We present our work on the identification of opinions and its components: the source, the topic and the message. We describe a rule-based system for which we achieved a recall of 74% and a precision of 94%. Experimentation with machine-learning techniques for the same task is currently underway.

## 1 Introduction

For some tasks in language processing such as Information Extraction or Q&A Systems, it is important to know the opinions expressed by different sources and their polarity, positive or negative, with respect to different topics. There are even commercial applications that provide this kind of service (http://www.jodange.com).

We here present a system for identifying opinions in Spanish texts. We define opinion as the report of someone's statement about any subject *( El investigador de la Politécnica afirma que el principal problema de este sistema es conseguir que sea fácil de usar / The researcher at the Politécnica asserts that the main problem with this system is making it easy to use)*, or as any mention of discourse participants' beliefs *(El PRI acepta participar en el debate / The PRI agrees to participate in the debate).*

As a first step, we study the impact of elements that typically introduce such expressions in written text. These elements are mainly verbs of communication *(decir, declarar / say, state)* but other verb classes (belief, agreement, appreciation) are also considered. In other cases, the opinions will be expressed through nouns *(opinión/opinion, declaración/statement)* or segments introduced by *según* (*according to*) or similar expressions. To complete the opinion, we identify its characteristic arguments: the source, the topic and the message.

In addition to recognizing an opinion, we try to determine its semantic orientation. To this end, we consider certain subjective elements and operators (reverse, intensifier, enhancing, neutralizing, etc.) which affect them. In this article, we present only results on the semantic orientation of opinion verbs, opinion nouns and topic introducers (*sobre/about, con respecto a/with respect to*, etc.).

There are many studies that address these issues: Pang and Lee (2008), for instance, discuss in



*Proceedings of the NAACL HLT 2010 Young Investigators Workshop on Computational Approaches to Languages of the Americas*, pages 54–61, Los Angeles, California, June 2010. ©2010 Association for Computational Linguistics

detail various concepts in the area of "Opinion Mining" or "Sentiment Analysis" and present the main proposals, resources and applications. For our work, which focuses on the identification of source, topic and message, we have mainly drawn on the following: the scheme for annotating opinions and emotions proposed by Wiebe, Wilson, and Cardie (2005); the work on opinion-holder (source) propositional opinion identification presented in (Bethard et al., 2004); a system for source identification using statistical methods (Choi et al, 2005); a method for opinion-holder and topic extraction from Kim and Hovy (2006); the study on the identification of source and target presented in (Ruppenhofer et al., 2008); and a work on topic annotation (Stoyanov and Cardie, 2008).

For our semantic orientation study, we have taken some concepts from Turney and Littman (2003) and analyzed some work on subjectivity operators (Polanyi and Zaenen, 2004; Moilanen and Pulman, 2007; Choi and Cardie, 2008).

In what follows, we briefly present the model that has been defined to represent opinions and two methods for their automatic recognition. First, we describe a rule-based system that incorporates lexical resources. This system, whose evaluation is detailed below, achieves a recall of 74% and a precision of 97%. During the evaluation process we produced an annotated corpus of 13,000 words, by manually correcting the system output. The second system, currently under development, involves the application of machine-learning techniques to the annotated corpus.

## 2 Opinion components

An opinion is composed of a predicative element and its characteristic arguments. The set of opinion predicates includes verbs, nouns and prepositions (or prepositional locutions). Verbs belong to various semantic classes: communication *(decir / say, declarar / state),* assessment *(criticar / criticize, felicitar / compliment),* belief (*creer / believe, opinar / think)* and acceptance *(aceptar / accept, rechazar / reject).*

These classes are similar to those proposed in (Asher et al., 2008), the main difference being that they include the class Sentiment but we do not. Nouns are generally derived from the aforementioned verbs (*opinión / opinion, declaración / statement, apoyo / support*). Some prepositions and prepositional locutions are *según, de acuerdo a, para / according to*.

The relevant arguments that we identified for the opinion predicates are, as already mentioned, source, topic and message. To establish this scheme we analysed syntactico-semantic schemes proposed in ADESSE[2] for selected verb classes (García-Miguel et al., 2005) and some of the Spanish FrameNet frames[3] (Subirats-Rüggeberg and Petruck., 2003), mainly the *opinion* frame whose frame elements include cognizer (source), topic and opinion (message) and the *communication* frame for which some elements are communicator (source), topic and message.

Our definition deviates from much of the literature on this subject because we limit our work to opinions introduced by an opinion predicate, as explained above, while many of the cited works identify all kinds of subjective expressions, mainly adjectives with positive or negative polarity, as with the *expressive subjective elements* described in (Wiebe et al., 2005).

As in our work we focus on finding the source, the message and the topic for each opinion, we ignore all the text fragments in which there is no evidence that the author is quoting or referring to other participants' opinions. These text fragments constitute the message, as defined above, stated by the text author. So, once our system has identified other participants' opinions, the remaining text should be attributed to the text author.

Identifying subjective elements is necessary in order to determine the semantic orientation of the opinion. We think the treatment of these elements within the author's message is similar to the treatment that must be applied within the message attributed to any other source. Such a treatment is not addressed in this work, since the semantic orientation study presented here is restricted to opinion predicates and topic introducers.

In some respects our work is related to that of (Bethard et al., 2004). For opinions introduced by opinion verbs, they identify the source (opinion holder) and the message (propositional opinion), restricting the study to messages that constitute subordinate clauses. However, we seek also to identify the explicit references to the topic and we consider not only verbs but also some nouns and prepositions such as *según / according to*. A further difference is that they distinguish propositions containing an opinion from those transmitting facts or predictions, whereas we do not make this distinction.

In our recognition of the topic we consider only explicit references to the opinion subject. We look for topic-introducing elements, such as *sobre / about, con respecto a / regarding, en contra de / against,* without trying to deduce the topic from the study of the message itself.

For this general scheme, there are different instances in which the arguments can take different forms. Thus, for some opinion verbs such as *rechazar / reject,* the message is usually empty. For other verbs the topic will be a noun phrase, such as *aceptar la propuesta / to accept the proposal,* while for others it will be a prepositional phrase, for example, *hablar de literatura / to speak about literature.*

### 2.1 Some opinion examples

In a standard reported speech utterance (1), the opinion predicate is a communication verb. The source is the subject of the verb and the message is contained in the subordinate clause. Normally, there is not a segment expressing the topic.

> (1) [El investigador de la Politécnica]f [afirma]p [que el principal problema de este sistema es conseguir que sea fácil de usar]m.
>
> (1) [The researcher at the Politécnica]f [said] p [that the main problem with this system is making it easy to use] m.

In (2), there is a verb that introduces referred speech in which a verbal act is mentioned, but the words uttered (message) are not reproduced (Maldonado, 1999).

> (2) [El abogado de Fernando Botero]$_s$ [habló]$_p$ [sobre el tema]$_t$ con Semana.
>
> (2) [The lawyer of Fernando Botero]$_s$ [spoke]$_p$ [about the subject]t with Semana.

However, we also found cases in which reported speech includes an explicit mention of the topic (3) and cases in which referred speech includes the uttered words (4). In both examples all the defined arguments are present in the text.

> (3) [Sobre la partitura]t [Ros Marbá]s [afirma]p [que es "enormemente teatral. Se define a los personajes desde la propia música, ...."]m.
> (3) [Concerning the score]t [Ros Marbá]s [said]p [it is "very theatrical. The characters are defined from the music itself, ....]m.
>
> (4) En una carta escrita por Dalí en Neuilly en abril de 1951, [el artista]s [habla]p [sobre su divina inspiración]t: ["Yo quería que ..."]m.
> (4) In a letter written by Dalí at Neuilly in April 1951, [the artist]s [talks]p [about his divine inspiration]t : ["I wanted to ..."]m.

As noted earlier, the opinion predicate can be a noun or a preposition such as *según / according to.* In (5), the source is the noun complement, introduced by *de / of.* In (6), the source is the noun phrase within the prepositional phrase headed by *según / according to.*

> (5) No tenemos por qué criticar las [declaraciones]p de [Elizardo Sánchez]s.
> (5) We need not criticize [Elizardo Sanchez']f [statements] p .
>
> (6) [Este sistema se utiliza en Estados Unidos desde 1982]m, [según]p [Roque Pifarré]f.
> (6) [This system has been used in the United States since 1982]m, [according to]p [Roque Pifarré]s.

Note that in (5) there is another opinion predicate, the verb *criticize,* occurring in a non-factive context. The factivity of events is not addressed in this work, but it can be expected to affect opinion recognition.

## 3 The rule-based system

We developed a rule-based system for the identification of the opinion elements. The system takes as input a pre-processed text using the POS-tagger Freeling (Atserias et al., 2006) and Clatex (Wonsever et al, 2006), a system that segments texts into propositions. Several rule modules are then applied, introducing XML annotations showing the identified opinions and their elements.

The following example illustrates the system output:

<opinion><menssage>Hasta el momento el virus H1N1 tiene una predominancia mayor que la de los demás virus en esos estudios</message>, <predicate>precisó</predicate><source>la ministra</source></opinion>.
<opinion><message>So far, the H1N1 virus has a higher prevalence than other viruses in these studies</message>, <predicate>said</predicate> <source>Minister</source></opinion>.

The rules are based on the contextual rules formalism defined by Wonsever and Minel (2004), including some further extensions. This type of rule allows the specification of contexts, exclusion zones, optionality, negation, and elimination of existing labels, among others. In addition, for each rule it is possible to check various conditions on its components, for example, membership in a list of words. For applying the rules we used a system implemented in Prolog.

The hand-written rules were derived from corpus analysis. They are grouped into modules according to the element they recognize: opinion predicate (verbs, nouns and prepositions), source, topic and message. There is also a final module that builds the entire opinion and some auxiliary modules: the complex noun phrase identifying module (*El director del Hospital Maciel, Daniel Parada / The director of the Hospital Maciel, Daniel Parada*) and the subjective elements and operators identifying module. Table 1 shows the number of rules contained in each module. In the next section we describe the source rules module.

| module | # rules |
|---|---|
| opinion predicate | 27 |
| source | 42 |
| topic | 22 |
| message | 8 |
| opinion | 37 |
| auxiliary | 7 |
| TOTAL | 143 |

Table 1: Number of rules in each module

### 3.1 Source rules

In order to show the rules features, we will describe the source module. Table 2 shows some (simplified) rules for source identification.

| | |
|---|---|
| fue1a | no(prep), <np>, (zone,3), verOp |
| fue1b | punt, verOp, (zone,3), <np> |
| fue1c | punt, verOp, (zone,3), prep, np, <np> |
| fue2 | verOpPart, "por", <np> |
| fue3a | nOp, "de", <np> |
| fue3b | <np>, verSup, op(det), nOp |
| fue3c | nOp, verSupPart, "por", <np> |
| fue4a | "según", op(verOp), <np> |
| fue4b | endS, "para", <np> |
| fue4c | "de acuerdo a", <np> |
| fue4d | "de acuerdo con", <np> |
| fue4e | "a juicio de", <np> |

Table 2 Simplified rules for source recognition. Notation used: np - nominal phrase; < > - element labeled by the rule; zone,x - exclusion zone up to x words; verOpFin - finite opinion verb; verOpPart - opinion verb, participle; nOp - opinion noun; verSup - support verb; endS - end of sentence; det - determiner; op - optionality operator

These rules assign the source tag to text segments that match the rule body (indicated by <> in the table). The elements that precede the body and those that follow it are the left and right contexts, respectively. In addition to assigning the tag, the rules assign values to some attributes:

- code of the rule that assigned the label
- syntactic structure (subject before verb / subject after verb / noun complement introduced by *de*)
- semantic orientation value (-, +, 0)

The three rules fue1 identify sources that are the subject of an opinion verb. We allow up to 3 words between the subject and the verb; these words cannot be verb, np, punctuation or conjunction (*<El senador> este martes dijo ... / <the senator> said Tuesday ...*). For rule fue1c we also allow a prepositional phrase (prep + np) between the source and the verb *(..., dijo ayer a la prensa <el senador> / ..., said yesterday to the reporters the senator).* As mentioned, we show simplified rules; the actual rules include other restrictions such as checking for subject-verb agreement.

Rule fue2 is applied when the opinion verb is in participle form and the source is an agent complement *(las palabras expresadas por el senador / the words uttered by the senator).*

The three rules fue3 concern noun phrases. The source is usually introduced by *de (las opiniones del senador / the senator's opinions)* but it is also common to find nouns in a support verb construction *(el senador emitió una declaración / the senator issued a statement).*

Finally, the five rules fue4 identify sources introduced by *según, para, de acuerdo a, de acuerdo con, a juicio de / according to.* When the source introducer is *según*, we can find an opinion verb between *según* and the source *(según el senador / según dijo el senador / according to the senator),* For the preposition *para / for*, preceding punctuation is required because of its high ambiguity.

### 3.2 Lexical Resources

Some of the rules, especially those for opinion predicate identification, rely heavily on lexical resources: lists of opinion verbs and nouns, person indicators *(señor, doctor, senador / Mr., Dr., senator),* institution indicators *(institución, hospital, diario / institution, hospital, journal),* support verbs *(plantear, emitir / make, deliver),* topic introducers *(sobre, con respecto a / about, with respect to),* positive subjective elements *(bueno, excelente, diversión / good, excellent, fun),* negative subjective elements *(malo, negativo, pesimista / bad, negative, pessimist),* and operators *(muy, extremadamente, a penas / very, extremely, just).*

In particular, the list of opinion verbs and nouns was manually created from corpora containing Spanish texts: Corin (Grassi et al., 2001), Corpus del Español (Davies, 2002) and a digital media corpus created for this study. Only those verbs and nouns that are frequently used in opinion contexts were included in the list, so as to minimize ambiguity. At the time of evaluation, the list comprised 86 verbs and 42 nouns.

#### 3.2.1 The opinion verbs and nouns list

For each verb or noun, we register its lemma and other information related to its syntactic and semantic properties.

For verbs, we record the following information:

- semantic orientation [-, 0, +]
- semantic role of the subject [source, topic]
- prepositions that introduce the subject.
- subordinate clause admitted (message)

For example, for the verb *decir / say*, the corresponding values are (0, source, [ ], yes) for the verb *apoyar / support*: (+, source, [a, np], no), for the verb *molestar / annoy:* (-, topic, [ ], no).

For nouns, the information of interest is:

- semantic orientation [-, 0, +]
- semantic role of the complement introduced by *de* [source, topic, ambiguous]

For example, for the noun *anuncio / announcement,* the corresponding values are (0, ambiguous). Note that this noun is ambiguous because the complement introduced by *de* can be either the source (*el anuncio del senador / the senator's announcement)* or the topic *(el anuncio de la extensión del plazo / the announcement about the deadline extension).* For the noun *comentario / comment* the values are (0,source) and for *apoyo / support* the values are (+, source).

The information associated to opinion predicates is taken into account when applying the rules. For example, the second attribute of the opinion noun is checked when rule fue3a is applied: if the attribute value is "source", the rule matches all np satisfying the remaining rule conditions, whereas if the attribute value is "ambiguous", the rule requires that the np contain a person or institution indicator. The rule does not apply if the attribute value is "topic".

Some of the message rules (not shown here) check that the final opinion verb attribute has the value "yes", indicating that it accepts a subordinate clause (dijo que ... / he said that ...). These rules label the proposition following the verb as a message. The proposition has already been segmented by Clatex.

The attribute that indicates which is the verb subject role is important in differentiating the rules shown in the table (fue1 to fue4), which only recognize verbs for which the subject role is source, from a set of additional rules (not shown in the table) that look for the source in the dative case, when the subject role is topic (*la propuesta gustó a los senadores / senators liked the proposal).*

### 3.3 Semantic orientation

For each element recognized, the rules assign a semantic orientation value. For the opinion predicate, source and topic this value comes from the lexical resources. For the message, this value is calculated from its subjective elements and operators. We consider that the final opinion semantic orientation can be calculated from the orientation values of its elements. We hypothesize that when the opinion predicate or the topic introducer are not neutral (they have a positive or negative semantic orientation) the complete opinion takes on the same value and there is no need to analyze the message. If these two elements are neutral the opinion semantic orientation must be obtained from the message.

To determine the message semantic orientation we carried out some experiments that are still ongoing. Semantic orientation values for opinion predicates are stated in the verb and noun lists, as mentioned. The semantic orientation for topic introducers is also stated in the corresponding list (*sobre / about* is neutral, *en contra de / against* is negative, etc.). The number of elements of this type is very limited. We did not study the source semantic orientation, in future work we will analyze expressions like *Los optimistas sostienen que ... / Optimists say that ....*

## 4 System evaluation

To evaluate the system we worked with a digital media corpus; the texts were taken from the same publications as those used to create the derivation corpus. The corpus contains 38 texts with an average of 300 words each, making a total size of approximately 13,000 words.

We applied the system to the entire corpus and performed a manual review of the output in order to evaluate the identification of the defined elements and also the complete opinion identification. We also made a partial semantic orientation evaluation, taking into account only opinion predicates and topic introducers' values and their effect on the complete opinion value.

In addition to assessing the rules performance, during the review stage the annotated corpus was manually corrected in order to obtain an opinion annotated corpus suitable for machine-learning. Table 3 shows the evaluation results. Rows represent:

- total: total number of elements in the text,
- corr-c: number of completely recognized items,
- corr-p: number of partially recognized elements,
- non-rec: number of unrecognized elements,
- incorr: number of marked segments which do not correspond to the item,
- PR: precision,
- REC-c: recall calculated using corr-c,
- REC-p: recall calculated using corr-p,
- F: F-measure.

| | **pred** | **sour** | **top** | **mess** | **opinion** |
|---|---|---|---|---|---|
| **total** | 281 | 212 | 74 | 243 | 302 |
| **corr-c** | 256 | 133 | 33 | 140 | 128 |
| **corr-p** | 0 | 20 | 13 | 64 | 104 |
| **no rec** | 25 | 57 | 28 | 39 | 70 |
| **incorr** | 23 | 11 | 2 | 10 | 14 |
| **PR** | 92 % | 93 % | 96 % | 95 % | 94 % |
| **REC-c** | 91 % | 63 % | 45 % | 58 % | 42 % |
| **REC-p** | 91 % | 72 % | 62 % | 84 % | 77 % |
| **F** | 91.5 % | 81 % | 75 % | 89 % | 85 % |

Table 3: System evaluation results.

Most opinion predicates present in the corpus are included in our opinion verbs and nouns list (91%).

Several sources and topics were partially recognized because the rules do not incorporate some complements (prepositional complements or subordinate clause) to the noun phrase.

Message is partially recognized when a pseudo-direct discourse is used (*Parada agregó que "la empresa reconoció que hubo un cálculo entre horas estimadas y horas reales y eso fue lo que pasó. Nosotros, primero empezamos a controlar a nuestro personal ..."*). This style is usually present in journalistic texts (Maldonado, 1999).

### 4.1 Semantic orientation evaluation

We recognized 25 non neutral opinion predicates in the corpus: 12 positive verbs and 14 negative verbs. One verb (*especular / speculate*) was incorrectly assigned a negative value, its means in this particular context is neutral.

We just found 3 non-neutral topic introducers, the 3 are negative.

The opinion predicates or topic introducers' semantic orientation values were assigned to the opinions containing them. This method for calculating opinion semantic orientation was correct in all cases (except for the verb *especular* that was incorrectly analyzed).

## 5 Machine-learning system

The evaluation system resulted in the generation of an annotated corpus, processed by the rule-based system and then manually reviewed and corrected. This corpus of about 13,000 words allows us to undertake some experiments applying machine-learning techniques.

We are currently experimenting with Conditional Random Fields, using the CRF++ tool (http://crfpp.sourceforge.net/). We are now determining the attributes to be considered for the training phase and defining the most appropriate templates for the kind of learning we need. While carrying out these prior tasks, we will extend the corpus using the same semi-automatic procedure as that already implemented.

## 6 Linguistic resources

Many of the linguistic resources needed to achieve our objectives have already been mentioned. Some of them were created especially in the context of this work and are available as a contribution to the development of Spanish text processing:

- opinion verbs and nouns lists with syntactic and semantic attributes,
- person and institution indicators lists,
- topic introducers list,
- subjective elements lists, created from available resources for Spanish (Redondo et al, 2007) and English (General Inquirer: www.wjh.harvard.edu), the latter translated into Spanish,
- subjective operators list.

We also used some resources that are available for Spanish, including:

- Freeling (POS-tagger),
- Clatex (propositions analyzer).

Freeling also provides a dependency parser that was not used here because the tests we carried out scored poorly in sentences containing opinions.

Resources such as a semantic role tagger or an anaphora resolution tool could no doubt improve our system, but as far as we know they are not available for Spanish.

As we did for the General Inquirer dictionary, we can apply machine translation to other English resources: subjective dictionaries and annotated corpora (Brooke et alt, 2009, Banea et alt, 2009). Tools for subjectivity analysis in English can be applied to a translated Spanish raw corpus (Banea et alt, 2009).

## 7 Conclusions

We have implemented a rule-based system for opinion identification in Spanish texts. We have also created some resources for Spanish: opinion verbs and nouns lists, subjective elements lists and an opinion annotated corpus. We think these resources are an important contribution to the development of Spanish text processing.

In our present work, we are experimenting with machine-learning techniques for recognizing opinion elements. The results will be compared with those obtained by the rule-based system. We hope to improve our results by combining rule-based and machine-learning modules.

## References


N. Asher, F. Benamara and Y. Mathieu. 2008. *Distilling Opinion in Discourse: A Preliminary Study. COLING – Posters.*

J. Atserias, B. Casas, E. Comelles, M. González, L. Padró and M. Padró. 2006. *FreeLing 1.3: Syntactic and semantic services in an open-source NLP library.* In Proceedings of the fifth international conference on Language Resources and Evaluation (LREC) ELRA.

Carmen Banea, Rada Mihalcea, Janyce Wiebe, Samer Hassan. 2008. *Multilingual Subjectivity Analysis Using Machine Translation.* Conference on Empirical Methods in Natural Language Processing (EMNLP).

J. Brooke, M. Tofiloski and M. Taboada. 2009. *Cross-Linguistic Sentiment Analysis: From English to Spanish.* RANLP 2009, Recent Advances in Natural Language Processing. Borovets, Bulgaria.

Steven Bethard, Hong Yu, Ashley Thornton, Vasileios Hatzivassiloglou, and Dan Jurafsky. 2004. *Automatic extraction of opinion propositions and their holders.* In AAAI Spring Symposium on Exploring Attitude and Affect in Text: Theories and Applications.

Yejin Choi, Claire Cardie, Ellen Riloff and Siddharth Patwardhan. 2005. *Identifying sources of opinions with conditional random fields and extraction patterns.* In Proceedings of the Conference on Human Language Technology and Empirical Methods in Natural Language Processing (Vancouver, British Columbia, Canada). Human Language Technology

Conference. Association for Computational Linguistics.

Yejin Choi and Claire Cardie. 2008. *Learning with Compositional Semantics as Structural Inference for Subsentencial Sentiment Analysis*. *EMNLP*.

Mark Davies. *2002. Corpus del español (100 millones de palabras, siglo XIII - siglo XX).* Disponible actualmente en http://www.corpusdelespanol.org.

J. García-Miguel, L. Costas and S. Martínez. 2005. *Diátesis verbales y esquemas construccionales. Verbos, clases semánticas y esquemas sintáctico-semánticos en el proyecto ADESSE*. Entre semántica léxica, teoría del léxico y sintaxis, 373-384.

Mariela Grassi, Marisa Malcuori, Javier Couto, Juan José Prada and Dina Wonsever. 2001. *Corpus informatizado: textos del español del Uruguay (CORIN)*, SLPLT-2 - Second International Workshop on Spanish Language Processing and Language Technologies - Jaén, España.

Soo-Min Kim and Eduard Hovy. 2006. *Extracting opinions, opinion holders, and topics expressed in online news media text*. In Proceedings of the Workshop on Sentiment and Subjectivity in Text (Sydney, Australia, July 22 - 22, 2006). ACL Workshops. Association for Computational Linguistics, Morristown, NJ, 1-8.

Concepción Maldonado. 1999. *Discurso directo y discurso indirecto.* In Ignacio Bosque and Violeta Demonte, *Gramática descriptiva de la lengua española (Entre la oración y el discurso. Morfología*), 3549-3596.

K. Moilanen and S. Pulman. 2007. *Sentiment Composition*. In *RANLP*.

Bo Pang and Lillian Lee. 2008. *Opinion Mining and Sentiment Analysis.* Foundations and Trends in Information Retrieval 2(1-2), pp. 1–135.

L. Polanyi and A. Zaenen. 2004. *Contextual Valence Shifters*. In AAAI spring Symposium on Attitude.

J. Redondo, I. Fraga, I. Padrón and M. Comesaña. 2007. *The Spanish Adaptation of ANEW (Affective Norms for English Words).* Behavior Research Methods, 39(3):600-605, Agosto.

Josef Ruppenhofer, Swapna Somasundaran and Janyce Wiebe. 2008. *Finding the Sources and Targets of Subjective Expressions*. The Sixth International Conference on Language Resources and Evaluation (LREC 2008).

Veselin Stoyanov and Claire Cardie. 2008. *Annotating Topics of Opinions.* Proceedings of the Sixth International Conference on Language Resources and Evaluation (LREC 2008), Marrakech, Morocco.

Carlos Subirats-Rüggeberg and Miriam R. L. Petruck. 2003. *Surprise: Spanish FrameNet!* In E. Hajicova, A. Kotesovcova & Jiri Mirovsky (eds.), Proceedings of CIL 17. CD-ROM. Prague: Matfyzpress.

P. Turney and M. Littman. 2003. *Measuring Praise and Criticism: Inference of Semantic Orientation from Association.* In ACM Transactions on Information Systems, 21:315--346.

Janyce Wiebe, Theresa Wilson and Claire Cardie. 2005. *Annotating expressions of opinions and emotions in language.* In Language Resources and Evaluation (formerly Computers and the Humanities), 39(2-3):165210.

Dina Wonsever and Jean-Luc Minel. 2004. Contextual Rules for Text Analysis. En Lecture Notes in Computer Science.

Dina Wonsever, Serrana Caviglia, Javier Couto and Aiala Rosá and. 2006. *Un sistema para la segmentación en proposiciones de textos en español*. In *Letras de hoje* 144 (41).

# A Machine Learning Approach for Recognizing Textual Entailment in Spanish

**Julio Javier Castillo**
National University of Córdoba
Ciudad Universitaria, 5000
Córdoba, Argentina
jotacastillo@gmail.com

## Abstract

This paper presents a system that uses machine learning algorithms for the task of recognizing textual entailment in Spanish language. The datasets used include SPARTE Corpus and a translated version to Spanish of RTE3, RTE4 and RTE5 datasets. The features chosen quantify lexical, syntactic and semantic level matching between text and hypothesis sentences. We analyze how the different sizes of datasets and classifiers could impact on the final overall performance of the RTE classification of two-way task in Spanish. The RTE system yields 60.83% of accuracy and a competitive result of 66.50% of accuracy is reported by train and test set taken from SPARTE Corpus with 70% split.

## 1 Introduction

The objective of the Recognizing Textual Entailment Challenge is determining whether the meaning of the Hypothesis (H) can be inferred from a text (T) (Ido Dagan et al., 2006). This challenge has been organized by NIST in recent years.

Another related antecedent was Answer Validation Exercise (AVE), part of Cross Language Evaluation Forum (CLEF), whose objective is to develop systems which are able to decide whether the answer to a question is correct or not (Peñas et al, 2006). It was a three year-old track, from 2006 to 2008.

AVE challenge was an evaluation framework for Question Answering (QA) systems to promote the development and evaluation of subsystems aimed at validating the correctness of the answers given by a QA system. The Answer Validation task must select the best answer for the final output. There is a subtask for each language involved in QA, the Spanish is one of these. Thus, AVE task is very similar to RTE (Recognition of Textual Entailments).

In this paper, we address the RTE task problem of determining the entailment value between Text and Hypothesis pairs in Spanish, applying machine learning techniques.

In the past, RTEs Challenges machine learning algorithms were widely used for the task of recognizing textual entailment (Marneffe et al., 2006; Zanzotto et al., 2007; Castillo, 2009) and they have reported goods results for English language. Also, our system applies machine learning algorithms to the Spanish.

We built a set of datasets based on public available datasets for English, together to SPARTE (Peñas et al, 2006), an available Corpus in Spanish. This corpus contains 2962 hypothesis with a document label and a True/False value indicating whether the document entails the hypothesis or not. Up to our knowledge, SPARTE corpus in the only corpus aimed at evaluating RTE systems in Spanish.

Finally, we generated a feature vector with the following components for both Text and Hypothesis: Levenshtein distance, a lexical distance based on Levenshtein, a semantic similarity measure Wordnet based, and the LCS (longest common



*Proceedings of the NAACL HLT 2010 Young Investigators Workshop on Computational Approaches to Languages of the Americas*, pages 62–67, Los Angeles, California, June 2010. 

substring) metric; in order to characterize the relationships between the Text and the Hypothesis.

The remainder of the paper is organized as follows. Section 2 shows the system description, whereas Section 3 describes the results of experimental evaluation and discussion of them. Section 4 discusses opportunities of collaboration. Finally, Section 5 summarizes the conclusions and lines for future work.

## 2 System Description

This section provides an overview of our system which is based on a machine learning approach for recognizing textual entailment to the Spanish. The system produces feature vectors for the available development data RTE3, RTE4, RTE5, and SPARTE(Peñas et al, 2006). Weka (Witten and Frank, 2000) is used to train classifiers on these feature vectors.

The SPARTE Corpus, was built from the Spanish corpora used at Cross-Language Evaluation Forum (CLEF) for evaluating QA systems during the years 2003, 2004 and 2005. This corpus contains 2962 hypothesis with a True/False value indicating whether the document entails the hypothesis or not.

Due to, all available dataset of PASCAL Text Analysis Conference were in English, we translated every dataset to Spanish by using an online translator engine[1]. So, we had a Spanish dataset but with some translation errors provided by the translator. It is important to note, that the "quality" of the translation is given by the Translator engine, and we suppose that the sense of the sentence should not be modified by the Translator. Indeed, it is the situation for the majority of the cases that we analyzed. The new datasets were named RTE3-Sp (Spanish), RTE4-Sp, and RTE5-Sp.

The following example is the pair number 799 from RTE3-Sp with False as entailment value.

Text:

*Otros dos marines, Tyler Jackson y Juan Jodka III, ya han se declaró culpables de asalto agravantes y conspiración para obstruir la justicia y fueron condenados a 21 meses y 18 meses, respectivamente.*

Hypothesis:

*Tyler Jackson ha sido condenado a 18 meses.*

This example shows a little noisy (and a minimal syntactic error) in the translation of the Text to Spanish (instead of "*ya han se declaró*" should be "ya se han declarado"); but the whole meaning was not changed.

Also, we show a pair example (pair id=3) taken from Sparte Corpus with False as entailment value:

Text: *¿Cuál es la capital de Croacia?*

Hypothesis :

*La capital de Croacia es ONU.*

In a similar way, all pairs from SPARTE belong to QA task and these are syntactically simpler than RTE's Corpus pairs.

Additionally, we generate the following development sets: RTE3-Sp+RTE4-Sp, and SPARTE-Bal+RTE3-Sp+RTE4-Sp in order to train with different corpus and different sizes. In all cases, RTE5-Sp TAC 2009 gold standard dataset was used as test-set.

Also, we did additional experiments with SPARTE, using cross-validation technique and percentage split method, in order to test the accuracy of our system taking only this corpus as development and training set.

### 2.1 Features

We experimented with the following four machine learning algorithms: Support Vector Machine (SVM), Multilayer Perceptron(MLP), Decision Trees(DT) and AdaBoost(AB).

The Decision Trees are interesting because we can see what features were selected from the top levels of the trees. SVM and AdaBoost were selected because they are known for achieving high performances, and MLP was used because it has achieved high performance in others NLP tasks.

We experimented with various settings for the machine learning algorithms, including only the results for the best parameters.

We generated a feature vector with the following components for every possible <T,H>: Levenshtein distance, a lexical distance based on Levenshtein, a semantic similarity measure Word-

[1] http://www.microsofttranslator.com/

net based, and the LCS (longest common substring) metric.

We chose only four features in order to learn the development sets, having into account that larger feature sets do not necessarily lead to improving classification performance because it could increase the risk of overfitting the training data.

Below the motivation for the input features: Levenshtein distance is motivated by the good results obtained as a measure of similarity between two strings. Using stems, this measure improves the Levenshtein over words. The lexical distance feature based on Levenshtein distance is interesting because works to a sentence level. Semantic similarity using WordNet is interesting because of the capture of the semantic similarity between T and H to sentence level. Longest common substring is selected because it is easy to implement and provides a good measure for word overlap.

## 2.2 Lexical Distance

The standard Levenshtein distance is a string metric for measuring the amount of difference between two strings. This distance quantifies the number of changes (character based) to generate one text string (T) from the other (H). The algorithm works independently from the language that we are analyzing.

We used a Spanish Stemmer that stems words in Spanish based on a modified version of the Snowball algorithm[2].

Additionally, by using Levenshtein distance we defined a lexical distance and the procedure is the following:

- Each string T and H are divided in a list of tokens.
- The similarity between each pair of tokens in T and H is performed using the Levenshtein distance over stems.
- The string similarity between two lists of tokens is reduced to the problem of "bipartite graph matching", performed using the Hungarian algorithm (Kuhn, 1955) over this bipartite graph. Then, we found the assignment that maximizes the sum of ratings of each token. Note that each graph node is a token of the list.

The final score is calculated by:

$$finalscore = \frac{TotalSim}{Max(Length(T), Length(H))}$$

Where:
TotalSim is the sum of the similarities with the optimal assignment in the graph.
Length (T) is the number of tokens in T.
Length (H) is the number of tokens in H.

## 2.3 Wordnet Distance

Since, all datasets are in Spanish, we need to convert <T, H> pair to English. In the case of RTEs-Sp datasets, this action will backward to the English language (source).

Our ideal case would be to use EuroWordNet[3] to obtain the semantic information that we need, but we won't be able to access to this resource.

Thus, WordNet is used to calculate the semantic similarity between T and H. The following procedure is applied:

1. Word sense disambiguation using the Lesk algorithm (Lesk, 1986), based on Wordnet definitions.

2. A semantic similarity matrix between words in T and H is defined. Words are used only in synonym and hyperonym relationship. The Breadth First Search algorithm is used over these tokens; similarity is calculated by using two factors: length of the path and orientation of the path.

3. To obtain the final score, we use matching average.

The semantic similarity between two words is computed as:

$$Sim(s,t) = 2 \times \frac{Depth(LCS(s,t))}{Depth(s) + Depth(t)}$$

Where: s,t are source and target words that we are comparing (s is in H and t is in T). Depth(s) is the shortest distance from the root node to the current node. LCS(s,t):is the least common subsume of s and t.

The matching average (step 3) between two sentences X and Y is calculated as follows:

$$MatchingAverage = 2 \times \frac{Match(X,Y)}{Length(X) + Length(Y)}$$

[2] http://snowball.tartarus.org/

[3] http://www.illc.uva.nl/EuroWordNet/

## 2.4 Longest Common Substring

Given two strings, T of length n and H of length m, the Longest Common Sub-string (LCS) problem (Dan, 1999) will find the longest string that is a substring of both T and H. It is found by dynamic programming.

$$lcs(T,H) = \frac{Length(MaxComSub(T,H))}{\min(Length(T), Length(H))}$$

# 3 Experimental Evaluation and Discussion of the Results

With the aim of exploring the differences among training sets and machine learning algorithms, we did many experiments looking for the best result to our system.

First, we converted the RTE4 and RTE5 datasets with Contradiction/Unknown/Entailment pair information to a binary True/False problem, named two-way problem.

Then, we used the following combination of datasets: RTE3-Sp, RTE4-Sp, RTE3-Sp+RTE4-Sp, SPARTE-Bal (balanced SPARTE Corpus with the same number of true and false cases), and SPARTE-Bal+ RTE3-Sp+RTE4-Sp. The training set SPARTE-Balanced was created by taking all true cases and randomly taking false cases, and then we build a balanced training set containing 1352 pairs, with 676 true and 676 false pairs.

We used four classifiers to learn every development set: (1) Support Vector Machine, (2) Ada Boost, (3) Multilayer Perceptron (MLP) and (4) Decision Tree using the open source WEKA Data Mining Software (Witten & Frank, 2005). In all the tables results we show only the accuracy of the best classifier.

The results obtained to predict RTE5-Sp in a two-way classification task are summarized in Table 1 below. In addition, table 2 shows our results reported in RTE two-way classification task by using with Cross Validation technique with 10 folds.

| *Dataset* | *Classifier* | *Accuracy%* |
|---|---|---|
| RTE3-Sp+RTE4-Sp | SVM | 60.83% |
| RTE3-Sp | SVM | 60.50% |
| RTE4-Sp | MLP | 60.50% |
| SPARTE-Bal+ RTE3-Sp+RTE4-Sp | MLP | 60.17% |
| SPARTE-Bal | DT | 50% |
| Baseline | - | 50% |

Table 1.Results obtained in two-way classification task.

| *Dataset* | *Classifier* | *Accuracy%* |
|---|---|---|
| SPARTE-Bal | DT | 68.19% |
| RTE3-Sp | SVM | 66.50% |
| RTE3-Sp+RTE4-Sp | MLP | 61.44% |
| RTE4-Sp | MLP | 59.60% |
| SPARTE-Bal+ RTE3-Sp+RTE4-Sp | AdaBoost | 56.83% |
| Baseline | - | 50% |

Table 2.Results obtained with Cross Validation 10 folds in two-way task.

The performance in all cases was clearly above those baselines. Only when using SPARTE-Bal we obtained a result equal to the baseline (50% true pairs and 50% false pairs).

The SPARTE-Balanced dataset yields the worst results, maybe because this dataset contains only pairs with QA task, and an additional reason, could be that SPARTE is syntactically simpler than PASCAL RTE. In that sense, some authors have reported low performance when using syntactically simpler datasets; for instance, by using BPI[4] dataset to predict RTEs datasets in English. Therefore, SPARTE seems to be not enough good training set to predict RTEs test sets.

The best performance of our system was achieved with SVM classifier with RTE3-Sp+RTE4-Sp dataset; it was 60.83% of accuracy. In the majority of the cases, SVM or MLP classifiers appear as 'favorite' in all classification tasks.

Surprisingly, in the two-way task, a slight and not statistical significant difference of 0.66% between the best and worst combination (except for SPARTE-Bal) of datasets and classifiers is found. So, it suggests that the combination of dataset and classifiers do not produce a strong impact predicting RTE5-Sp, at least, for these feature sets.

[4] http://www.cs.utexas.edu/users/pclark/bpi-test-suite/

Also, we observed that by including SPARTE-Bal to RTE3-Sp+RTE4-Sp dataset, the performance slightly decreases, although this difference was not statistical significant.

The results obtained in table 2(and table 4) with SPARTE-Bal and decision tree algorithm, are the best for cross-validation experiments. In fact, an accuracy of 68.19% was obtained, which is 18.19% bigger than the result obtained in table 1, and was statistical significant.

Finally, we assessed our system only over the SPARTE Corpus. First, we used cross validation technique with ten folds over SPARTE-Bal, testing over our four classifiers. Then, we tested SPARTE-Bal by splitting the corpus in training set (70%), and test set (30%).

The results are shown in the tables 4 and 5 below.

| *Classifier* | *Accuracy%* |
|---|---|
| DT | 68.19% |
| MLP | 62.64% |
| AdaBoost | 61.31% |
| SVM | 60.35% |
| Baseline | 50% |

Table 4.Results obtained with Cross Validation 10 folds in two-way task to predict SPARTE.

| *Classifier* | *Accuracy%* |
|---|---|
| DT | 66.50% |
| AdaBoost | 62.31% |
| SVM | 59.60% |
| MLP | 52.70% |
| Baseline | 50% |

Table 5.Results obtained with SPARTE with split 70%.

The results on cross-validation are better than those obtained on test set, which is most probably due to overfitting of classifiers.

Table 5 shows a good performance of 66.50%, predicting test set and using Decision trees. These results are opposed to the bad performance reported by SPARTE to predict RTEs datasets. Here, in fact, the syntactic complexity and original task do not change between train and test set; and it seems to be the main problem with the low performance of SPARTE in Table 1.

## 3.1 Related Work

Up to our knowledge, there are not available results of other teams that used SPARTE to predict RTE, or used RTEs applied to Spanish. However, some comparison with other results for Spanish could be done in AVE Challenge (Alberto Téllez-Valero et al., 2008; Ferrández et al., 2008; Castillo, 2008), but we will need to modify our system to test AVE 2008 test set and computing different metric for the ranking of the result.

On the other hand, comparing the results obtained with English in RTE5 TAC Challenge, we obtained a result not statistical significant with respect to the median score for English systems that is 61.17% of accuracy. Also, our system could be compared to independent-language RTE systems.

To finish, we think that several improvements could be done in order to improve the accuracy of the system, using syntactic features, more semantic information, and new external resources such as Acronyms database.

# 4 Opportunities for Collaboration

Our work is oriented to create a Textual Entailment System. Such system could be used by another system or teams of others Universities, as an internal module.

The entailment relations between texts or strings are very useful for a variety of Natural Language Processing applications, such as Question Answering, Information Extraction, Information Retrieval and Document Summarization.

For example, a RTE module could be used in a Question Answering system, where the answer of a question must be entailed by the text that supports the correctness of the answer; or an Automatic Summarization system could eliminate the passages whose meaning is already entailed by other passages and, by this way, reduce the size of the passages.

In addition, a question answering system could be enhanced by a RTE module, and also, these results are useful as Answer Validation System.

Our system was designed having in mind the interoperation among systems. Thus, the system inputs accept files in .xml format, and the output is text plain files and .xml files.

On the other hand, one of the resources that would allow this work advance is the EuroWordnet, because it could provide additional semantic information improving our semantic features, and so the performance of our system. Due to being an expensive and not freely available resource, we are avoiding using it, but we expect to be able to use it in the future. In section 3, we used Wordnet in order to obtain the relationship between two different concepts. Since Wordnet includes only synsets for English and not for Spanish, we have translated the <t,h> pairs to English using the online Microsoft Bing translator[5], in order to use Wordnet. As a result, a loss of performance was obtained. We believe that the use of EuroWordNet could benefit our semantic features.

Currently, we are keeping improving our system, and we are looking forward to get opportunities for collaboration with other teams of all the Americas.

## 5 Conclusion and Future work

In this paper we present an initial RTE System based for the Spanish language, based on machine learning techniques that uses some of the available textual entailment corpus and yields 60.83% of accuracy.

One issue found is that SPARTE Corpus seems to be not useful to predict RTEs-Sp datasets, because of the syntactic simplicity and the absence of task information different to QA task.

On the other hand, we found that a competitive result of 66.50%acc is reported by train and test set taken from SPARTE Corpus.

Future work is oriented to experiment with additional lexical and semantic similarities features and to test the improvements they may yield. Also, we must explore how to decrease the computational cost of the system. Our plan is keeping applying machine learning algorithms, testing with new features, and adding new source of knowledge.

## References


Luisa Bentivogli, Ido Dagan, Hoa Trang Dang, Danillo Giampiccolo, and Bernardo Magnini. 2009. *The Fifth PASCAL Recognizing Textual Entailment Challenge.* In proceedings of Textual Analysis Conference (TAC). NIST, Maryland USA.

Adrian Iftene, Mihai-Alex Moruz.2009. *UAIC Participation at RTE5,* TAC 2009, Gaithersburg, Maryland, USA.

S. Mirkin, R. Bar-Haim, J. Berant, I. Dagan, E. Shnarch, A. Stern, and I. Szpektor.2009. *Bar-Ilan University's submission to RTE5,* TAC 2009, Gaithersburg, Maryland, USA.

Castillo, Julio. *Sagan in TAC2009: Using Support Vector Machines in Recognizing Textual Entailment and TE Search Pilot task.* TAC 2009, Gaithersburg, Maryland, USA.

Marie-Catherine de Marneffe, Bill MacCartney, Trond Grenager, Daniel Cer, Anna Rafferty and Christopher D. Manning. 2006. *Learning to distinguish valid textual entailments.* RTE2 Challenge, Italy.

F. Zanzotto, Marco Pennacchiotti and Alessandro Moschitti.2007. *Shallow Semantics in Fast Textual Entailment Rule Learners,* RTE3, Prague.

Ian H. Witten and Eibe Frank. 2005. "Data *Mining: Practical machine learning tools and techniques"*, 2nd Edition, Morgan Kaufmann, San Francisco, USA.

Anselmo Peñas, Alvaro Rodrigo, Felisa Verdejo. *SPARTE, a Test Suite for Recognising Textual Entailment in Spanish.* Cicling 2006, Mexico.

Peñas A., Rodrigo A., Sama V., and Verdejo F. *Overview of the Answer Validation Exercise 2006*, In-Working notes for the Cross Language Evaluation Forum Workshop (CLEF 2006), September 2006, Spain.

Ido Dagan, Oren Glickman and Bernardo Magnini. *The PASCAL Recognising Textual Entailment Challenge.* In Quiñonero-Candela, J.; Dagan, I.; Magnini, B.; d'Alché-Buc, F. (Eds.) Machine Learning Challenges. Lecture Notes in Computer Science , Vol. 3944, pp. 177-190, Springer, 2006.

M. Lesk. *Automatic sense disambiguation using machine readable dictionaries: How to tell a pine cone from a ice cream cone.* In SIGDOC '86, 1986.

Harold W. Kuhn, *The Hungarian Method for the assignment problem*, Naval Research Logistics Quarterly. 1955

Alberto Téllez-Valero, Antonio Juarez-Gonzalez, Manuel Montes-y-Gomez, Luis Villasenior-Pineda. *INAOE at QA@CLEF 2008:Evaluating Answer Validation in Spanish Question Answering.* CLEF 2008.

Julio J. Castillo. *The Contribution of FaMAF at QA@CLEF 2008.Answer ValidationExercise.*CLEF 2008.

Oscar Ferrández, Rafael Muñoz, and Manuel Palomar. *A Lexical Semantic Approach to AVE.* CLEF 2008.


[5] http://www.microsofttranslator.com/

# The emergence of the modern concept of introspection: a quantitative linguistic analysis

**I. Raskovsky**
Department of Computer Science
University of Buenos Aires
Pabellón I, Ciudad Universitaria
Buenos Aires, C1428EGA, Argentina
iraskovsky@dc.uba.ar

**D. Fernández Slezak**
Department of Computer Science
University of Buenos Aires
Pabellón I, Ciudad Universitaria
Buenos Aires, C1428EGA, Argentina
dfslezak@dc.uba.ar

**C.G. Diuk**
Department of Psychology
Princeton University
Princeton, NJ 08540, USA
cdiuk@princeton.edu

**G.A. Cecchi**
Computational Biology Center
T.J. Watson IBM Research Center
Yorktown Heights, NY 10598, USA
gcecchi@us.ibm.com

**Abstract**

The evolution of literary styles in the western tradition has been the subject of extended research that arguably has spanned centuries. In particular, previous work has conjectured the existence of a gradual yet persistent increase of the degree of self-awareness or introspection, i.e. that capacity to expound on one's own thought processes and behaviors, reflected in the chronology of the classical literary texts. This type of question has been traditionally addressed by qualitative studies in philology and literary theory. In this paper, we describe preliminary results based on the application of computational linguistics techniques to quantitatively analyze this hypothesis. We evaluate the appearance of introspection in texts by searching words related to it, and focus on simple studies on the Bible. This preliminary results are highly positive, indicating that it is indeed possible to statistically discriminate between texts based on a semantic core centered around introspection, chronologically and culturally belonging to different phases. In our opinion, the rigurous extension of our analysis can provide not only a stricter statistical measure of the evolution of introspection, but also means to investigate subtle differences in aesthetic styles and cognitive structures across cultures, authors and literary forms.

## 1 Introduction

The evolution of literary styles in the western tradition has been the subject of extended research that arguably has spanned centuries. In particular, previous work has conjectured the existence of a gradual yet persistent increase of the degree of self-awareness or *introspection*, i.e. that capacity to expound on one's own thought processes and behaviors, reflected in the chronology of the classical literary texts. This type of question has been traditionally addressed by qualitative studies in philology and literary theory. In this paper, we describe preliminary results based on the application of computational linguistics techniques to quantitatively analyze this hypothesis.

The striking differences between the Iliad and the Oddysey in the way the characters' behaviors are attributed to divine intervention, or to the individual's volition, has been pointed out by numerous scholars (Onians, 1988; Dodds, 1951; Adkins, 1970; De Jong and Sullivan, 1994). However, not until the highly influential work of Marshall McLuhan (McLuhan, 1962) and Julian Jaynes (Jaynes, 2000) was it pointed out that these changes may reflect not just artistic or even cultural tendencies, but profound alterations in the mental structure of those who wrote, collected and assimilated the stories. While



*Proceedings of the NAACL HLT 2010 Young Investigators Workshop on Computational Approaches to Languages of the Americas*, pages 68–75, Los Angeles, California, June 2010. 

McLuhan argued for a materialistic effect of the type of medium (the linearity of written language, the holistic nature of the moving image) on the organization of thoughts (linear or integrative, respectively), Jaynes proposed a more radical hypothesis: a relatively abrupt transition from a "bicameral mind", where one hemisphere produced god-like commands that the other followed blindly, to the modern mind with its ability of self-awareness. Moreover, Jaynes boldly suggested that this transition may have been accompanied by a physical process that altered the relationship between the hemispheres, and changed culture permanently. Since its publication, *The origins of consciousness in the breakdown of the bicameral mind* has been highly influential inside and outside scientific quarters, as well as a source of continuing controversy (Cavanna et al., 2007).

Whether brought about by nature or nurture, however, Jaynes presents compelling arguments about the effects of this transition, including stylistic changes throughout the other foundational text of the western world, the Bible. Simply put, a less radical version of Jaynes' hypothesis would state that, within the judeo-greco-christian cultural tradition, there exists an "arrow of time" pointing to increasing *introspection*. The question we set out to answer in the present manuscript is to what extent it is possible to analyze, quantitatively, this hypothesis.

The widespread availability of classic and modern literary texts has paved the road to a wide variety of linguistic studies. Matters of literary style and structure are necessarily more controversial, although the recent work of F. Moretti (Moretti, 2005) has shown that it is indeed possible to quantify the subtle variations in the structure of the novel over temporal periodizations and geographical locations. In any event, given that our intention is to complete a preliminary study of feasibility, we focus here on capturing the textual traces of words or lexical structures that can be reasonably argued to reflect introspective thinking on the part of the characters, using techniques from machine learning and computational linguistics.

## 2 Materials and methods

We downloaded selected texts representative of different ages in literature from the MIT classic texts archive (Daniel C. Stevenson, 2010), based on references in Jaynes' book (Jaynes, 2000). The selected texts are: the Iliad and the Odyssey (approx. 1200 BC to 900 BC), The Bible (approx. 1400 BC to AD 200), Lucretius' On the Nature of Things (99 BC - 55 BC), St. Augustine's Confessions (AD 397 - AD 398), Shakespear's The Merchant of Venice (AD 1596 - AD 1598), Hamlet (approx. AD 1600), Macbeth (AD 1603 - AD 1607) and Othello (AD 1603), Cervantes' Quixote (AD 1605 - AD 1615), Jean Austen's Mansfield Park (AD 1814), Emma (AD 1815) and Persuasion (AD 1816) and Proust's Time Regained (AD 1927).

On this preliminary study, we focused on extremely simple techniques to test our hypothesis. We have implemented a series of basic routines to analyze the frequency of certain words related to introspection, selected by hand. We used very simple regular expressions to search over the text: `think+`, `thought`, `myself`, `mind+`, `feel+` and `felt`. The search was conducted on 10,000-words windows starting from the beginning of the text moving towards the end in 2,000-words steps. Also, the appearance of references to God in the Bible was measured. In this case, we looked for: `lord`, `god` and `almighty`; all searches done case insensitive. In order to control for the possible increase of these selected words as a trivial consequence of an increase in the overall linguistic richness or expressiveness of the text, we also computed the total number of distinct words for each step.

As an alternative approach, we applied a data-driven method to extract the semantic structure of texts, namely topic modeling (Blei, 2009). We utilized the implementation of the *mallet* package (McCallum, 2002), an off-the-shelf tool, generating 100 topics through 10,000 Gibbs sampling rounds. The topics were then manually inspected for their semantic relevance to the issue at hand, i.e. introspection.

## 3 Results

The preliminary results are highly positive, indicating that it is indeed possible to statistically discriminate between texts based on a semantic core cen-

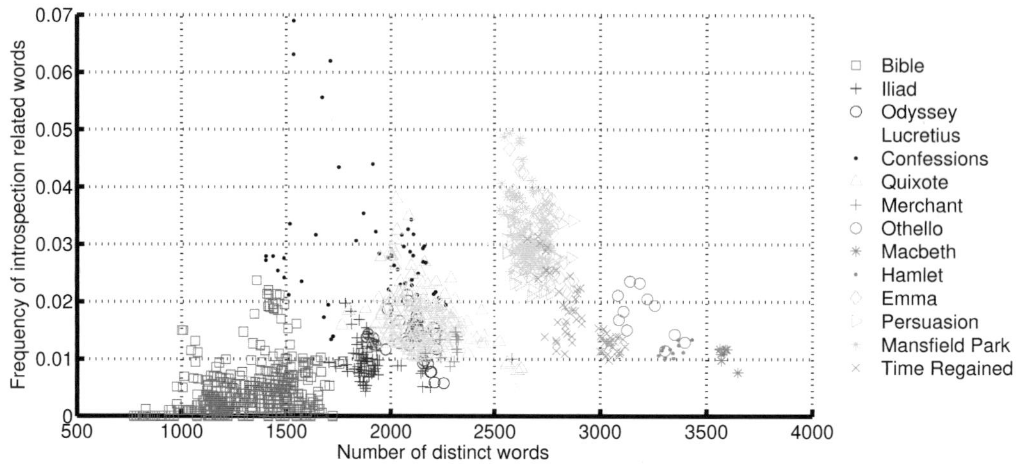


Figure 1: Frequency of words related to introspection versus the amount of different words. Each text is identified by a unique color; each point represents a 10,000-words window.

tered around introspection, chronologically and culturally belonging to different phases. In figure 1 we show the frequency of words related to introspection versus the amount of different words, for all the texts we chose. Each author is identified by a unique color; each text is identified by an unique symbol; each point represents a 10,000-words window. The frequency is calculated as count over the number of different words in the 10K windows. To summarize this information and provide statistical value to our analysis, we present in figure 2 the mean and standard deviation for each of the selected texts.

We clearly observe how different texts are disjoint in the graph, both in amount of different words used in each window, as well as the frequency of introspection. This is the case for the Iliad and the Odyssey, confirming that our preliminary measure captures the semantic differences between both pieces. We also observe a trend between some of the sections of the Bible (we will return to this below), to the Homeric texts, Lucretius, Cervantes and Austen, roughly following a chronological order. St. Augustine's *Confessions* is an exception of this trend, as it shows a higher frequency than Cervantes. However, given that *Confessions* is considered the first auto-biography work in the Western tradition, the high value of our introspection measure is to some extent a validation of its pertinence. A more noticeable exception is Shakespear's oeuvre, that seems to consist of very differentiated clusters for each piece. Taken together, however, the ensemble average of his work seems to fall in line with the global temporal order. It is beyond the scope of our manuscript to discuss the nuances of the work of The Bard, but our analytic approach may provide new tools to the ongoing Shakespearean scholarship. Finally, our analysis seems to really break down for Proust, as one intuitively would expect a much higher measure of introspection, even more so considering that he displays significant richness in terms of the number of distinct words in the text. This failure is clearly an indication of the limitations of our current approach, which as it stands may only not be applicable to modern or contemporary literature.

The Bible is of particular interest for this work, as it was written in parts along a wide time interval (taking into account the Old and New Testaments). It enables us to analyze the "arrow of time" of introspection within a relatively coherent framework, even though a vast and in most cases unknown host of writers and compilers gave this text its present shape, and the relationship between textual linearity and chronological order is certainly not simple. Be it as it may, for our purposes we only require that this relationship be monotonic in a statistical sense, which we assume to be the case for the Bible. In figure 3 we show the frequency of introspection along different *periods* of the Bible. The text was divided into 6 pieces of the same length; purposefully, no semantic division was performed. Introspection increases towards the more modern sections of the

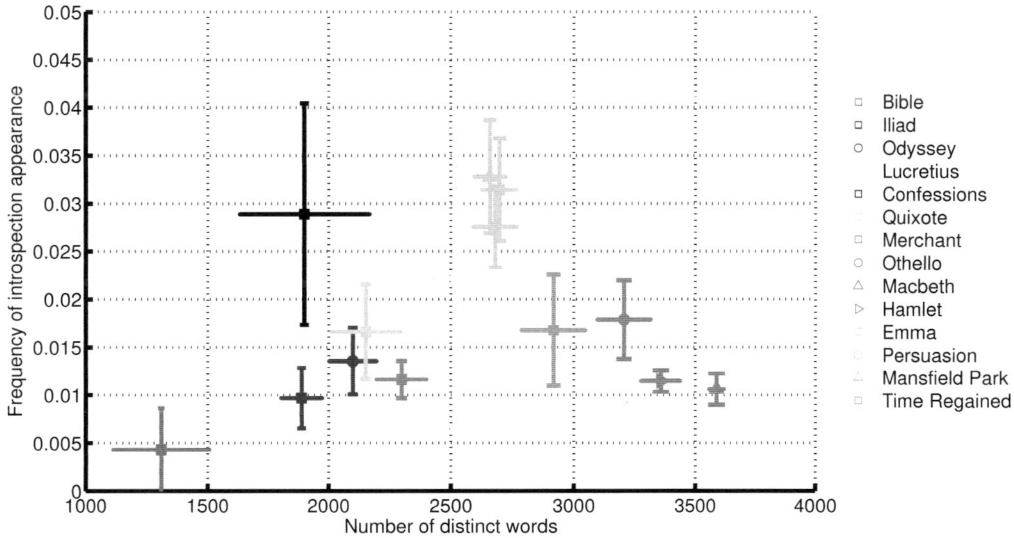


Figure 2: Frequency of words related to introspection versus the amount of different words. Each text is identified by a unique color. Error bars shows the standard deviation in both axis.

text, confirming our initial hypothesis. Note that the lexical richness (number of distinct words) of the last period, that includes the New Testament, seems to be part of the same plateau as the 3rd, 4th and 5th. Another interesting aspect is how introspection and citations to God evolve along the lexical, pseudo-chronological order the the Bible's test. Figure 4 shows the appearance of introspection and mentions to God over 10,000-words windows. We observe a significant increase in introspection as the lexical order moves ahead, while at the same time the references to God show a weaker, yet clearly discernible trend to diminish. This is precisely the analytic counterpart of the phenomenology on which Jaynes based his hypothesis.

Another avenue of research involves developing and applying more sophisticated tools of textual analysis, in order to capture the presence of relevant passages of introspection using data-driven approaches. In particular, we have done a preliminary study using Topic Modeling (Blei, 2009), a technique that uses probabilistic models to uncover the underlying semantic structure of a text or a collection of documents. In topic modeling, a *topic* is a collection of keywords that are automatically extracted as highly descriptive of a document. As described in the Methods section, we utilized the *mallet* package implementation, choosing 100 topics to be uncovered. This package produces *approximate* inference and therefore different runs may yield different results. In each run, we observed a handful of topics (between 3 and 6, approximately) that contained words related to introspection, such as the `mind`, `think` and `feel` roots. The following topic, selected as a representative from one of the *mallet* runs, was identified based only on the presence of `mind`, although some of the other words may also be relevant for the purpose of revealing introspective activity (`soul` and `desire`):

| | | | |
|---|---|---|---|
| soul | love | yea | desire |
| mind | hate | sought | loveth |
| measure | fair | pleasant | nay |
| keepeth | hungry | satisfied | excellent |
| occasion | rejoicing | desired | |

Figure 5 presents the frequency with which this topic of interest is considered the main topic by mallet, as a running average for every 100 lines of the Bible. A simple linear regression shows that this topic becomes more frequent towards the end of the text, and mirrors the results obtained with the more hand-crafted approach. This result, while preliminary (there is a good number of parameters to explore in setting up topic modeling), is highly promising, as topic modeling provides a link with the vast literature of statistical semantic analysis.

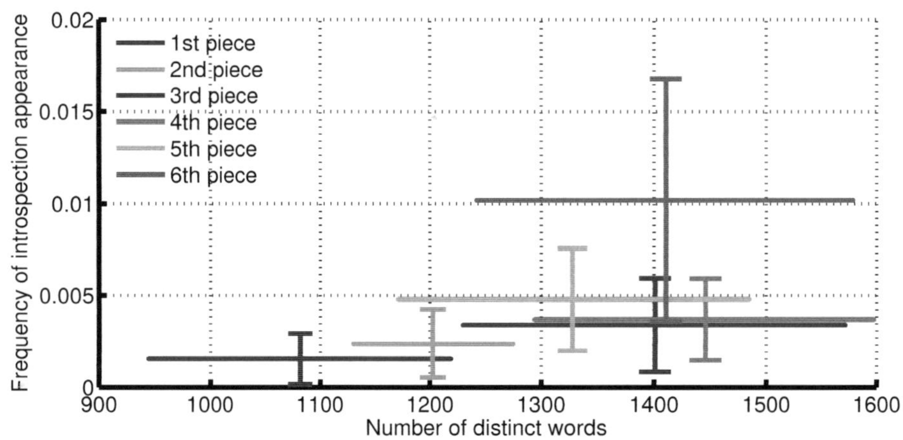


Figure 3: Frequency of words related to introspection versus the amount of different words in the Bible, divided in 6 pieces of the same length.

## 4 Conclusions

Previous work in the evolution of literary styles in the Western tradition has conjectured the existence of a gradual yet persistent increase of the degree of *introspection*. In particular, the ideas of Marshall McLuhan and Julian Jaynes suggest the hypothesis that these changes reflect profound and permanent alterations in the cognitive structures of the culture. We set out to investigate to what extent it is possible to analyze, quantitatively, this hypothesis. We focused on Homeric and Biblical texts, given their cultural preeminence, and utilized relatively simple analytic techniques to measure the degree of introspection along the texts, assuming they reflect, however imperfectly, a certain chronological order.

The result of measuring word frequencies is highly positive, indicating that it is indeed possible to statistically discriminate between texts based on a semantic core centered around introspection, chronologically and culturally belonging to different phases. However, our analysis seems to really break down for Proust, as one intuitively would expect a much higher measure of introspection. This failure is clearly an indication of the limitations of our current approach, which as it stands may only not be applicable to modern or contemporary literature.

Our analysis on the Bible is of particular interest. It enables us to analyze the "arrow of time" of introspection within a relatively coherent framework, and the relationship between textual linearity and chronological order is certainly not simple. Another interesting aspect is how introspection and citations to God evolve along the test, with a significant increase in introspection as the lexical order moves ahead, while references to God show a weaker, yet clearly discernible trend to diminish.

As an alternative approach, in order to capture the presence of relevant passages of introspection using a data-driven method, we applied topic modeling. We observed a handful of topics that contained words related to introspection. The analysis of the Bible under this technique mirrors the results obtained with the more hand-crafted approach.

While the analysis presented can only be considered an initial step towards a systematic characterization of the textual correlate of the concept of introspection, the simplicity of our methods and the clarity of the results support our initial hypothesis, and validate our approach. In our opinion, the rigorous extension of our analysis can provide not only a stricter statistical measure of the evolution of introspection, but also a means to investigate subtle differences in aesthetic styles and cognitive structures across cultures, authors and literary forms (i.e. the novel, cf. (Moretti, 2005)).

## 5 Outlook

Given the necessarily broad, integrative nature of any approach to introspection, there is a number of different alternatives we are currently exploring to expand our analysis, with an emphasis on inter-

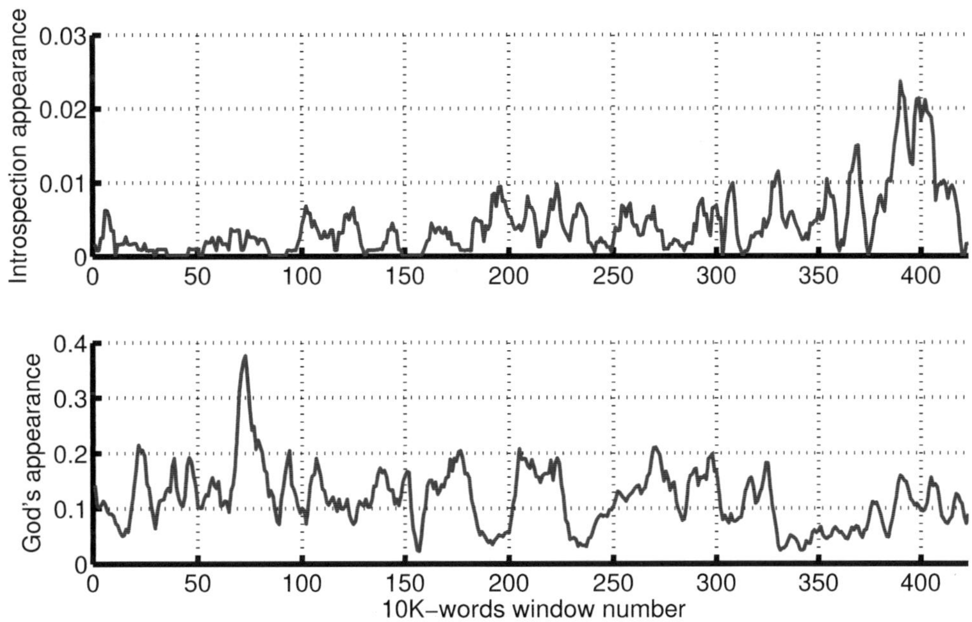


Figure 4: Frequency of words related to introspection and God versus the 10,000-words window number.

disciplinary perspectives.

A first step is systematizing the routines for filtering, processing and analysis of the texts. We will incorporate more terms related to introspection captured in the structure of Wordnet, and eventually also incorporate as part of the analysis elements of the graphical structure that underlies this database (Sigman and Cecchi, 2002). Some interesting developments in this area are the measures of semantic similarity between concepts (Budanitsky and Hirst, 2006; Pedersen et al., 2004; Patwardhan et al., 2003). This measure may result useful for classifying the different topics acquired using topic modeling, taking into account the *similarity* of the words related to introspection, as an extension to the semantic relationships established by Wordnet and the various dictionaries and thesaurii currently available as databases.

We will also incorporate the notion of *concept drift* to our topic modeling, expecting it to account for the temporal evolution of the use of introspection. A promising proposal for this purpose is that of Dynamic Topic Modeling. We are particularly interested in approaches that require minimal a priori intervention; we expect that a dynamic model with an unconstrained number of topics, as opposed to the fixed number of topics proposed in the original paper (Blei and Lafferty, 2006), may lead more naturally to the identification of potential transitions along the text. This approach is not straightforward to implement, and may require the development of an appropriate statistical model.

Another step will be a more careful and principled selection and categorization of our text corpus. While the techniques at hand enable the analysis of massive amounts of data, we will select our texts based on their cultural and historical relevance in a more systematic way. Comparing different cultures and ages results in an interesting challenge. We are specifically interested in the replication of the results presented here in the case of the aboriginal American cultures. The concept of introspection appears in many classic American texts such as the Popol Vuh and the Chilam Balam; however, their compilation by European scholars and translation to different languages may not keep the essence of the original texts. A robust systematization of our technique will allow us to analyze texts in different languages easily. We look forward to compare the measures of introspection between texts in their native languages in contrast with its appearance in their translations. Moreover, this may help with the conservation of se-

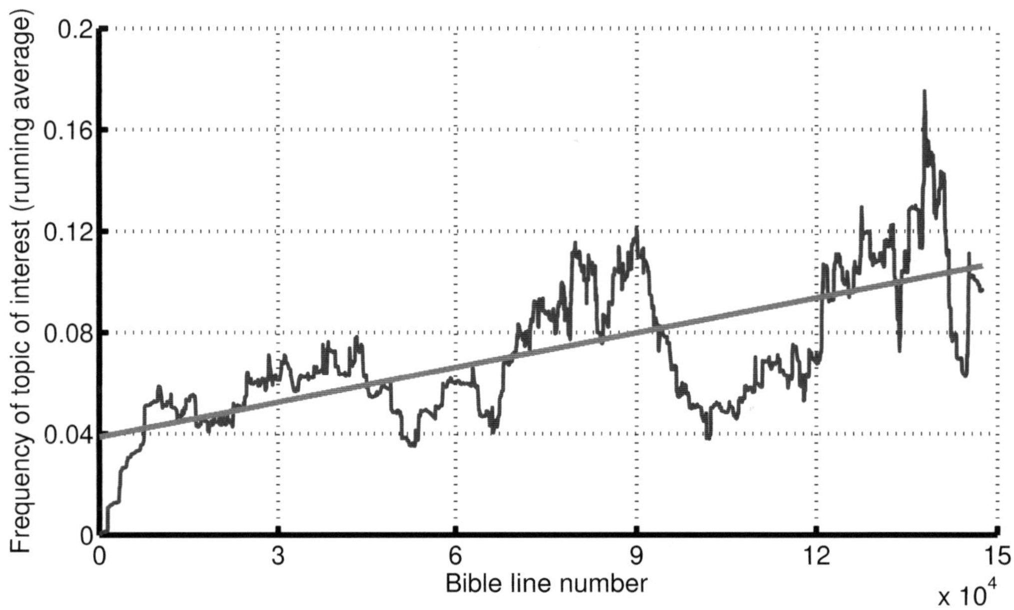


Figure 5: Frequency of Introspection topic as the main topic for each section of the Bible, as a running average every 100 lines.

lected concepts along translations of texts. This line of research will require the interaction with experts in early American philology.

Finally, it is important to note that the analytical techniques proposed here, namely the quantification of psychological concepts embedded in the text, can be used as tools for pedagogical and psychiatric evaluation (Lombardo et al., 2007). This will require a consorted effort with psychologists and psychiatrists to collect and organize personal narrations by patients, as well as the compilation of texts already available in the literature, in particular by people suffering from schizophrenia and depression.

In summary, we believe the results presented here will provide a rich source of multi-disciplinary follow-up and derived lines of research around statistical measurements of psychological features in text, within and beyond the concept of introspection.

## References


Adkins, A. (1970). *From the many to the one: a study of personality and views of human nature in the context of ancient Greek society, values and beliefs*. Constable & Company Limited.

Blei, D. (2009). *Text Mining: Theory and Applications (A. Srivastava and M. Sahami editors)*, chapter Topic Models. Taylor and Francis.

Blei, D. and Lafferty, J. (2006). Dynamic topic models. In *ICML '06: Proceedings of the 23rd international conference on Machine learning*, pages 113–120, New York, NY, USA. ACM.

Budanitsky, A. and Hirst, G. (2006). Evaluating wordnet-based measures of lexical semantic relatedness. *Computational Linguistics*, 32(1):13–47.

Cavanna, A., Trimble, M., Cinti, F., and Monaco, F. (2007). The "bicameral mind" 30 years on: a critical reappraisal of Julian Jaynes hypothesis. *Functional Neurology*, 22(1):11–15.

Daniel C. Stevenson, W. A. (last accessed: Feb. 27th, 2010). Mit classics. `http://classics.mit.edu/`.

De Jong, I. and Sullivan, J. (1994). *Modern critical theory and classical literature*. Brill Academic Pub.

Dodds, E. (1951). *The Greeks and the Irrational*. Berkeley: Univ. of California Press.

Jaynes, J. (2000). *The origin of consciousness in the breakdown of the bicameral mind*. Mariner Books.

Lombardo, M., Barnes, J., Wheelwright, S., and Baron-Cohen, S. (2007). Self-Referential Cognition and Empathy in Autism. *PLoS ONE*, 2(9):e883.

McCallum, A. (2002). Mallet: A machine learning for language toolkit. http://mallet.cs.umass.edu.

McLuhan, M. (1962). *The Gutenberg galaxy: The making of typographic man*. Routledge & Kegan Paul.

Moretti, F. (2005). *Graphs, Maps, Trees: Abstract models for a literary history*. Verso Books.

Onians, R. (1988). *The origins of European thought about the body, the mind, the soul, the world, time, and fate: new interpretations of Greek, Roman and kindred evidence also of some basic Jewish and Christian beliefs*. Cambridge University Press.

Patwardhan, S., Banerjee, S., and Pedersen, T. (2003). Using measures of semantic relatedness for word sense disambiguation. *Lecture notes in computer science*, pages 241–257.

Pedersen, T., Patwardhan, S., and Michelizzi, J. (2004). Wordnet:: similarity-measuring the relatedness of concepts. In *Proceedings of the National Conference on Artificial Intelligence*, pages 1024–1025.

Sigman, M. and Cecchi, G. (2002). Global organization of the wordnet lexicon. *Proceedings of the National Academy of Sciences*, 99(3):1742.

# Combining CBIR and NLP for Multilingual Terminology Alignment and Cross-Language Image Indexing

**Diego A. Burgos Herrera**
Translation and New Technologies Group
University of Antioquia
Calle 67 No. 53-108 – Bloque 11
burgos.diego@gmail.com

## Abstract

In this paper, an overview of an approach for cross-language image indexing and multilingual terminology alignment is presented. Content-Based Image Retrieval (CBIR) is proposed as a means to find similar images in target language documents in the web and natural language processing is used to reduce the search space and find the image index. As the experiments are carried out in specialized domains, a systematic and recursive use of the approach is used to align multilingual terminology by creating repositories of images with their respective cross-language indices.

## 1 Introduction

Images, as representation of real world entities, constitute a *sine qua non* prerequisite for a number of language tasks. For instance, children as well as foreign language learners often resort to images in order to concretize lexical learning through associative processes (cf. Bloom, 2000: 57).

Likewise, human translators particularly benefit a lot from images when dealing with specialized texts. For example, a word-based image search is a very useful technique to enhance understanding of the source text and achieve precision in the target text. In the context of online resources, a site with the image of a device provides the translator not only with an illustration of the object, but also with hyperlinks to websites containing relevant information.

However, for an integral usage of images as a supportive resource for automated language processes, comprehensive indexed image databases as well as wide-coverage lists of suitable index terms are required. The availability of such lists and the material to index images are language dependent. For instance, for English, considerably more resources are available than for Spanish. A study carried out by Burgos (2006) with bilingual Spanish-English terminological dictionaries revealed that the average of retrieved Spanish documents per term from the web was dramatically lower (7,860) than the average of retrieved English documents (246,575). One explanation to this is the huge size of the web search space for English and the little search space for Spanish. However, another reason is that Spanish terms found in traditional terminological dictionaries could not be of conventional usage among experts and do not represent what is actually contained in the search space. Therefore, more suitable index terms must be looked for.

In the present work, content-based image retrieval (CBIR) is proposed as a means for multilingual terminology retrieval from the web with the purpose of aligning a multilingual glossary and building up an image index. The main goal of this research is to exploit the co-occurrence of images and terms in specialized texts which has been called the bimodal co-occurrence (BC). Experiments have been done so far for English and Span-



*Proceedings of the NAACL HLT 2010 Young Investigators Workshop on Computational Approaches to Languages of the Americas*, pages 76–83, Los Angeles, California, June 2010. 

ish with a few observations in other languages, e.g., Portuguese. Figure 1 shows a forecast of the whole system.

The following section provides references on previous work and suggests that the use of terminology for indexing specialized domain images in a bilingual or multilingual setting has not been discussed in previous literature. Section 3 describes the bimodal co-occurrence (BC) hypothesis with more detail. Section 4 provides an overview of how CBIR supports image indexing and term alignment and includes an outline of the procedure to select candidate indices through concrete / abstract discrimination. Section 5 presents the current appeals and needs of this research and section 6 sketches the future work.

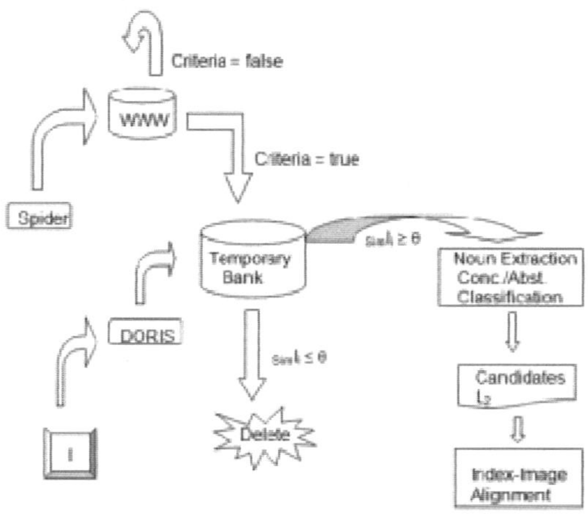


Figure 1. Forecast of the system. A spider is launch to the Internet. Websites fulfilling predefined criteria are temporarily saved and their images analyzed by DORIS. If an image in the website presents feature values within a threshold determined by the example image features, nouns are extracted and classified from the surrounding text to make up a list of candidate target terms which could designate the object in the website's image. Finally, index-image alignment is carried out.

## 2 Related Research

The particular nature of this research where linguistic and visual representations converge to make up a bimodal co-occurrence which is intended to be exploited for multilingual term retrieval from the web requires the support of diverse specialized knowledge to be applied along the image-based multilingual term retrieval proposed here. As a consequence, the required processes will be framed within or related to the fields and subfields of cross-language information retrieval, cross-language retrieval from image collections, image-term alignment, image annotation and content-based image retrieval.

Many of the latest contributions on the above mentioned fields have been presented in widely known events such as the Text Retrieval Conference (TREC), the Cross-Language Evaluation Forum (CLEF), the Language Resource Evaluation Conference (LREC), the Special Interest Group in Information Retrieval (SIGIR) Conference or the Symposium on String Processing and Information Retrieval (SPIRE), among others.

For work related to cross-language image retrieval which deals with the problem of retrieving images from multilingual collections, see Clough et al. (2006), Clough et al. (2005), Clough (2005), Bansal et al. (2005), Daumke et al. (2006), Izquierdo-Beviá et al. (2005) or Peinado et al. (2005).

Likewise, for standard and alternatives proposals for Content-Based Image Retrieval systems, the reader can check DORIS (Jaramillo and Branch, 2009b), CIRES[1] (Iqbal and Aggarwal, 2003), QBIC[2] (Flickner *et al.*, 1995), PHOTOBOOK[3] (Pentland *et al.*, 1996), IMATCH[4] and VisualSEEk[5] (Smith and Chang, 1996), Nakazato et al. (2003) or Iqbal and Aggarwal (2003). On the other hand, for a detailed description of the CBIR standard technology, see Urcid Pliego (2003), Geradts (2003) or Rui et al. (1999) who present concrete information on the main features for CBIR as well as on some related systems and research. For web-based CBIR related work, see Carson et al. (2002), Yi et al., (2000), Chang et al. (1997), Tollmar et al. (2004) or Drelie et al. (2007). An updated review, compilation of CBIR techniques, real world applications, evaluation techniques and interesting references can be found in Datta et al. (2008).

Content and Text-Based Cross-Language Image Retrieval works can be found in Alvarez et al. (2005), Besançon et al. (2005), Besançon and Mil-

[1] http://amazon.ece.utexas.edu/~qasim/research.htm

[2] http://domino.research.ibm.com/comm/pr.nsf/pages/rsc.qbic.html

[3] http://vismod.media.mit.edu/vismod/demos/photobook/

[4] http://www.photools.com/

[5] http://www.ctr.columbia.edu/~jrsmith/html/pubs/acmmm96/acmfin.html

let (2006), Chang and Chen (2006) or Deselaers et al. (2006).

Image Annotation contributions can be reviewed in Barnard et al. (2003), Cheng et al. (2005), Liu et al. (2006), Qiu et al. (2006), Rahman et al. (2005), Florea et al, (2006), Güld et al. (2006), Petkova and Ballesteros (2005), Müller et al. (2006) or Li and Wang (2003).

Finally, some image-term alignment work has been presented in Burgos and Wanner (2006), Declerck and Alcantara (2006); Li and Wang (2003); Barnard and Forsyth (2001); Pastra (2006) and Wang et al. (2004).

## 3 BC Hypothesis

The starting point of this proposal is the BC hypothesis which can be defined as follows.

We assume language independent bimodal co-occurrence of images and their index terms in the corpus. This implies that if an image occurs in a document of the corpus, the corresponding index term will also occur in the same document (see Figure 2).

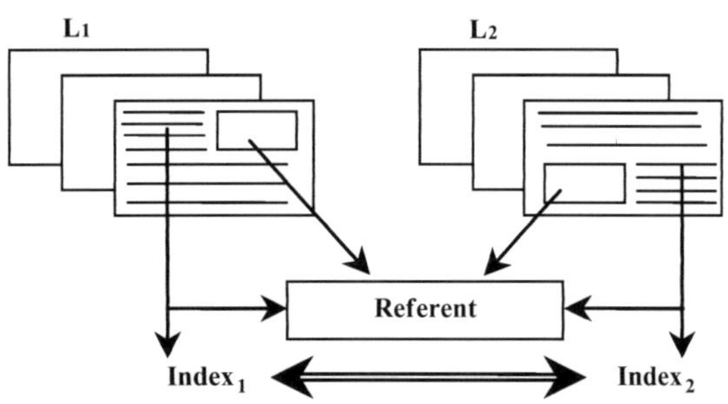


Figure 2. Representation of the BC-hypothesis

Figure 2 also suggests the BC in a bilingual setting. That is, when there is an image of an object in the source language corpus along with its index term there should also be an image of the same object along with its index term in the target language corpus. This means that matching both images would get the two equivalent terms closer. Table 1 shows an example of the bilingual setting of the BC. Both bimodal pairs (image and term) were extracted from manually tracked websites. It is an example of two manually matched images taken from two different language websites which also serve to illustrate how cross-language equivalences between index terms can be established.

| | Source (English) | Target (Spanish) |
|---|---|---|
| Image | 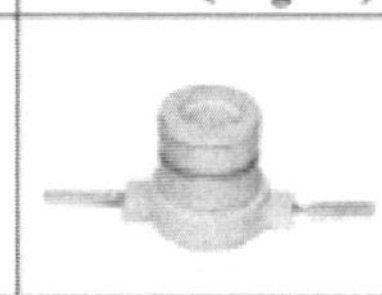 |  |
| Index | Slip-Ring FD 3G 26.9 mm | Colector Ford 3G |

Table 1. BC-hypothesis for indexing in a bilingual setting.

In order to prove this BC assumption with some more representative data, a preliminary empirical study (carried out initially for English) was carried out. A sub-corpus of 20 noun phrases[6] designating concrete entities from the automotive industry was extracted from an issue of the Automotive Engineering International Online[7] journal's Tech Briefs section and used to retrieve documents from the web. The first 10 results (i.e., web pages) for each term were stored. Each of the web pages was manually analyzed to check the BC. The result was that the 20 terms confirmed the BC-hypothesis in 145 sites (out of 200) which means a 72.5% of positive cases.

## 4 CBIR-Based Image indexing

In order to make the most of the BC, it is necessary to automate the process of image matching and image indexing. The fact of matching two images coming from different language documents generates comparable corpora (i.e., topic related) and increases the probability of aligning two equivalent terms by reducing the search space. To do so, we use DORIS, a Domain-ORiented Image Searcher (Jaramillo and Branch, 2009a). DORIS is a JAVA application to retrieve visual information which uses both geometric and Zernike moments based on texture and shape information contained in images. DORIS performance reaches a 90% of precision (Jaramillo and Branch, 2009b).

For the image indexing, we first start from a source language indexed image. An internet segment in the target language is delimited as the search space whose images are compared with the source language image using DORIS. When a

[6] See (Quirk et al., 1985: 247) or (Bosque, 1999: 8-28, 45-51) with respect to the interpretation of the concept 'concrete noun'.

[7] Cf. http://www.sae.org/automag/, state January, 2006.

positive image matching occurs, the target language document containing the matched image is marked as a potential location of the target language index term.

Given that more noise results from a large search space, the size of the image database is usually one of the major concerns in CBIR applications. In our work, we observed that the first problem to tackle is the appropriate definition of the web segment that will constitute the search space. Therefore, scalability and quality issues will be initially addressed by systematically predefining the websites which could contain the image and therefore the target term. In this regard, and as a starting point, the Open Directory Project[8] is used to define our search space. This way, not only categories but also languages can be filtered. For example, the url http://www.dmoz.org/Business/Automotive/ leads to the *automotive* category which contains subcategories and sites in English. On the other hand, following the url http://www.dmoz.org/World/Español/Negocios/Industrias/Automotriz/ which specifies the language, the user finds subcategories and sites of the category *automotriz* for Spanish.

The image database size and quality will depend on this definition. Uniformity is more likely, for example, within the photographs of the same site than between the images of two or more sites. Likewise, there will be greater variance of image characteristics between the images of two different domains than within the images of the same domain, and so on.

Current results were achieved using DORIS. The observations made so far with respect to matching of images on the web suggest that some positive matches in rather homogeneous search spaces provided enough target index term locations to pursue index candidate selection.

## 4.1 Index Candidate Selection

As it has been suggested, BC can be used for monolingual or bilingual indexing. Once this setting has been decided and the target image has been located as described in the previous section, the index candidate selection can be carried out but, before, it is possible to reduce even more the search space for the index term location by parsing the text surrounding the target image and extracting the noun phrases (NP).

We distinguish NPs from other sort of phrases by means of a chunker. Once all NPs have been extracted, some normalization is done in order to optimize the coming noun classification stage. The cleaning consists of removing determiners at the beginning of the phrase; lemmatization (if appropriate); discarding NPs whose head noun is an acronym[9]; splitting Saxon possessives, and deleting proper nouns and numbers:

*three development objectives --> development objective*
*FSE's single direct injector --> single direct injector*

Given the nature of the association, we are focusing, that is image-term alignment, the list of remaining NPs can be additionally pruned by classifying nouns intro concrete and abstract[10].

Classifying nouns as denoting an *abstractum* or a *concretum* is not a trivial task and cannot be widely covered in this paper because of the limited space. It can be said, however, that for noun classification, some approaches have been considered here. For example, remarkable contributions were made particularly by Bullinaria (2008), Katrenko and Adriaans (2008), Peirsman et al. (2008), Shaoul and Westbury (2008), Van de Cruys (2008) and Versley (2008). They use word space and syntactic models which, in some cases, behave very well.

As for the present study experimentation concerning noun classification, three approaches were tested. The number one used non-linguistic variables, the number two was based on syntactic patterns and the number three used lexical semantics information taken from WordNet (Fellbaum, 1998). The automatic semantic annotation was done by the SuperSenseTagger (Ciaramita, 2006). In fact, it is the latter approach the one that yielded the best results with a precision of 88.6% (for detailed information, see Burgos, 2009).

[8] http://dmoz.org/

[9] NPs with acronyms as HN are not included at this stage of the work since often do not reveal whether they designate concrete or abstract entities – which could hinder further validation.

[10] The experiments in this stage so far have been done for English.

|  | Concrete | Abstract | No annotation | No analysis |
|---|---|---|---|---|
| Concrete | 81 | 14 | 1 | 4 |
| Abstract | 8 | 90 | 0 | 2 |

Table 2. Results of noun classification for 100 concrete nouns and 100 abstract nouns. The first two columns/rows show the confusion matrix

These figures suggest that out of 95 concrete nouns, 81 were correctly annotated, and that out of 98 abstract nouns, 90 were annotated with the right sense.

### 4.2 Index-Image Alignment

With a 90% of precision in image matching and an 88.6% of precision in the noun classification task, we assume a high probability of having the right image with a reduced list of index candidates.

Now, the indexing process can be simplified if the image file name matches any of the candidates. For cases where such matching does not occur, the following procedure is proposed.

For indexing the target image, each candidate is used to query the image database (e.g., Google) for images. For each candidate, the 20 first retrieved images are compared with the target image using DORIS. When a positive image match occurs, the original image is indexed with the candidate that was used to retrieve from the web the image that yielded the positive image match. Table 4 illustrates this procedure by an example. In the example, the images retrieved by *steering wheel* and *air filter* did not match with the original image, but one of the images retrieved by *cylinder head* did. Therefore, the original image is indexed as *cylinder head.*

| **NP** | **Google Images** | **Original image** | **Matching (+/-)** | **New index** |
|---|---|---|---|---|
| steering wheel | ☼ → <br> ☼ → | <br> ⇮ | – <br> – | <br> – |
| cylinder head | ◙ → <br> ⇮ → <br> OBJ → | <br> ⇮ <br> | – <br> + <br> – | ⇮ <br> cylinder head |
| air filter | ۞ → <br> ۞ → | <br> ⇮ | – <br> – | <br> – |

Table 3. Illustration of the monolingual image-index alignment procedure.

## 5 Discussion

The approach shows that image indices can be assigned taking into account usage, specificity and geographical variants. The fact of indexing the image with a term retrieved from its context assures that the index term is being used. Moreover, this technique tries to retrieve the appropriate degree of specificity that the index of a specific domain image is expected to present – which is often determined by the number of modifiers of multiword expressions. Likewise, even for specialized discourse, indices should respond to geographical variants. This aspect can be controlled by specifying country domains.

## 6 Appeals and needs

This work could be incorporated with projects dealing with the access to existing information bases by providing multilingual and multimodal extensions to them. For instance, assistive technology databases (e.g. EASTIN) or patent retrieval engines (cf. Codina et al., 2008) which contain a great deal of visual content.

Content-Based Image Retrieval (CBIR) is an important contribution to multimodal information retrieval. In addition, pairing images with equivalent multilingual terminology has become a matter of interest, particularly in specialized domains. This work could integrate CBIR and natural language processing (NLP) techniques so that images can be used as language independent representations to help in finding documents of textual or ontology descriptions.

Our approach can be especially useful for web users who do not know the structure of the classification system to successfully search or when they do not know the language and special terminology of the information base.

Thus, this work can be integrated to other systems in order to provide cross-lingual retrieval and machine translation for both queries and documents and to enable visualization support for query formulation and document content presentation.

Given the nature of this research's products, they can be included into the scope of multilinguality by combining CBIR and cross-language information retrieval technology. A link to terminological databases can also be established so they can be automatically fed with entries and visual content.

As for this research needs, an adaptation of the SST to Spanish would be really valuable. The SST has already been ported to Italian which represents an interesting experience to take into account.

On the other hand, optimization and integration of the research modules such as a web crawler and an interface for CBIR and noun classification are still pending.

## 7 Future work

Given that not all process stages of the proposal presented in this paper have been completely integrated and automated, an overall evaluation has not been possible so far. Future work aims at integrating DORIS in modules for index candidate selection and index-image alignment. The goal is to be able to compile multilingual specialized glossaries after systematic and recursive exploration of well delimited web segments and storage of images with their respective cross-language indices. Likewise, some other methods to improve discrimination between concrete and abstract nouns will be researched. The above cited related works in this line have not been tested yet for our proposal, but, for future work, they will be taken into account provided that these models rely on local information and it certainly represents an advantage for this specific task[11]. Even if linguistic specific features are hard to find in both classes of nouns, they are not completely discarded. Finally, further experiments will be carried out with other domains than automotive engineering.

## Acknowledgments

This study is part of a wider research work being carried out by the author within the framework of his PhD thesis at the IULA, Universitat Pompeu Fabra, Barcelona, Spain. It was partially supported by a grant from the Government of Catalonia according to resolution UNI/772/2003 of the Departament d'Universitats, Recerca i Societat de la Informació dated March 10th, 2003.

The author is very grateful with the anonymous reviewers of this paper as well as with Leo Wanner and Stefanos Vrochidis for their valuable comments.

[11] From a theoretical and experimental point of view, Altarriba et al. (1999) provide concreteness, context availability, and imageability ratings and word associations for abstract, concrete, and emotion words. These ratings may be used to further research in areas such as retrieval of abstract and concrete nouns.

## References

Altarriba, J.; Bauer, L. M. & Benvenuto, C. (1999), 'Concreteness, context availability, and imageability ratings and word associations for abstract, concrete, and emotion words', *Behavior Research Methods, Instruments, & Computers* **31**(4), 578-602.

Alvarez, C.; Oumohmed, A. I.; Mignotte, M. & Nie, J.Y. (2005), *Multilingual Information Access for Text, Speech and Images*, Springer Berlin / Heidelberg, Berlin, chapter Toward Cross-Language and Cross-Media Image Retrieval, pp. 676-687.

Bansal, V.; Zhang, C.; Chai, J. Y. & Jin, R. (2005), *Multilingual Information Access for Text, Speech and Images*, Springer Berlin / Heidelberg, Berlin, chapter MSU at ImageCLEF: Cross Language and Interactive Image Retrieval, pp. 805-815.

Barnard, K. & Forsyth, D. (2001), Learning the semantics of words and pictures, *in* 'Proceedings of the International Conference on Computer Vision', pp. 408--415.

Barnard, K.; Duygulu, P.; Forsyth, D.; de Freitas, N.; Blei, D. M. & Jordan, M. I. (2003), 'Matching Words and Pictures', *Journal of Machine Learning Research* **3**, 1107–1135.

Besançon, R. & Millet, C. (2006), Using Text and Image Retrieval Systems: Lic2m Experiments at ImageCLEF 2006, *in* 'Working notes of the CLEF 2006 Workshop'.

Besançon, R.; Hede, P.; Moellic, P.A. & Fluhr, C. (2005), *Multilingual Information Access for Text, Speech and Images*, Springer Berlin / Heidelberg, Berlin, chapter Cross-Media Feedback Strategies: Merging Text and Image Information to Improve Image Retrieval, pp. 709-717.

Bloom, P. (2000), *How Children Learn the Meanings of Words*, MIT Press.

Bosque, I. (1999). El nombre común. In Bosque, I., Demonte, V. (eds) *Gramática descriptiva de la lengua castellana*. Madrid: Espasa Calpe, pp. 3-75.

Bullinaria, J. A. (2008), Semantic Categorization Using Simple Word Co-occurrence Statistics, *in* Baroni Marco; Evert Stefan & Lenci Alessandro, ed.,'ESSLLIWorkshop on Distributional Lexical Semantics'.

Burgos, D. & Wanner, L. (2006), Using CBIR for Multilingual Terminology Glossary Compilation and Cross-Language Image Indexing, *in* 'Proceedings of the Workshop on Language Resources for Content-based Image Retrieval', pp. 5-8.

Burgos, D. (2006). Concept and Usage-Based Approach

for Highly Specialized Technical Term Translation. In Gotti, M., Sarcevic, S. (eds) 2006. *Insights into Specialized Translation*. Bern: Peter Lang.

Burgos, D. (2009) "Clasificación de nombres concretos y abstractos para extracción terminológica". In *La terminología y los usuarios de la información: puntos de encuentro y relaciones necesarias para la transferencia de la información*. 4, 5 and 6 of May, 2009. Medellin, Colombia. ISBN: 978-958-714-251-8 .

Carson, C., Belongie, S., Greenspan, H., Malik, J. (2002). Blobworld: Image Segmentation Using Expectation-Maximisation and its Application to Image Querying. *IEEE Trans. Pattern Analysis and Machine Intelligence* 24(8), pp. 1026-1038.

Chang, S., Smith, J. R., Beigi, M., Benitez, A. (1997). Visual Information Retrieval from Large Distributed Online Repositories. *Communications of the ACM* 40(12). 63-71.

Chang, Y.C. & Chen, H.H. (2006), Approaches of Using a Word-Image Ontology and an Annotated Image Corpus as Intermedia for Cross-Language Image Retrieval, *in* 'Working notes of the CLEF 2006 Workshop'.

Chen, F., Gargi, U., Niles, L., Schutze, H. (1999). Multi-Modal Browsing of Images in Web Documents. *Document Recognition and Retrieval VI, Proceedings of SPIE* 3651, pp. 122-133.

Chen, Y., Wang, J. Krovetz, R. (2003). CLUE: Cluster-Based Retrieval of Images by Unsupervised Learning. *IEEE Transactions on Image Processing*, Vol. 14 (8) pp. 1187-1201.

Cheng, P.C.; Chien, B.C.; Ke, H.R. & Yang, W.P. (2005), NCTU_DBLAB@ImageCLEF 2005: Automatic annotation task, *in* 'Working Notes of the CLEF Workshop 2005'.

Ciaramita, M. & Altun, Y. (2006), Broad-Coverage Sense Disambiguation and Information Extraction with a Supersense Sequence Tagger, *in* 'Proceedings of the Conference on Empirical Methods in Natural Language Processing'.

Clough, P. (2005), *Multilingual Information Access for Text, Speech and Images*, Springer Berlin / Heidelberg, Berlin, chapter Caption and Query Translation for Cross-Language Image Retrieval, pp. 614-625.

Clough, P.; Grubinger, M.; Deselaers, T.; Hanbury, A. & Müller, H. (2006), Overview of the ImageCLEF 2006 photographic retrieval and object annotation tasks, *in* 'Working notes of the CLEF 2006 Workshop'.

Clough, P.; Müller, H. & Sanderson, M. (2005), *Multilingual Information Access for Text, Speech and Images*, Springer Berlin / Heidelberg, Berlin, chapter The CLEF 2004 Cross-Language Image Retrieval Track, pp. 597-613.

Codina, J.; Pianta, E.; Vrochidis, S.; Papadopoulos, S. (2008) 'Integration of Semantic, Metadata and Image search engines with a text search engine for patent retrieval', Semantic Search 2008 Workshop, Tenerife, Spain, 2 June.

Datta, R.; Joshi, D.; Li, J. & Wang, J. Z. (2008), 'Image retrieval: Ideas, influences, and trends of the new age', *ACM Comput. Surv.* **40**(2), 1--60.

Daumke, P.; Paetzold, J. & Markó, K. (2006), Morphosaurus in ImageCLEF 2006: The effect of subwords on biomedical IR, *in* 'Working notes of the CLEF 2006 Workshop'.

Declerck, T. & Alcantara, M. (2006), Semantic Analysis of Text Regions Surrounding Images in Web Documents, *in* 'Proceedings of the Workshop on Language Resources for Content-based Image Retrieval', pp. 9-12.

Deselaers, T.; Weyand, T. & Ney, H. (2006), Image Retrieval and Annotation Using Maximum Entropy, *in* 'Working notes of the CLEF 2006 Workshop'.

Fellbaum, C. (1998), *WordNet: An Electronic Lexical Database*, MIT Press, Cambridge.

Gelasca, E. D.; Ghosh, P.; Moxley, E.; Guzman, J. D.; Xu, J.; Bi, Z.; Gauglitz, S.; Rahimi, A. M. & Manjunath, B. S. (2007), 'CORTINA: Searching a 10 Million + Images Database'.

Güld, M. O.; Thies, C.; Fischer, B. & Lehmann, T. M. (2006), Combining global features for content-based retrieval of medical images, *in* 'Working notes of the CLEF 2006 Workshop'.

Iqbal, I. & Aggarwal, J. K. (2003), Feature Integration, Multi-image Queries and Relevance Feedback in Image Retrieval, *in* '6th International Conference on Visual Information Systems (VISUAL 2003)', pp. 467-474.

Izquierdo-Beviá, R.; Tomás, D.; Saiz-Noeda, M. & Vicedo, J. L. (2005), University of Alicante in ImageCLEF2005, *in* 'Working Notes of the CLEF Workshop 2005'.

Jaramillo, G. & Branch, J. (2009), 'Recuperación de Imágenes por Contenido Utilizando Momentos', *Revista Iteckne* **5**(2).

Jaramillo, G. E. & Branch, J. W. (2009), Recuperación Eficiente de Información Visual Utilizando Momentos, *in* 'XXXV Conferencia Latinoamericana de Informática - CLEI 2009'.

Katrenko, S. & Adriaans, P. (2008), Qualia Structures and their Impact on the Concrete Noun Categorization Task, *in* Baroni Marco; Evert Stefan & Lenci Alessandro, ed.,'ESSLLIWorkshop on Distributional Lexical Semantics'.

Li, J. & Wang, J. Z. (2003), 'Automatic Linguistic Indexing of Pictures by a Statistical Modeling Approach', *IEEE TRANSACTIONS ON PATTERN ANALYSIS AND MACHINE INTELLIGENCE* **25**(9), 1075-1088.

Liu, J.; Hu, Y.; Li, M. & Ying Ma, W. (2006), Medical Image Annotation and Retrieval Using Visual Features, *in* 'Working notes of the CLEF 2006 Workshop'.

Müller, H.; Gass, T. & Geissbuhler, A. (2006), Performing image classification with a frequency–based information retrieval schema for ImageCLEF 2006, *in* 'Working notes of the CLEF 2006 Workshop'.

Pastra, K. (2006), Image-Language Association: are we looking at the right features?, *in* 'Proceedings of the Workshop on Language Resources for Content-based Image Retrieval', pp. 40-43.

Peinado, V.; López-Ostenero, F. & Gonzalo, J. (2005), UNED at ImageCLEF 2005: Automatically Structured Queries with Named Entities over Metadata, *in* 'Working Notes of the CLEF Workshop 2005'.

Peirsman, Y.; Heylen, K. & Geeraerts, D. (2008), Size Matters: Tight and Loose Context Definitions in English Word Space Models, *in* Baroni Marco; Evert Stefan & Lenci Alessandro, ed.,'ESSLLIWorkshop on Distributional Lexical Semantics'.

Petkova, D. & Ballesteros, L. (2005), Categorizing and Annotating Medical Images by Retrieving Terms Relevant to Visual Features, *in* 'Working Notes of the CLEF Workshop 2005'.

Qiu, B.; Xu, C. & Tian, Q. (2006), Two-stage SVM for Medical Image Annotation, *in* 'Working notes of the CLEF 2006 Workshop'.

Quirk, R., Greenbaum, S., Leech, G. Svartvik, J. (1985). *A Comprehensive Grammar of the English Language*. London: Longman.

Rahman, M. M.; Desai, B. C. & Bhattacharya, P. (2005), Supervised Machine Learning based Medical Image Annotation and Retrieval, *in* 'Working Notes of the CLEF Workshop 2005'.

*Routledge English Technical Dictionary*. Copenhaguen: Routledge. 1998.

Shaoul, C. & Westbury, C. (2008), Performance of HAL-like word space models on semantic clustering, *in* Baroni Marco; Evert Stefan & Lenci Alessandro, ed.,'ESSLLIWorkshop on Distributional Lexical Semantics'.

Shen H.T., Ooi B.C., Tan K.L. (2000). Giving Meanings to WWW Images. In: *Proceedings of the 8th ACM international conference on multimedia*, 30 October - 3 November 2000, Los Angeles, pp 39-48

Tsai, C. (2003). Stacked Generalisation: a Novel Solution to Bridge the Semantic Gap for Content-Based Image Retrieval. *Online Information Review*, Vol. 27 (6), pp. 442-445.

Van de Cruys, T. (2008), A Comparison of Bag of-Words and Syntax-based Approaches for Word Categorization, *in* Baroni Marco; Evert Stefan & Lenci Alessandro, ed.,'ESSLLIWorkshop on Distributional Lexical Semantics'.

Versley, Y. (2008), Decorrelation and Shallow Semantic Patterns for Distributional Clustering of Nouns and Verbs, *in* Baroni Marco; Evert Stefan & Lenci Alessandro, ed.,'ESSLLIWorkshop on Distributional Lexical Semantics'.

Wang, X. J.; Ma, W.Y. & Li, X. (2004), Data-driven approach for bridging the cognitive gap in image retrieval, *in* 'Proceedings of the 2004 IEEE International Conference on Multimedia and Expo (ICME 2004)', pp. 2231-2234.

Yeh, T., Tollmar, K., Darrell, T. (2004). Searching the Web with Mobile Images for Location Recognition. *IEEE Computer Society Conference on Computer Vision and Pattern Recognition* (CVPR'04), Vol. 2, pp. 76-81.

# IRASubcat, a highly customizable, language independent tool for the acquisition of verbal subcategorization information from corpus

**Ivana Romina Altamirano** and **Laura Alonso i Alemany**
Grupo de Procesamiento de Lenguaje Natural
Sección de Ciencias de la Computación
Facultad de Matemática, Astronomía y Física
Universidad Nacional de Córdoba
Córdoba, Argentina
romina.altamirano@gmail.com, alemany@famaf.unc.edu.ar

## Abstract

IRASubcat is a language-independent tool to acquire information about the subcategorization of verbs from corpus. The tool can extract information from corpora annotated at various levels, including almost raw text, where only verbs are identified. It can also aggregate information from a pre-existing lexicon with verbal subcategorization information. The system is highly customizable, and works with XML as input and output format.

IRASubcat identifies patterns of constituents in the corpus, and associates patterns with verbs if their association strength is over a frequency threshold and passes the likelihood ratio hypothesis test. It also implements a procedure to identify verbal constituents that could be playing the role of an adjunct in a pattern. Thresholds controlling frequency and identification of adjuncts can be customized by the user, or else they are given a default value.

## 1 Introduction and Motivation

Characterizing the behavior of verbs as nuclear organizers of clauses (the so-called subcategorization information) is crucial to obtain deep analyses of natural language. For example, it can significantly reduce structural ambiguities in parsing (Carroll et al., 1999; Carroll and Fang, 2004), help in word sense disambiguation or improve information extraction (Surdeanu et al., 2003). However, the usual construction of linguistic resources for verbal subcategorization involves many expert hours, and it is usually prone to low coverage and inconsistencies across human experts.

Corpora can be very useful to alleviate the problems of low coverage and inconsistencies. Verbs can be characterized by their behavior in a big corpus of the language. Thus, lexicographers only need to validate, correct or complete this digested information about the behavior of verbs. Moreover, the starting information can have higher coverage and be more unbiased than if it is manually constructed. That's why automatic acquisition of subcategorization frames has been an active research area since the mid-90s (Manning, 1993; Brent, 1993; Briscoe and Carroll, 1997).

However, most of the approaches have been adhoc for particular languages or particular settings, like a determined corpus with a given kind of annotation, be it manual or automatic. To our knowledge, there is no system to acquire subcategorization information from corpora that is flexible enough to work with different languages and levels of annotation of corpora.

We present IRASubcat, a tool that acquires information about the behaviour of verbs from corpora. It is aimed to address a variety of situations and needs, ranging from rich annotated corpora to virtually raw text (because the tags to study can be selected in the configuration file). The characterization of linguistic patterns associated to verbs will be correspondingly rich. The tool allows to customize most of the aspects of its functioning, to adapt to different requirements of the users. Moreover, IRASubcat is platform-independent and open source, available for download at http://www.irasubcat.com.ar.

IRASubcat input is a corpus (in xml format) with examples of the verbs one wants to characterize, and its output is a lexicon where each verb is associated with the patterns of linguistic constituents that reflect its behavior in the given corpus, an approxima-



*Proceedings of the NAACL HLT 2010 Young Investigators Workshop on Computational Approaches to Languages of the Americas*, pages 84–91, Los Angeles, California, June 2010. ©2010 Association for Computational Linguistics

tion to its subcategorization frame. Such association is established when the verb and pattern co-occur in corpus significantly enough to pass a frequency test and a hypothesis test.

In the following section we discuss some previous work in the area of subcategorization acquisition from corpora. Then, Section 3 presents the main functionality of the tool, and describe its usage. Section 4 details the parameters that can be customized to adapt to different experimental settings. In Section 5 we outline the functionality that identifies constituents that are likely to be adjuncts and not arguments, and in Section 6 we describe the procedures to determine whether a given pattern is actually part of the subcategorization frame of a verb. Section 7 presents some results of applying IRASubcat to two very different corpora. Finally, we present some conclusions and the lines of future work.

## 2 Previous Work

We review here some previous work related to acquisition of subcategorization information from corpora, focussing on the constraints of the approach and corpora to learn with. We specially mention approaches for languages other than English.

The foundational work of (Brent, 1993) was based on plain text (2.6 million words of the Wall Street Journal (WSJ, 1994)). Since the corpus had no annotation, verbs were found by heuristics. He detected six frame types and filtered associations between verbs and frames with the binomial hypothesis test. This approach obtained 73.85% f-score in an evaluation with human judges.

Also in 1993, (Ushioda et al., 1993) exploited also the WSJ corpus but only the part that was annotated with part-of-speech tags, with 600.000 words. He studied also six frame types and did not distinguishing arguments and adjuncts.

The same year, (Manning, 1993) used 4 million words of the New York Times (Sandhaus, ), selected only clauses with auxiliary verbs and automatically analyzed them with a finite-state parser. He defined 19 frame types, and reported an f-score of 58.20%.

Various authors developed approaches assuming a full syntactic analysis, which was usually annotated manually in corpora (Briscoe and Carroll, 1997; Kinyon and Prolo, 2002). Others associated syntactic analyses to corpora with automatic parsers (O'Donovan et al., 2005).

Various approaches were also found for languages other than English. For German, (Eckle-Kohler, 1999) studied the behaviour of 6305 verbs on automatically POS-tagged corpus data. He defined linguistic heuristics by regular expression queries over the usage of 244 frame types.

(Wauschkuhn, 1999) studied 1044 German verbs. He extracted maximum of 2000 example sentences for each verb from a corpus, and analyzed them with partial (as opposed to full) syntactic analysis. He found valency patterns, which were grouped in order to extract the most frequent pattern combinations, resulting in a verb-frame lexicon with 42 frame types.

(Schulte im Walde, 2000) worked with 18.7 million words of German corpus, found 38 frame types. She used the Duden das Stilwörterbuch(AG, 2001) to evaluate results and reported f-score 57,24% with PP and 62,30% without.

Many other approaches have been pursued for various languages: (de Lima, 2002) for Portuguese, (Georgala, 2003) for Greek, (Sarkar and Zeman, 2000) for Czech, (Spranger and Heid, 2003) for Dutch, (Chesley and Salmon-Alt, 2006) for French or (Chrupala, 2003) for Spanish, to name a few.

## 3 General description of the tool

IRASubcat takes as input a corpus in XML format. This corpus is expected to have some kind of annotation associated to its elements, which will enrich the description of the patterns associated to verbs. The minimal required annotation is that verbs are marked. If no other information is available, the form of words will be used to build the patterns. If the corpus has rich annotation for its elements, the system can build the patterns with the value of attributes or with a combination of them, and also with combinations with lexical items. The only requirements are that verbs are marked, and that all linguistic units to be considered to build the patterns are siblings in the XML tree.

The output of IRASubcat is a lexicon, also in XML format, where each of the verbs under inspection is associated to a set of subcategorization patterns. A given pattern is associated to a given verb if the evidence found in the corpus passes certain tests. Thresholds for these tests are defined by the user, so that precision can be priorized over recall or the other way round. In all cases, information about the evidence found and the result of each test is provided, so that it can be easily assessed whether the threshold for each test has the expected effects, and it can be modified accordingly.

The lexicon also provides information about frequencies of occurrence for verbs, patterns, and their co-occurrences in corpus.

Moreover, IRASubcat is capable of integrating the output lexicon with a pre-existing one, merging information about verbs and patterns with information that had been previously extracted, possibly from a different corpus or even from a hand-built lexicon. The only requirement is that the lexicon is in the same format as IRASubcat output lexicon.

## 4 A highly customizable tool

IRASubcat has been designed to be adaptable in a variety of settings. The user can set the conditions for many aspects of the tool, in order to extract different kinds of information for different representational purposes or from corpora with different kinds of annotation. For example, the system accepts a wide range of levels of annotation in the input corpus, and it is language independent. To guarantee that any language can be dealt with, the corpus needs to be codified in UTF-8 format, in which virtually any existing natural language can be codified.

If the user does not know how to customize these parameters, she can resort to the default values that are automatically provided by the system for each of them. The only information that needs to be specified in any case is the name of the tag marking verbs, the name of the parent tag for the linguistic units that characterize patterns and, of course, the input corpus.

The parameters of the system are as follows:

- The user can provide a list of verbs to be described, so that any other verb will not be considered. If no list is provided, all words marked as verb in the corpus will be described.
- The scope of patterns can be specified as a window of n words around the words marked as verbs, where n is a number specified by the user. It can also be specified that all elements that are siblings of the verb in the XML tree are considered, which is equivalent to considering all elements in the scope of the clause, if that is the parent node of the verb in an annotated corpus. By default, a window of 3 sibling nodes at each side of the verb is considered.
- It can be specified that patterns are completed by a dummy symbol if the context of occurrence of the verb does not provide enough linguistic elements to fill the specified window length, for example, at the end of a sentence. By default, no dummy symbol is used.
- It can be specified whether the order of occurrence of linguistic units should be taken into account to characterize the pattern or not, depending of the meaning of word order in the language under study. By default, order is not considered.
- We can provide a list of the attributes of linguistic units that we want to study, for example, syntactic function, morphological category, etc. Attributes should be expressed as an XML attribute of the unit. It can also be specified that no attribute of the unit is considered, but only its content, which is usually the surface form of the unit. By default, an attribute named "sint" will be considered.
- We can specify whether the content of linguistic units will be considered to build patterns. As in the previous case, the content is usually the surface form of the unit (lexical form). By default, content is not considered.
- A mark describing the position of the verb can be introduced in patterns. By default it is not considered, to be coherent with the default option of ignoring word order.
- It can be specified that, after identifying possible adjuncts, patterns with the same arguments are collapsed into the same pattern, with all their characterizing features (number of occurrences, etc.). By default, patterns are not collapsed.
- The number of iterations that are carried out on patterns to identify adjuncts can be customized,

by default it is not considered because by default patterns are not collapsed.

- The user can specify a minimal number of occurrences of a verb to be described. By default, the minimal frequency is 0, so all verbs that occur in the corpus are described.
- A minimal number of occurrences of a pattern can also be specified, with the default as 0.
- The user can specify whether the Log-Likelihood Ratio hypothesis test will be applied to test whether the association between a verb and a pattern cannot be considered a product of chance. By defect, the test is used (and the output will be 90, 95, 99 or 99.5 when the co-ocurrence have that confiability) .

## 5 Identification of adjuncts

One of the most interesting capabilities of IRASubcat is the identification of possible adjuncts. Adjuncts are linguistic units that do not make part of the core of a subcategorization pattern (Fillmore, 1968). They are optional constituents in the constituent structure governed by a verb. Since they are optional, we assume they can be recognized because the same pattern can occur with or without them without a significant difference. IRASubcat implements a procedure to identify these units by their optionality, described in what follows. An example of this procedure is shown in Figure 1.

First, all patterns of a verb are represented in a trie. A trie is a tree-like structure where patterns are represented as paths in the trie. In our case, the root is empty and each node represents a constituent of a pattern, so that a pattern is represented by concatenating all nodes that are crossed when following a path from the root. Each node is associated with a number expressing the number of occurrences of the pattern that is constructed from the root to that node. Constituents are ordered by frequency, so that more frequent constituents are closer to the root.

In this structure, it is easy to identify constituents that are optional, because they are topologically located at the leaves of the trie and the number of occurrences of the optional node is much smaller than the number of occurrences of its immediately preceding node.

We have experimented with different ratios between the frequency of the pattern with and without the constituent to identify adjuncts. We have found that adjuncts are usually characterized by occurring in leaves of the trie at least for 80% of the patterns of the verb.

Once a constituent is identified as an adjunct, it is removed from all patterns that contain it within the verb that is being characterized at the moment. A new trie is built without the adjunct, and so new adjuncts may be identified. This procedure can be iterated until no constituent is found to be optional, or until a user-defined number of iterations is reached.

When an adjunct is removed, the original pattern is preserved, so that the user can see whether a given pattern occurred with constituents that have been classified as adjuncts, and precisely which constituents.

When this data structure is created, the sequential ordering of constituents is lost, in case it had been preserved in the starting patterns. If the mark signalling the position of the verb had been introduced, it is also lost. However, order and position of the verb can be recovered in the final patterns, after adjuncts have been identified.

## 6 Associating patterns to verbs

One of the critical aspects of subcategorization acquisition is the association of verbs and patterns. How often must a pattern occur with a verb to make part of the subcategorization frame of the verb? To deal with this problem, different approaches have been taken, going from simple co-occurrence count to various kinds of hypothesis testing (Korhonen et al., 2000).

To determine whether a verb and a pattern are associated, IRASubcat provides a co-occurrence frequency threshold, that can be tuned by the user, and a hypothesis test, the Likelihood Ratio test (Dunning, 1993). We chose to implement this test, and not others like the binomial that have been extensively used in subcategorization acquisition, because the Likelihood Ratio is specially good at modeling unfrequent events.

To perform this test, the null hypothesis is that the distribution of an observed pattern '$M_j$' is independent of of the distribution of verb '$V_i$'.

Figure 1: Example of application of the procedure to identify adjuncts.

1. A starting set of patterns:
   `[NP DirObj PP-with], [NP DirObj], [NP DirObj], [NP DirObj PP-with],[NP DirObj] y [NP DirObj PP-for]`
2. Pattern constituents are ordered by frequency:
   `NP > DirObj > PP-with > PP-for`
3. Constituents in patterns are ordered by their relative frequency:

```
[NP DirObj PP-with]
[NP DirObj]
[NP DirObj]
[NP DirObj PP-with]
[NP DirObj]
[NP DirObj PP-for]
```

4. A trie is built with patterns:

```
[NP DirObj] ->3
[NP DirObj PP-with] ->2
[NP DirObj PP-for] ->1
```

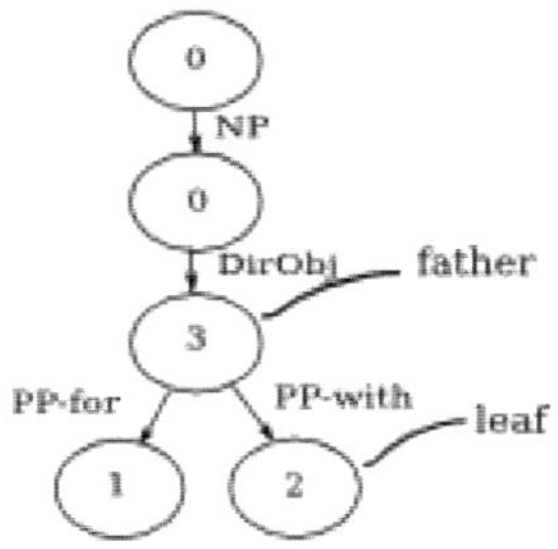


5. Leafs in the trie are "DirObj","PP-with" and "PP-for". Since DirObj also occurs in the trie in a position other than leaf, it will not be considered as an adjunct in this iteration. In contrast, both PP-with and PP-for fulfill the conditions to be considered adjuncts, so we prune the patterns the trie, which will now have the single pattern, which forms a trie with 2 adjuncts (with information about the number of occurrences of each adjunct constituent):

```
[NP DirObj {PP-with:1 PP-for:2}]
```

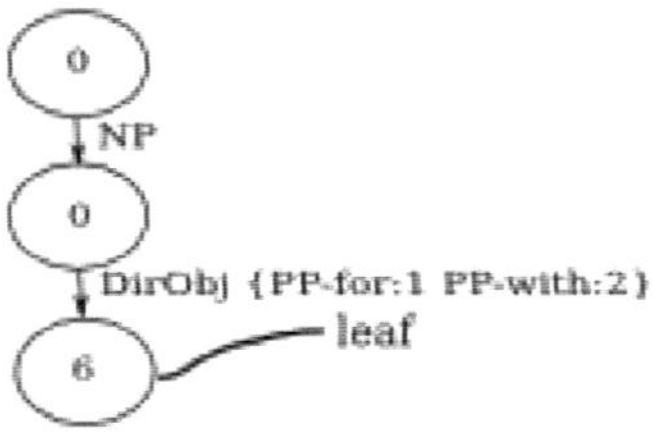


6. If the trie has been modified in this iteration, we go back to 2. If no modification has been operated, the procedure ends.

Moreover, the user can also specify a minimum number of occurrences of a verb to be taken into consideration, thus ruling out verbs for which there is not enough evidence in the corpus to obtain reliable subcategorization information.

## 7 Examples of applications

We have applied IRASubcat to two very different corpora in order to test its functionalities.

We have applied it to the SenSem corpus (Castellón et al., 2006), a corpus with 100 sentences for each of the 250 most frequent verbs of Spanish, manually annotated with information of verbal sense, syntactical function and semantic role of sentence constituents, among other information. From all the available information, we specified as input parameter for IRASubcat to consider only the syntactic function of sentence constituents. Thus, the expected output was the syntactic aspect of subcategorization frames of verbs. We worked with the verbal sense as the unit.

We compared the patterns associated to each verbal sense by IRASubcat with the subcategorization frames manually associated to the verbs at the a lexical data base of SenSem verbs[1]. We manually inspected the results for the 20 most frequent verbal senses. Results can be seen at Table 1. We found that the frequency threshold was the best filter to associate patterns and verbs, obtaining an f-measure of 74%. When hypothesis tests were used as a criterion to filter out associations of patterns with verbal senses, performance dropped, as can be seen in the lower rows of Table 1.

We also applied IRASubcat to an unannotated corpus of Russian. The corpus was automatically POS-tagged with TreeTagger (Schmid, 1994). We applied IRASubcat to work with parts of speech to build the patterns.

We manually inspected the patterns associated to prototypical intransitive ("*sleep*"), transitive ("*eat*") and ditransitive ("*give*") verbs. We found that patterns which were more strongly associated to verbs corresponded to their prototypical behaviour. For example, the patterns associated to the verb "*eat*" reflect the presence of a subject and a direct object:

| Pattern | occurrences | % Likelihood Ratio Test |
|---|---|---|
| ['V', 'Nn'] | 5 | 99 |
| ['V', 'C'] | 5 | 95 |
| ['V', 'R'] | 4 | did not pass |
| ['V', 'Nn', 'C', 'Q'] | 3 | 95 |
| ['V', 'V', 'Nn', 'Nn'] | 3 | 99 |
| ['V', 'Nn', 'Na'] | 3 | 99,5 |
| ['Nn', 'C'] | 3 | 90 |
| ['V', 'Nn', 'Nn'] | 3 | 99 |
| ['V', 'R', 'Q'] | 2 | 95 |
| ['V', 'Nn', 'An'] | 2 | 99 |

For more details on evaluation, see (Altamirano, 2009).

## 8 Conclusions and Future Work

We have presented a highly flexible tool to acquire verbal subcategorization information from corpus, independently of the language and level of annotation of the corpus. It is capable of identifying adjuncts and performs different tests to associate patterns with verbs. Thresholds for these tests can be set by the user, as well as a series of other system parameters. Moreover, the system is platform-independent and open-source[2].

We are currently carrying out experiments to assess the utility of the tool with two very different corpora: the SenSem corpus of Spanish, where sentences have been manually annotated with information about the category, function and role of the arguments of each verb, and also a raw corpus of Russian, for which only automatic part-of-speech tagging is available. Preliminary results indicate that, when parameters are properly set, IRASubcat is capable of identifying reliable subcategorization information in corpus.

As future work, we plan to integrate evaluation capabilities into the tool, so that it can provide precision and recall figures if a gold standard subcategorization lexicon is provided.

## Acknowledgments

This research has been partially funded by projects KNOW, TIN2006-15049-C03-01 and *Representation of Semantic Knowledge* TIN2009-14715-C04-03 of the Spanish Ministry of Education and Cul-

[1]The lexical data base of SenSem verbs can be found at http://grial.uab.es/adquisicio/.

[2]IRASubcat is available for download at http://www.irasubcat.com.ar

| applied filter | Precision | Recall | F-measure |
|---|---|---|---|
| Frequency | .79 | .70 | **.74** |
| likelihood ratio 90% | .42 | .46 | .39 |
| likelihood ratio 95% | .38 | .42 | .32 |
| likelihood ratio 99% | .31 | .36 | .22 |
| likelihood ratio 99.5% | .25 | .28 | .14 |

Table 1: Performance of IRASubcat to acquire subcategorization information from the SenSem corpus, for the 20 most frequent verbal senses, as compared with manual association of subcategorization patterns with verbal senses. Performance with different filters is detailed: only the most frequent patterns are considered, or only patterns passing a hypothesis test are considered.

ture, and by project PAE-PICT-2007-02290, funded by the National Agency for the Promotion of Science and Technology in Argentina.

## References

Bibliographisches Institut & F. A. Brockhaus AG, editor. 2001. *Duden das Stilwörterbuch*. Dudenverlag.

I. Romina Altamirano. 2009. Irasubcat: Un sistema para adquisición automática de marcos de subcategorización de piezas léxicas a partir de corpus. Master's thesis, Facultad de Matemática, Astronomía y Física, Universidad Nacional de Córdoba, Argentina.

Michael R. Brent. 1993. From grammar to lexicon: unsupervised learning of lexical syntax. *Comput. Linguist.*, 19(2):243–262.

Ted Briscoe and John Carroll. 1997. Automatic extraction of subcategorization from corpora. pages 356–363.

J. Carroll and A. Fang. 2004. The automatic acquisition of verb subcategorisations and their impact on the performance of an HPSG parser. In *Proceedings of the 1st International Joint Conference on Natural Language Processing (IJCNLP)*, pages 107–114.

J. Carroll, G. Minnen, and T. Briscoe. 1999. Corpus annotation for parser evaluation. In *Proceedings of the EACL-99 Post-conference Workshop on Linguistical ly Interpreted Corpora*, pages 35–41, Bergen, Norway.

Irene Castellón, Ana Fernández-Montraveta, Glòria Vázquez, Laura Alonso, and Joanan Capilla. 2006. The SENSEM corpus: a corpus annotated at the syntactic and semantic level. In *5th International Conference on Language Resources and Evaluation (LREC 2006)*.

Paula Chesley and Susanne Salmon-Alt. 2006. Automatic extraction of subcategorization frames for french.

Grzegorz Chrupala. 2003. Acquiring verb subcategorization from spanish corpora. Master's thesis, Universitat de Barcelona.

Erika de Lima. 2002. The automatic acquisition of lexical information from portuguese text corpora. Master's thesis, Institut für Maschinelle Sprachverarbeitung, Universität Stuttgart.

Ted Dunning. 1993. Accurate methods for the statistics of surprise and coincidence. *COMPUTATIONAL LINGUISTICS*.

Judith Eckle-Kohler. 1999. Linguistic knowledge for automatic lexicon acquisition from german text corpora.

Charles J. Fillmore. 1968. The case for case. In E. Bach and R. T. Harms, editors, *Universals in Linguistic Theory*. Holt, Rinehart, and Winston, New York.

Effi Georgala. 2003. A statistical grammar model for modern greek: The context-free grammar.

Alexandra Kinyon and Carlos A. Prolo. 2002. Identifying verb arguments and their syntactic function in the penn treebank. pages 1982–1987.

Anna Korhonen, Genevieve Gorrell, and Diana McCarthy. 2000. Statistical filtering and subcategorization frame acquisition. In *Proceedings of the 2000 Joint SIGDAT conference on Empirical methods in natural language processing and very large corpora*, pages 199–206, Morristown, NJ, USA. Association for Computational Linguistics.

Christopher D. Manning. 1993. Automatic acquisition of a large subcategorization dictionary from corpora. pages 235–242.

Ruth O'Donovan, Michael Burke, Aoife Cahill, Josef van Genabith, and Andy Way. 2005. Large-scale induction and evaluation of lexical resources from the penn-ii and penn-iii treebanks. volume 31, pages 329–365.

Evan Sandhaus, editor. *New York Times*.

Anoop Sarkar and Daniel Zeman. 2000. Automatic extraction of subcategorization frames for czech. pages 691–697.

H. Schmid. 1994. Probabilistic part–of–speech tagging using decision trees. In *Proceedings of the Conference on New Methods in Language Processing*, pages 44–49, Manchester, UK.

Sabine Schulte im Walde. 2000. Clustering verbs semantically according to their alternation behaviour. In *COLING'00*, pages 747–753.

Kristina Spranger and Ulrich Heid. 2003. A dutch chunker as a basis for the extraction of linguistic knowledge.

Mihai Surdeanu, Sanda Harabagiu, John Williams, and Paul Aarseth. 2003. Using predicate arguments structures for information extraction. In *Proceedings of the 41st Annual Meeting of the Association for Computational Linguistics (ACL 2003)*.

Akira Ushioda, David A. Evans, Ted Gibson, and Alex Waibel. 1993. The automatic acquisition of frequencies of verb subcategorization frames from tagged corpora. pages 95–106.

Oliver Wauschkuhn. 1999. Automatische extraktion von verbvalenzen aus deutschen text korpora. Master's thesis, Universität Stuttgart.

WSJ, editor. 1994. *Wall Street Journal*.

# The TermiNet Project: an Overview

**Ariani Di Felippo**
Interinstitutional Center for Research and Development in Computational Linguistics (NILC)/
Research Group of Terminology (GETerm), Federal University of São Carlos (UFSCar)
Rodovia Washington Luís, km 235 - SP-310
CP 676, 13565-905, São Carlos, SP, Brazil
ariani@ufscar.br

## Abstract

Linguistic resources with domain-specific coverage are crucial for the development of concrete Natural Language Processing (NLP) systems. In this paper we give a global introduction to the ongoing (since 2009) TermiNet project, whose aims are to instantiate a generic NLP methodology for the development of terminological wordnets and to apply the instantiated methodology for building a terminological wordnet in Brazilian Portuguese.

## 1 Introduction

In knowledge-based Natural Language Processing (NLP) systems, the lexical knowledge database is responsible for providing, to the processing modules, the lexical units of the language and their morphological, syntactic, semantic-conceptual and even illocutionary properties (Hanks, 2004).

In this scenario, there is an increasing need of accurate general lexical-conceptual resources for developing NLP applications.

A revolutionary development of the 1990s was the Princeton WordNet (WN.Pr) (Fellbaum, 1998), an online reference lexical database built for North-American English that combines the design of a dictionary and a *thesaurus* with a rich ontological potential.

Specifically, WN.Pr is a semantic network, in which the meanings of nouns, verbs, adjectives, and adverbs are organized into "sets of cognitive synonyms" (or synsets), each expressing a distinct concept. Synsets are interlinked through conceptual-semantic (i.e., hypernymy[1]/hyponymy[2], holonymy/meronymy, entailment[3], and cause[4]) and lexical (i.e., antonymy) relations. Moreover, WN.Pr encodes a co-text sentence for each word-form in a synset and a concept gloss for each synset (i.e., an informal lexicographic definition of the concept evoked by the synset).

The success of WN.Pr is largely due to its accessibility, linguistic adequacy and potential in terms of NLP. Given that, WN.Pr serves as a model for similarly conceived wordnets in several languages. In other words, the success of WN.Pr has determined the emergence of several projects that aim the construction of wordnets for other languages than English or to develop multilingual wordnets (the most important project in this line is EuroWordNet) (Vossen, 2002).

Many recent projects with the objective of (i) integrating generic and specialized wordnets (e.g., Magnin and Speranza, 2001; Roventini and Marinelli, 2004; Bentivogli et al., 2004), (ii) enriching generic wordnets with terminological units (e.g., Buitelaar and Sacaleanu, 2002) or (iii) constructing terminological wordnets (e.g.: Sagri et al., 2004; Smith and Fellbaum, 2004) have shown that con-

[1] The term Y is a hypernym of the term X if the entity denoted by X is a (kind of) entity denoted byY.
[2] If the term Y is a hypernym of the term X then the term X is a hyponym of Y.
[3] The action A1 denoted by the verb X entails the action A2 denoted by the verb Y if A1 cannot be done unless A2 is, or has been, done
[4] The action A1 denoted by the verb X causes the action A2 denoted by the verb Y.



*Proceedings of the NAACL HLT 2010 Young Investigators Workshop on Computational Approaches to Languages of the Americas*, pages 92–99, Los Angeles, California, June 2010. 

crete NLP application must be able to comprehend both expert and non-expert vocabulary.

Despite the existence of a reasonable number of terminological wordnets, there is no a general methodology for building this type of lexical database. Thus, motivated by this gap and by the fact that Brazilian Potuguese (PB) is a resource-poor language, the two-years TermiNet project has been developed since September 2009.

This paper gives an overview of the TermiNet project. Accordingly, in Section 2 we brief describe the original WN.Pr design that motivated the project. In Section 3 we present the aims of the TermiNet project and its methodological approach. In Section 4 we depict the current state of the project. In Section 5 we describe future work, and in Section 6 we outline potential points for collaboration with researchers from the rest of the Americas.

## 2 Princeton WordNet and its Design

WN.Pr contains information about nouns, verbs, adjectives and adverbs in North-American English and is organized around the notion of a *synset*. As mentioned, a synset is a set of words with the same part-of-speech that can be interchanged in a certain context. For example, {car; auto; automobile; machine; motorcar} form a synset because they can be used to refer to the same concept. A synset is often further described by a concept gloss[5], e.g.: "4-wheeled; usually propelled by an internal combustion engine".

Finally, synsets can be related to each other by the conceptual-semantic relations of hyperonymy/hyponymy, holonymy/meronymy, entailment and cause, and the lexical relation of antonymy.

In the example, taken from WN.Pr (2.1), the synset {car; auto; automobile; machine; motorcar} is related to:

(i) more general concepts or the hyperonym synset: {motor vehicle; automotive vehicle};
(ii) more specific concepts or hyponym synsets: e.g. {cruiser; squad car; patrol car; police car; prowl car} and {cab; taxi; hack; taxicab}; and
(iii) parts it is composed of: e.g. {bumper}; {car door}, {car mirror} and {car window}.

[5] An informal lexicographic definition of the concept evoked by the synset.

WN.Pr also includes an English co-text sentence for each word-form in a synset, and a semantic type for each synset.

Based on WN.Pr design, Brazilian Portuguese WordNet (WordNet.Br or WN.Br) project launched in 2003 departed from a previous lexical resource: the Brazilian Portuguese Thesaurus (Dias-da-Silva et al, 2002). The original WN.Br database is currently being refined, augmented, and upgraded. The improvements include the encoding of the following bits of information in to the database: (a) the co-text sentence for each word-form in a synset; (b) the concept gloss for each synset; and (c) the relevant language-independent hierarchical conceptual-semantic relations.

The current WN.Br database presents the following figures: 11,000 verb forms (4,000 synsets), 17,000 noun forms (8,000 synsets), 15,000 adjective forms (6,000 synsets), and 1,000 adverb forms (500 synsets), amounting to 44,000 word forms and 18,500 synsets (Dias-da-Silva et al, 2008).

## 3 The TermiNet Project

The TermiNet ("Terminological WordNet") project started in September 2009 and shall be finished finish in August 2011. It has been developed in the laboratory of the Research Group of Terminology[6] (GETerm) in Federal University of São Carlos (UFSCar) with the collaboration of the Interinstitutional Center for Research and Development in Computational Linguistics[7] (NILC/University of São Paulo) researchers.

The TermiNet project has two main objectives. The first is to instantiate the generic NLP methodology, proposed by Dias-da-Silva (2006), for developing terminological databases according to the WN.Pr model. Such methodology distinguishes itself by conciliating the linguistic and computational facets of the NLP researches. The second is to apply the instantiated methodology to build a terminological wordnet or terminet[8] in BP, since BP is a resource-poor language in NLP for which domain-specific databases in wordnet format have not been built yet.

It is important to emphasize that the main terminological resources in BP, which are availa-

[6] http://www.geterm.ufscar.br/

[7] http://www.nilc.icmc.usp.br

[8] In the TermiNet project, a terminological wordnet database is called "terminet".

ble through the OntoLP[9] website, are in fact (formal) ontologies or taxonomies. There is no nological WordNet-like database in BP.

In order to achieve its objectives, TermiNet has, apart from the project leader (Prof. Ariani Di Felippo), an interdisciplinary team that includes six undergraduate students: five from Linguistics and one from Computer Science courses. The Linguistics students are responsible for specific linguistic tasks in the project, such as: (i) *corpus* compilation, (ii) candidate terms extraction, (iii) synonymy identification, and (iv) semantic-conceptual relations extraction (hypernymy/hyponymy). The responsability of the Computer Science student is to support the automatic processing related to the linguistic (e.g., *tagging, parsing,* term extraction, etc.) and linguistic-computational domains during the initial stages of the project.

Moreover, the project counts with the collaboration of four PhD researchers from NILC. Specifically, TermiNet has the support of Prof. Gladis Maria de Barcellos Almeida, a specialist in terminological research and the coordinator of GETerm; Prof. Maria da Graças Volpe Nunes, the coordinator of NILC and one of the most important Brazilian NLP researchers; Prof. Sandra Aluisio, a specialist in *corpus* construction, and Prof. Thiago Pardo, who has interests in the development of lexical resources for the automatic processing of BP.

### 3.1 Instantiation of the NLP Tree-Domain Methodology

Based on Expert Systems development, Dias-da-Silva (2006) established a three-domain approach methodology to develop any research in NLP domain, assuming a compromise between Human Language Technology and Linguistics (Dias-da-Silva, 1998).

The linguistic-related information to be computationally modeled is likened to a rare metal. So, it must be "mined", "molded", and "assembled" into a computer-tractable system (Durkin, 1994). Accordingly, the processes of designing and implementing a terminet lexical database have to be developed in the following complementary domains: the linguistic domain, the linguistic-computational domain, and implementational or computational domain.

[9] http://www.inf.pucrs.br/~ontolp/downloads.php

*(a) The Linguistic-related Domain*

In this domain, the lexical resources and the lexical-conceptual knowledge are mined. More specifically, the research activities in the linguistic domain are divided in two processes: the selection of the lexical resources for building the terminet database, and the specification of the lexical-conceptual knowledge that characterize a terminet.

The linguist starts off these procedures by delimitating the specialized domain that will be encoded in wordnet format.

According to Almeida and Correia (2008), dealing with an entire specialized domain is a very problematic task because the domains (e.g.: Materials Engineering) in general are composed of subdomains (e.g.: Ceramic Materials, Polymers and Metals) with different characteristics, generating a large universe of sources from which the lexical-conceptual knowledge will have to be mined.

Consequently, the authors present some criteria that may lead to delimitate a specialized domain: (i) the interest of the domain experts by terminological products (in this case, by a terminet); (ii) the relevance of the domain in the educational, social, political, economic, scientific and/or technological scenarios, and (iii) the availability of specialized resources in digital format from which the lexical-conceptual knowledge will be extracted. After delimitating the domain, it is necessary to select the lexical resources describe in (iii). According to Rigau (1998), the two main sources of information for building wide-coverage lexicons for NLP systems are: structured resources (e.g.: conventional monolingual and bilingual dictionaries, *thesauri,* taxonomies, vocabularies, etc.) and unstructured resources (i.e., *corpora*[10]).

Due to the unavailability of reusing structured resources, the *corpora* have become the main source of lexical knowledge (Nascimento, 2003; Agbago and Barrière, 2005; Cabré et al., 2005; Almeida, 2006). The increasing use of *corpora* in terminological researches is also due to the fact that "el carácter de término no se da per se, sino en función del uso de una unidad léxica en un contexto expresivo y situacional determinado" (Cabré, 1999: 124). Thus, in the TermiNet project, the *cor-*

[10] "A corpus is a collection of pieces of language text in electronic form, selected according to external criteria to represent, as far as possible, a language or language variety as a source of data for linguistic research" (Sinclair, 2005).

*pus* is considered the main lexical resource that can be used to construct a terminet.

Although there are available several specialized *corpora*, the development of a terminet of certain domains may require the compilation of a *corpus*.

Based on the assumptions of Corpus Linguistics (Aluisio and Alemida, 2007), the construction of a *corpus* must follow three steps: (i) the *corpus* projection, i.e., the specification of the *corpus* typology according to the research purposes; (ii) the compilation of the texts that will compose the *corpus*, and (iii) the pre-processing of the *corpus* (i.e., conversion, clean-up, manipulation, and annotation of the texts).

From the *corpus,* the specialized knowledge will be extracted, i.e., the terminological units (or terms), the lexical relations, and the conceptual-semantic relations[11].

As mentioned in previous sections, the lexical units are organized into four syntactic categories in WN.Pr: verbs, nouns, adjectives and adverbs. Given the relevance of nouns in the organization of any terminology (i.e., the set of all terms related to a given subject field or discipline), we decided to restrict the construction of a terminet to the category of nouns. In other words, a terminet database, in principle, will only contain information about concepts lexicalized by nouns. Additionally, it will only encode the hyperonymy/hyponymy relations, which are the most important conceptual-semantic relations between nouns. The co-text sentence for each word-form in a synset and the concept gloss for each synset will not be focused in building a terminet.

As the TermiNet a *corpus*-based project, we will apply approaches and strategies to automatically recognize and extract candidate terms and relations from *corpus*.

In order to better understand the automatic candidate terms and extraction, it can be useful to identify two mainstream approaches to the problem. In the first approach, statistical measures have been proposed to define the degree of *termhood* of candidate terms, i.e., to find appropriate measures that can help in selecting good terms from a list of candidates. In the second approach, computational terminologists have tried to define, identify and recognize terms looking at pure linguistic properties, using linguistic filtering techniques aiming to identify specific syntactic term patterns (Bernhard, 2006; Pazienza et al., 2005; Cabré et al., 2001).

Once extrated, the candidate terms have be validated. Two validation estrategies will be considered in the TermiNet project. The first strategy consists on manually validating by domain experts. The second consists on automatically comparing the list of candidate terms with a list of lexical unities extracted from a general *corpus* in BP.

The automatic acquisition of hyperonym/hyponymy relation from *corpus* is commonly based on linguistic methods. These methods look for linguistic clues that indisputably indicate the relation of interest (Hearst, 1992). The linguistic clues are basically lexico-syntactic patters such as: [NP such {NP,}*{(or|and)} NP] (e.g., "works by such authors as Herrick, and Shakespeare"). The hierarchical relations extrated from *corpus* are commonly validated by domain experts.

*(b) The Linguistic-Computational Domain*

In this domain, the overall information selected and organized in the preceding domain is molded into a computer-tractable representation; in the case of a WordNet-like database, the computer-tractable representation is based on the notions of:

- *word form* – a orthographic representation of an individual word or a string of individual words joined with underscore characters;
- *synset* – a set of words built on the basis of the notion of synonymy in context, i.e. word interchangeability in some context;
- *lexical matrix* – associations of sets of word forms and the concepts they lexicalize;
- *relational pointers* – formal representations of the relations between the word forms in a synset and other synsets; synonymy of word forms is implicit by inclusion in the same synset; hyperonymy always relates one synset to another, and is an example of a semantic relation; hyperonymy, in particular, is represented by reflexive pointers (i.e., if a synset contains a pointer to another synset, the other synset should contain a corresponding reflexive pointer back to the original synset).

*(c) The Computational Domain*

In this domain, the computer-tractable representations are assembled by utilities (i.e., a computational tool to create and edit lexical knowledge). In

[11] The glosses and co-text sentences will not be specificied in the TermiNet projet.

other words, it is generated, in this domain, the terminet database. The software tool that we will use to generate the terminet database is under investigation.

## 4 TermiNet: Past and Current Stages of Development

The project, which started in September 2009, is still in its early stages. Consequently, the research tasks that have been developed so far are those related to the linguistic domain. As described in Section 3.1a, there are several linguistic tasks in the TermiNet project. Two of them – the delimitation of the specialized domain and the *corpus* projection – are completed. In subsections 4.1 and 4.2, we present these finished processes and in 4.3 we focus on the current activity.

### 4.1 Delimitation of the specialized domain

DE is conventionally defined as "*any educational or learning process or system in which the teacher or instructor is separated geographically or in time from his or her students or educational resources*".

According to the second Brazilian Yearbook of Statistics on Open and Distance Education (Anuário Brasileiro Estatístico de Educação Aberta e a Distância[12]), in 2007 there were approximately 2,5 millions of students enrolled in accredited DE courses, from basic to graduate education, in 257 accredited institutions. The number of students in DE courses has grown 24.9% in relation to 2006. Thus, we can see the relevance of the DE modality in Brazil. Despite the relevance of the DE in the Brazilian educational (and political) scenario, there is no a lexical-conceptual representation of this domain, especially in a machine-readable format.

Consequently, the instantiated methodology will be validated by building DE.WordNet (DE.WN), a specialized wordnet of the Distance Education (or Distance Learning) domain in BP. The construction of such database has been supported by domain experts from the "Open University of Brazil" (Universidade Aberta do Brasil – UAB) project of the Federal University of São Carlos (UFSCar).

DE.WN can be integrated into the wordnet lexical database for BP, the WordNet.Br (Dias-da-Silva et al., 2008), enriching it with domain specific knowledge.

### 4.2 *Corpus* projection

Following the assumptions of Corpus Linguistics described in Section 3, the *corpus* of DE domain has been constructed according to the steps: (i) *corpus* projection, (ii) *corpus* compilation, and (iii) the pre-processing of the texts.

The *corpus* typology in the TermiNet project was specified based on: (i) the conception of "*corpus*", (ii) the type of lexical resource to be built, and (iii) the project decisions (Di Felippo and Souza, 2009).

The *corpus* definition or conception is commonly related to three criteria: *representativeness, balance* and *authenticity*.

According to the *representativeness* criterion, we have been compiled a representative *corpus* of the DE domain. There have been many attempts to set the size, or at least establish a minimum number of texts, from which a specialized *corpus* may be compiled. To satisfy the *representativeness* criterion, we have been constructed a medium-large *corpus,* with at least 1 million of words.

In a specialized *corpus,* it is important to gather texts from different genres (i.e. technical-scientific, scientific divulgation, instructional, informative, and technical-administrative) and media (i.e, newswire, books, periodicals, etc.). Following the *balance* and *authenticity* criteria, we have been constructed a *corpus* with a balanced number of real texts per genre.

Besides, the format of the lexical database (i.e. a terminet) determined some characteristics of the *corpus*. Specifically, the *corpus* has to be synchronic/ contemporary, since a wordnet (terminological or not) encodes synchronic lexical-conceptual knowledge. The *corpus* has only to store written texts, since wordnets are lingwares for written language processing. Finally, the *corpus* in the TermiNet project has only to store texts from a specialized domain and in one language.

Additionally, some project decisions determined other characteristics of the *corpus*. Two initial decisions in the project were: (i) to apply semi-automatic methods of lexical-conceptual knowledge extraction, and (ii) to share the resources and results of the TermiNet project with Computational Linguistics community. As a consequency of the project decision described in (i), the *corpus* will be

[12] http://www.abraead.com.br/anuario/anuario_2008.pdf

annotated with part-of-speech (PoS) information, since some automatic extraction methods require it. As a consequency of the decision presented in (ii), the *corpus* will be available and usable as widely as possible on the *web*.

Finally, we also decided that once the *corpus* has been assembled, it will not be changed until the first version of DE.WN is ready.

Based on the typology proposed by Giouli and Peperidis (2002), the Table 1 summarizes the characteritics of the *corpus* previously described.

| | |
|---|---|
| **Modality** | Written *corpus* |
| **Text Type** | Written *corpus* |
| **Medium** | Newspapers, books, journals, manuals and others |
| **Language coverage** | Specialized *corpus* |
| **Genre/register** | Technical-scientific, scientific divulgation, instructional, informative and, technical-administrative |
| **Language variables** | Monolingual *corpus* |
| **Markup** | Annotated *corpus* (PoS annotation) |
| **Production Community** | Native speakers |
| **Open-endedness** | Closed *corpus* |
| **Historical variation** | Synchronic *corpus* |
| **Availability** | Online *corpus* |

**Table 1.** The *corpus* design.

The specialized domain and *corpus* typology were specified by the undergraduate student responsible for the *corpus* compilation under the supervision of a PhD in Linguistics (leader of the project).

### 4.3 *Corpus* compilation

Currently, one undergraduate student from Linguistics has been compiled the *corpus*. Specifically, the *corpus* compilation comprises two processes: (i) the selection of resources and (ii) the collect of texts from these resources.

In the TermiNet project, the web is the main source for collecting texts of DE. The choice of web reflects the fact that web has become an unprecedented and virtually inexhaustible source of authentic natural language data for researchers in linguistics.

Although there are many computational tools that assist in gathering a considerable amount of texts on the web, the selection/collection of texts has been followed a manual process, which is composed of three steps: (i) to access a webpage whose content is important for compiling the *corpus*, (ii) to search the texts on the webpage by search queries as "distance education" and "distance learning", and (iii) to save the text files on the computer.

In the pre-processing step, the text files in a non-machine readable format (e.g. pdf) are manually converted to text format (txt), which is readable by machines. This process is important because the lexical-conceptual knowledge will be (semi)automatically extracted from the *corpus,* and the extraction tools require a *corpus* whose texts are in *txt* format.

Data corrupted by the conversion or even unnecessary to the research (e.g. references, information about filliation, etc.) are excluded during the cleaning process. After that, the metadata or external information (e.g. authorship, publication details, genre and text type, etc.) on each text are being automatically annotated and encoded in a header. In the TermiNet project, we are using the header editor available at the "Portal de Corpus" website[13].

## 5 Future Work

According to the three-domain methodology, future steps will involve the following tasks of the linguistic domain: candidate terms and relations extraction (and validation).

In the TermiNet project, two specific software tools constructed based on lingustic approaches will be used to extract candidate terms from the DE *corpus*: $E_X ATO_{LP}$ (Lopes et al., 2009) and OntoLP (Ribeiro Jr., 2008). Additionally, we intend to extract the terms from *corpus* using the NSP (Ngram Statistics Package) tool (Bannerjee and Pedersen, 2003), i.e., a flexible and easy-to-use software tool that supports the identification and analysis of Ngrams.

To extract the hyperonymy and hyponymy relations, we will also use the OntoLP, which is a tool, actually a plug-in, for the ontologies editor Protégé[14], a widely used editor in the scientific community and which gives support to the construction of ontologies. The process of automatic

[13] http://www.nilc.icmc.usp.br:8180/portal/

[14] http://protege.stanford.edu/

ontology construction in the OntoLP tool also englobes the identification of hierarchical relation between the terms.

The synonymy relation will be also recognized and extracted automatically from the *corpus*. However, the automatic extraction method of such lexical relation is still under investigation.

After the acquisition of all lexical-conceptual information, we will develop the tasks or processes of the linguistic-computational and computational domains.

Among the expected results of the TermiNet projet are: (i) a methodological framework for building a specific type of *lingware*, i.e. terminological wordnets; (ii) a specialized *corpus* of the DE domain; (iii) a terminological lexical database based on the WN.Pr format of the DE domain. Moreover, there is the possibility of extending the WN.Br database through the inclusion of specialized knowledge.

Besides the benefits to NLP domain, the DE.WN may also contribute to the development of standard terminographic products (e.g., glossary, dictionary, vocabulary, etc.), of the DE domain since the organization of the lexical-conceptual knowledge is an essential step in building such products.

## 6 Collaborative Opportunities

We consider our experience in developing a terminet in BP as the major contribution that we can offer to other researchers in Latin America. Since the resources (i.e., *corpus* and lexical database) and tools (i.e., terms and relations extractors) that we have been used are language-dependent, they cannot be used directly for Spanish and English. But, we are willing to share our expertise on (i) compiling a terminological *corpus,* (ii) automatically extracting lexical-conceptual knowledge from *corpus,* and (iii) constructing a terminet database in order to develop similar projects for Spanish and English.

We are really interested in actively taking part in joint research projects that aim to construct terminological lexical database for Spanish or English, especially in *wordnet* format.

Collaboration of researchers from the USA that were directly involved in the development of wordnet databases (terminological or not), willing to share their experience and tools, would be welcome.

We would appreciate collaboration from researchers in the USA specifically in relation to computational programs or software tools used in building WordNet-like lexical database, which are responsible for the computer-tractable representation described in 3.1(b). The current WN.Br editing tool, which was originally designed to aid the linguist in carrying out the tasks of building synsets, selecting co-text sentences from *corpora*, and writing synset concept glosses, has been modified to aid the linguistic in carrying out the task of encoding conceptual relations. However, this editor is just able to deal with the hypernymy/hyponymy relations when they are inherited from WN.Pr through a conceptual-semantic alignment strategy (Dias-da-Silva et al, 2008). So, the WN.Br editor is not the most appropriate tool to TermiNer project tasks. Consequently, contributions to develop "a kind of" Grinder[15] for TermiNet would be welcome. We would also appreciate collaboration from re-searchers in the USA in relation to methodological approaches to enriching generic wordnets with terminological units.


## Acknowledgments

We thank the Brazilian National Council for Scientific and Technological Development (CNPq) (471871/2009-5), and the State of São Paulo Research Foundation (FAPESP) (2009/06262-1) for supporting the TermiNet project. We also thank the NAACL HLT Young Investigators Workshop referees, who helped make this paper better.


## References


Adriana Roventini and Rita Marinelli. 2004. Extending the Italian Wordnet with the specialized language of the maritime domain. In: *Proceedings of the 2nd International Global Wordnet Conference.* Masaryk University, Brno, 193-198.

Akakpo Agbago and Caroline Barrière. 2005. Corpus construction for Terminology. In: *Proceedings of the Corpus Lingustics Conference.* Birmingham, 14-17.

Bento Carlos Dias-da-Silva. 2006. Bridging the gap between linguistic theory and natural language processing. In: *Proceedings of the 16th International*


[15] This is the most important program used in building WN.Pr. Lexicographers make their additions and changes in the lexical source files, and the Grinder takes those files and converts them into a lexical database (in *wordnet* format).

*Congress of Linguistics,* 1997. Oxford: Elsevier Sciences, 1998, 1-10.

Bento Carlos Dias-da-Silva. 2006. O estudo linguístico-computacional da linguagem. *Letras de Hoje*, 41(2): 103-138.

Bento Carlos Dias-da-Silva, Ariani Di Felippo and Maria G. V. Nunes. 2008. The automatic mapping of Princeton Wordnet lexical-conceptual relations onto the Brazilian Portuguese Wordnet database. In: *Proceedings of the 6th LREC.* Marrakech, Morocco.

Bento Carlos Dias-da-Silva, Mirna Fernanda de Oliveira, Hélio Roberto de Moraes. 2002. Groundwork for the development of the Brazilian Portuguese Wordnet. In: *Proceedings of the 3rd International Conference Portugal for Natural Language Processing* (PorTal). Faro, Portugal. Berlin: Springer-Verlag, 189-196.

Bernardo Magnini and Manuela Speranza. 2001. Integrating generic and specialized wordnets. In: *Proceedings of the Conference on Recent Advances in Natural Language Processing*. Bulgaria.

Christiane Fellbaum (ed.). 1998. *Wordnet: an electronic lexical database*. The MIT Press, Ca, MA: 423p.

Delphine Bernhard. 2006. Multilingual term extraction from domain-specific corpora using morphological structure. In: *Proceedings of the 11th European Chapter Meeting of the ACL*, Trento, Italy, 171-174.

German Rigau Claramunt. 1998. *Automatic acquisition of lexical knowledge from MRDs*. PhD Thesis. Departament de Llenguatges i Sistemes Informàtics, Barcelona.

Gladis Maria Barcellos de Almeida. 2006. A Teoria Comunicativa da Terminologia e a sua prática. *Alfa*, 50:81-97

Gladis Maria de Barcellos Almeida and Margarita Correia. 2008. Terminologia e corpus: relações, métodos e recursos. In: Stella E. O. Tagnin and Oto Araújo Vale (orgs.). *Avanços da Lingüística de Corpus no Brasil*. 1 ed. Humanitas/FFLCH/USP; São Paulo, volume 1, 63-93.

Gladis Maria Barcellos de Almeida, Sandra Maria Aluisio and Leandro H. M. Oliveira. 2007. O método em Terminologia: revendo alguns procedimentos. In: Aparecida N. Isquerdo and Ieda M. Alves. (orgs.). *Ciências do léxico: lexicologia, lexicografia, terminologia*. 1 ed. Editora da UFMS/Humanitas: Campo Grande/São Paulo, volume 3, 409-420.

John Durkin. 1994. *Expert Systems: Design and Development.* Prentice Hall International, London, 800p.

John Sinclair, J. 2005. Corpus and text: basic principles. In: Martin Wynne (ed.). *Developing linguistic corpora: a guide to good practice.* Oxbow Books: Oxford, 1-16. Available at http://ahds.ac.uk/linguistic-corpora/

Lucelene Lopes, Paulo Fernandes, Renata Vieira and Gustavo Fedrizzi. 2009. ExATOlp - an automatic tool for term extraction from Portuguese language corpora. In: *Proceedings of the LTC'09*, Poznam, Poland.

Luisa Bentivogli, Andrea Bocco and Emanuele Pianta. 2004. ArchiWordnet: integrating Wordnet with domain-specific knowledge. In: *Proceedings of the 2nd International Global Wordnet Conference*. Masaryk University, Brno, 39-47.

Luiz Carlos Ribeiro Jr. 2008. *OntoLP: construção semi-automática de ontologias a partir de textos da língua portuguesa*. MSc Thesis, UNISINOS, 131p.

Maria Fernanda Bacelar do Nascimento. 2003. O papel dos corpora especializados na criação de bases terminológicas. In: I. Castro and I. Duarte (orgs.). *Razões e emoções, miscelânea de estudos em homenagem a Maria Helena Mateus*. Imprensa Nacional-Casa da Moeda: Lisboa, volume II, 167-179.

Maria Tereza Cabré. 1999. *La terminología: representación y comunicación: elementos para una teoría de base comunicativa y otros artículos*. Institut Universitari de Linguística Aplicada: Barcelona.

Maria Tereza Cabré, Anne Condamines and Fidelia Ibekwe-SanJuan. 2005. Application-driven terminology engineering. *Terminology*, 11(2):1-19.

Maria Tereza Cabré, Rosa Estopà and Jordi Vivaldi Palatresi. 2001. Automatic term detection: a review of current systems, In: Didier Bourigault et al. (eds.). *Recent Advances in Computational Terminology*. John Benjamins Publishing Co: Amsterdam & Philadelphia, 53-87.

Maria Teresa Pazienza, Marco Pennacchiotti and Fabio Massimo Zanzotto. 2005. Terminology extraction: an analysis of linguistic and statistical approaches. *Studies in Fuzziness and Soft Computing*, 185:255-280.

Maria Teresa Sagri, Daniela Tiscornia and Francesca Bertagna. 2004. Jur-Wordnet. In: *Proceedings of the 2nd International Global Wordnet Conference*. Masaryk University, Brno, 305-310.

Marti A. Hearst, M. 1992. Automatic acquisition of hyponyms from large text corpora. In: *Proceedings 14th of the International Conference on Computational Linguistics*. Nantes, 539-545.

Paul Buitelaar and Bogdan Sacaleanu. 2002. Extending synsets with medical terms. In: *Proceedings of the 1st International Global Wordnet Conference*. Mysore, India, 2002.

Piek Vossen (ed.). 2002. EuroWordnet general document (Version 3–Final). Available at: http://www.vossen.info/docs/2002/EWNGeneral.pdf.

Satanjeev Banerjee and Ted Pedersen. 2003. The Design, Implementation, and Use of the Ngram Statistics Package. In: *Proceedings of the Fourth International Conference on Intelligent Text Processing and Computational Linguistics*. Mexico City.

# Automated Detection of Language Issues Affecting Accuracy, Ambiguity and Verifiability in Software Requirements Written in Natural Language

**Allan Berrocal Rojas, Gabriela Barrantes Sliesarieva**
Escuela de Ciencias de la Computación e Informática
Universidad de Costa Rica, San José, Costa Rica
{allan.berrocal,gabriela.barrantes}@ecci.ucr.ac.cr

## Abstract

Most embedded systems for the avionics industry are considered safety critical systems; as a result, strict software development standards exist to ensure critical software is built with the highest quality possible. One of such standards, DO-178B, establishes a number of properties that software requirements must satisfy including: *accuracy*, *non-ambiguity* and *verifiability*. From a language perspective, it is possible to automate the analysis of software requirements to determine whether or not they satisfy some quality properties. This work suggests a bounded definition for three properties (*accuracy*, *non-ambiguity* and *verifiability*) considering the main characteristics that software requirements must exhibit to satisfy those objectives. A software prototype that combines natural language processing (NLP) techniques and specialized dictionaries was built to examine software requirements written in English with the goal of identifying whether or not they satisfy the desired properties. Preliminary results are presented showing how the tool effectively identifies critical issues that are normally ignored by human reviewers.

## 1 Introduction

Software requirements play a critical role in the software life cycle. It has been observed that poorly written software requirements often lead to weak and unpredictable software applications (Wilson et al., 1997). Besides, the cost of fixing errors increases exponentially throughout the different phases of software development (Galin, 2004; Leffingwell and Widrig, 2003). In other words, it is less expensive to fix an error in the software requirements phase than it is to fix the same error during the integration or verification phase.

Embedded systems for the avionics industry are developed following particularly rigorous restrictions due to strict safety and availability constraints that need to be satisfied during air or ground operations. DO-178B (RTCA, 1992) is a recognized standard for development of safety critical embedded systems. It is widely used by software certification authorities such as FAA (*Federal Aviation Association*), and it establishes some guidelines and quality objectives for each phase of a software development effort. In particular, the standard estates that software requirements must be *accurate*, *verifiable*, and *non-ambiguous*.

### 1.1 Software Quality

Milicic suggests that software quality can be understood as conformity with a given specification (Milicic et al., 2005). This definition is in total agreement with DO-178B, which requires that software is designed, built, and tested following approved standards for each phase of the development cycle.

Extrapolating the previous definition, one can argue that quality of software requirements can be understood as the degree to which software requirements also comply with a given specification. In other words, in order to produce high quality software requirements, one needs to ensure that they satisfy the criteria established in a software requirements standard.

In the case of software requirements written in natural language (NL), some of the criteria can be addressed from a linguistic perspective, observing certain types of language constructs and language usage in general that may represent violations against desired quality criteria in a standard.



*Proceedings of the NAACL HLT 2010 Young Investigators Workshop on Computational Approaches to Languages of the Americas*, pages 100–108, Los Angeles, California, June 2010. 

### 1.2 Overview of Research Goals

The overall objective of this research was to identify some of the linguistic elements that one can observe to determine whether or not software requirements written in natural language[1] comply with three specific properties established by DO-178B: *accuracy*, *verifiability* and *non-ambiguity*. Those linguistic elements can be seen as rules in an expert system, so that requirements are said to be compliant with their quality objectives when they satisfy all rules. They are said to be non-compliant with their quality objectives when rules are not satisfied.

In this research, linguistic elements were identified and independently validated by professionals in the field of software verification. Later on, a software prototype capable of examining a list of requirements was built to automatically detect when requirements do not satisfy a given rule.

The main contribution of this research is that it provides a quantitative evaluation of the target requirements. More specifically, based on the number of satisfied and non satisfied rules, the prototype scores each requirement in a 1 to 10 scale. The tool also provides additional information (qualitative analysis) to the user indicating the root of the problem when a given rule is not satisfied, as well as possible ways to fix the issue.

### 1.3 Justification

The author's experience in the field of requirements verification suggests that the task of reviewing a set of requirements for compliance with properties such as *accuracy*, *verifiability* and *non-ambiguity* is a non trivial task. This is particularly true when the reviewer lacks the proper training and tools. Some of the known difficulties for this process are:

- It requires linguistic (e.g. grammar, semantics) and technical knowledge from a reviewer.
- There is no warranty that two or more reviewers will produce the same findings for the same input (mostly due to the informal nature of NL).
- The process is error prone since reviewers become fatigued after some time.
- The process is time consuming, which directly affects budget and schedule performance.

Having a tool that partially automates the process of reviewing software requirements may represent significant improvements in the overall software life cycle process. Even when current developments in computational linguistics do not provide a complete solution for the problem at hand, a partial approach is still valuable producing numerous advantages such as:

- Linguistic and technical knowledge is input into the system in a cumulative manner, reducing dependency on highly qualified personnel.
- Results are reproducible for any given set of inputs, reducing inconsistencies while adding reliability to the results.
- Review time is significantly reduced.

## 2 Related Work

Significant work has been done in the area of software requirements analysis. Lami (Lami et al., 2004) classifies these efforts in three groups. A first group consists of preventive techniques that need to be applied during the process of writing requirements. Those techniques normally trigger checklists that are enforced by a person with no support from tools, see for instance (Firesmith, 2003). Another group consists of restrictive techniques that limit the degree of language freedom when writing requirements. One example in this group is Fuchs (Fuchs et al., 1998) who introduces ACE (Attempto Controlled English), a restricted subset of English with a restricted grammar and domain specific vocabulary. Requirements can be written in natural language with enough expressive power. They are later translated into first order predicate logic to be processed formally by a computer program.

The last group of efforts consists of analytic techniques that perform automated analysis of requirements once they have been produced. The following are two relevant projects in this group. Wilson (Wilson et al., 1997) developed a tool named ARM that performs automated analysis of a requirements document. The tool focuses on lexical analysis to detect specific keywords such as vague adverbs and

[1] This research assumes requirements are written in English.

vague adjectives that are not desired. Different from our work, ARM also checks that the document itself complies with a specific format. Then, Lami (Lami et al., 2004) described a systematic method for automated analysis of requirements detecting deficiencies such as ambiguity, inconsistencies, and incompleteness. A tool named QuARS implements the suggested methodology and appears to be a good contribution in this area [2].

## 3 Theoretical Framework

This section provides a basic explanation of some concepts that are commonly used in the field of software verification. Emphasis will be made on concepts related to the software engineering field in an attempt to set the grounds for the investigation. Other linguistic related concepts will be mentioned along the paper assuming the reader has basic understanding of them.

### 3.1 Software Life Cycle

A Software Life Cycle Model or Software Development Model consists of a group of concepts and well coordinated methodologies that guide the software development process from beginning to end (Galin, 2004). The classic software life cycle model (a.k.a. *the waterfall model*) consists of linear sequence of activities or phases that take place during a software development effort.

In the **Requirements elicitation phase**, a detailed description of what the software shall do is produced. Although there are various methods, a natural language description in the form of a list of statements is widely used to produce requirements.

A **software requirement** is a condition or characteristic that a system must possess to satisfy a contract, a standard, a formal specification or other applicable regulation (IEEE, 1990).

In simple words, a software requirement explains how the system should behave or react given a specific set of inputs and initial conditions. While not true for all software applications, in the avionics industry, all software functionalities are required to be fully deterministic. This means that the system must behave exactly the same all the time for a given set of inputs and initial conditions. This is why correctness of requirements is so critical.

The following section briefly comments on three of the properties that requirements must satisfy to meet quality objectives. Although there are many such properties, we focus on three whose detection is partially automated in this research.

### 3.2 Quality Properties for Software Requirements

To meet quality objectives, software requirement must be *accurate*, *non-ambiguous* and *verifiable*. This section provides a brief explanation of these terms in the context of software verification. Additionally, it describes the main language elements used in this research to automatically detect when software requirements do not satisfy a given property.

#### 3.2.1 Ambiguity

A word or phrase is said to be ambiguous when it has more than one possible meaning causing confusion or uncertainty. Similarly, software requirements are said to be ambiguous when they admit more than one possible interpretation. An ambiguous requirement is notably incompatible with the goal of producing deterministic software.

Berry (Berry, 2003) distinguishes six major forms of ambiguity in software requirements: lexical, syntactical, semantic, pragmatic, vagueness and language error. In this research, we focused on lexical, syntactic, vagueness, and language errors since this group covers common deficiencies that show in requirements.

One form of syntactical ambiguity occurs when requirements fail to group logical conditions (e.g. AND, OR) with appropriate punctuation marks or explicit parenthesis. In the following example, for instance, it is not clear what the conditions are for the system to enter into normal mode: "*The system shall enter Normal mode when SDI field on label 227 equals 2 <u>or</u> SSM in label 268 equals 3 <u>and</u> WOW is true <u>or</u> AIR is false.*"

Vague adverbs usually modifying nouns (such as: *acceptable, high, low, fast, in/sufficient, normal, similar* and many others) also create ambiguous requirements like the following: "*The system shall allow the operator to adjust volume to an <u>acceptable</u> level.*"

[2]The author has not been able to use QuARS yet.

Finally, non deterministic constructs such as *and/or, any, not limited to* also create ambiguity in requirements, such as the following case: "*The system shall display altitude and/or temperature at the bottom line of the screen.*"

### 3.2.2 Accuracy

In a requirement, accuracy refers to how concise and precise a requirement is specified. Accuracy should be present not only in the content but also in the structure of a requirement.

In terms of structure, a requirement must clearly distinguish between at least two parts: condition and action. A requirement with a clear action and no condition opens a possibility to think that the specified action is permanent (which is rarely the case). On the other hand, by definition, there can not exist a requirement with no action.

For instance, the following requirement is inaccurate: "*The system shall clear the DMA shared space,*" since no one knows when the action must occur.

In terms of content, a requirement must include clear and detailed information about the condition and the action that is being described. Accurate requirements also include explicit units for physical values as well as tolerances and thresholds for numerical computations.

For instance, the following requirement is inaccurate "*The system shall send ARINC label 251 every 50 ms,*" but adding a tolerance value solves the issue as in "*The system shall send ARINC label 251 every 50 ms +/- 5ms.*"

Non deterministic adverbs usually modifying verbs (such as: *continually, periodically, regularly* and others) also create inaccurate requirements like the following: "*The system shall periodically perform CBITE.*"

Finally, there are a number of general verbs that should be avoided in requirements since they create inaccurate descriptions. Some of these verbs are: *process, monitor, support, check* among others. For instance, it is not clear to see the software action that this requirement implies: "*The system shall monitor responses from the slave processor.*"

### 3.2.3 Verifiability

A requirement is said to be verifiable if it is possible to create and execute a test to demonstrate that the software behaves exactly as specified in the requirement.

Sometimes a test can not be executed primarily because of hardware or test equipment limitations. In other cases, conflicts or inconsistencies between requirements are revealed which prevent a test from being performed. However, another group of requirements become non verifiable due to language usage errors.

For instance, by definition requirements are meant to describe actions that the system shall perform. In that sense, a requirement must not describe anything that the system shall not perform. To illustrate, a requirement such as the following is *non verifiable*: "*The system shall not enter INTERACTIVE mode when WOW is false.*" The reason is that a tester can not expect any specific system action during a test for this requirement.

Furthermore, requirements using the adverbs *always* and *never* are also *non-verifiable* since a test for them would require infinite time. Similarly, the term *only* must be used correctly when modifying the main action (verb) of the requirement. For example, the requirement "*The system shall only display invalid data in red color*" implies that the only action this system performs is "*display invalid data in red color.*" The intended meaning is probably "*The system shall display only invalid data in red color.*"

Finally, some requirements contain verbs that imply actions that a software application can not perform; instead, these are usually human-specific tasks that are incorrectly assigned to software. Some of these verbs are: *determine, ignore, consider, analyse* and others. One example of wrong usage is "*The system shall consider fault history during CBITE.*"

As mentioned in section 1.2, one objective was to provide a quantitative evaluation of a set of requirements against three properties: *accuracy, ambiguity* and *verifiability*. With that goal in mind, section 4.1 introduces some of the formulations that will be used to perform the evaluation of the requirements against the selected properties.

## 4 Research Foundation

To accomplish the general objectives described in section 1.2, section 4.1 introduces a semi-formal nomenclature used to express the various situations when a requirement either satisfies or violates any of the desired properties. This nomenclature is valuable for it allows to represent various situations in a symbolic and summarized way. Section 4.2 describes the process followed to select the criteria against which the software requirements will be evaluated for quality.

### 4.1 Proposing General Nomenclature

We will use the term *element* to refer to individual linguistics elements or rules as mentioned in section 1.2. Similarly, the term *attribute* refers to quality properties: *accuracy*, *ambiguity* and *verifiability*.

To represent the attribute *ambiguity*, we define the set $\Lambda = \{\lambda_1, \lambda_2, ..., \lambda_k\}$ with $k \in \mathbb{N}_{\geq 1}$ where each $\lambda_i$ is an element that reveals a non compliance for the attribute of *ambiguity* by a given requirement. For instance, let's assume $\lambda_1 =$ "*A requirement must not use vague or general adverbs to describe an action,*" then, if we apply $\lambda_1$ to the requirement $R_1 =$ "*The system shall allow the operator to adjust volume to an acceptable level,*" we conclude that $R_1$ is *ambiguous* since the adverb "*acceptable*" is vague. In that case we say that $R_1$ does not satisfy $\lambda_1$.

For *accuracy* we define $\Gamma = \{\gamma_1, \gamma_2, ..., \gamma_r\}$ with $r \in \mathbb{N}_{\geq 1}$, and for *verifiability* we define $\Upsilon = \{\upsilon_1, \upsilon_2, ..., \upsilon_s\}$ with $s \in \mathbb{N}_{\geq 1}$ in an analogous way. Summarizing, we define:

$$X_1 = \Lambda \quad , \quad X_2 = \Gamma \quad , \quad X_3 = \Upsilon$$

where $X_i = \{\epsilon_1, \epsilon_2, ..., \epsilon_n\}$ and each $\epsilon_i$ is an *element* that tells us if a requirement does not satisfy a specific attribute.

We propose the following notation to represent situations where requirements fail to satisfy an element.

- When a requirement $R_e$ meets the restriction imposed by an element $\epsilon_k$, we say that $R_e$ *satisfies* $\epsilon_k$, and we write $R_e \odot \epsilon_k$.

- When a requirement $R_e$ does not meet the restriction imposed by an element $\epsilon_k$, we say that $R_e$ *does not satisfy* $\epsilon_k$, and we write $R_e \oslash \epsilon_k$.

- When the restriction imposed by an element $\epsilon_k$ is not applicable for a requirement $R_e$, we say that $\epsilon_k$ *is not applicable* for $R_e$ and we write $R_e \oplus \epsilon_k$

Notice how the expressions $R_e \odot \epsilon_k$ , $R_e \oslash \epsilon_k$ and $R_e \oplus \epsilon_k$ can be seen as logical predicates for a binary relation. For instance, we could read the first expression as $\odot(R_e, \epsilon_k)$ or $\text{SATISFIES}(R_e, \epsilon_k)$ .

However, computing the degree in which a requirement satisfies an attribute is not a binary relation. For instance, a requirement can meet some restrictions and not others; besides, some restrictions are more critical than others.

For a more objective evaluation, a scale from 0 to 10 is proposed. Each element $\epsilon_1, \epsilon_2, ..., \epsilon_n$ in $X_i$ is assigned a value or score so that the scores for all elements in an attribute add up to 10 and $score(\epsilon_i) = p$ , $p \in \mathbb{R}^+_{10}$ (where $\mathbb{R}^+_{10} = [0, 10]$). Values are assigned depending on the criticality and type of error revealed by each element. Summarizing:

$$\sum_{j=1}^{|X_i|} score(\epsilon_j) = 10 \quad \text{where } \epsilon_j \in X_i \text{ and } X_i \in \{\Lambda, \Gamma, \Upsilon\} \tag{1}$$

Now, in order to **evaluate** a requirement $R_e$ in regards to an attribute, we define $\theta$: $(R) \rightarrow \mathbb{R}^+_{10}$:

$$\theta(R_e, X_i) = [10 - \sum_{j, R_e \oslash \epsilon_j} score(\epsilon_j)] = [\sum_{j, R_e \odot \epsilon_j} score(\epsilon_j)] \quad \text{where } \epsilon_j \in X_i \tag{2}$$

Notice how we write $\theta$ using either predicate *does not satisfy* $\oslash$ or *satisfies* $\odot$. In both cases, when an element *is not applicable* $\oplus$ to a requirement, we assume that the requirement *satisfies* such element.

To understand the meaning of $\theta$, suppose that $x = \theta(R_e, \Gamma)$ is the score a requirement $R_e$ gets when it is evaluated against a given attribute, let's say *accuracy*.

- When $x = 10$ we say that $R_e$ satisfies $\Gamma$ and we write $R_e \odot \Gamma$. $R_e$ is accurate, since it meets all the restrictions imposed by each element in $\Gamma$.

- When $x = 0$ we say that $R_e$ does not satisfy $\Gamma$ and we write $R_e \oslash^0 \Gamma$. $R_e$ is not accurate, since it does not meet any of the restrictions imposed by elements in $\Gamma$.

- When $0 < x < 10$ we say that $R_e$ does not satisfy $\Gamma$ with a degree $x$ and we write $R_e \oslash^x \Gamma$. $R_e$ meets some of the restrictions imposed by elements in $\Gamma$ but not all. In this case, the closer $x$ is to 10, the better the requirement will be[3].

Finally, to get a requirement's overall score against all three attributes, we define a function $\phi : (R) \rightarrow \mathbb{R}^+_{10}$ as follows:

$$\phi(R_k) = \frac{\sum_{i=1}^{3} \theta(R_k, X_i)}{3} \quad \text{where } X_i \in \{\Lambda, \Gamma, \Upsilon\} \tag{3}$$

$\phi$ is the arithmetic mean of the scores a requirement gets against each attribute h$X_i$ in (2). The overall score is a measure of a requirement's quality, and it could be used potentially to estimate costs in a software project.

To understand $\phi$ suppose $x = \phi(R_k)$ is the score a requirement $R_k$ gets when it is evaluated against all three attributes (*ambiguity*, *accuracy* and *verifiability*) using all elements in $\{\Lambda, \Gamma, \Upsilon\}$.

- When $x = 10$, we say that $R_k$ is *accurate*, *verifiable* and *non-ambiguous* since $R_k \odot X_i \quad \forall_{X_i} \in \{\Lambda, \Gamma, \Upsilon\}$.

- When $x = 0$ we say that $R_k$ is *inaccurate*, *non-verifiable* and *ambiguous* since $R_k \oslash X_i \quad \forall_{X_i} \in \{\Lambda, \Gamma, \Upsilon\}$.

- When $0 < x < 10$, we say that $R_k$ is either *inaccurate*, *non-verifiable* or *ambiguous* since it does not satisfy at least one element in $\{\Lambda, \Gamma, \Upsilon\}$. In this case, $\theta$ provides more information about the weakness detected in $R_k$.

The value of the suggested notation comes from the fact that we can now produce quantitative evaluations of requirements, as opposed to common qualitative evaluations. The following sections briefly describe a bottom up process we followed to select evaluation criteria for the prototype that was built.

[3]We will use either notation $\oslash$ or $\oslash^x$ to indicate that a requirement does not satisfy an attribute and the degree $x$ is not relevant.

### 4.2 Selecting Criteria for Evaluation

The process of selecting the elements for each attribute was conducted in a series of steps that are summarized below. The objective of our approach was to provide a selection of elements that satisfied three main goals. The first goal was to have representative and useful selection within the field of software verification. The second goal was that the selection could be independently validated by a group of professionals in the field. And finally, the third goal was that the selection of elements refers to weaknesses that can be automatically detected by a software.

The following is a summary of the process that was followed to select the criteria to evaluate requirements.

1. A list of elements was first suggested by the author based on relevant literature and his own experience in software verification for embedded systems. The list contained 19 elements (10 for *accuracy*, 5 for *ambiguity* and 4 for *verifiability*).

2. Five elements were filtered out as they were not candidates to be automated. Feasible candidates were those that could be automated using techniques such as parsing, tagging, regular expressions, and specialized dictionaries like WordNet (Miller, 1993) and VerbNet (Kipper, 2005). The list ended with 6 elements in *accuracy*, 4 in *ambiguity* and 4 in *verifiability*.

3. The author suggested an initial value or score for each element in the list.

4. Both the element selection and the value distribution were independently validated by a group of three professionals with demonstrable experience in software verification[4].

5. A numerical model was prepared based on the proposed approach described in section 4.1. This is already a contribution since the evaluation of the requirements could be done manually in case no tool had been created.

[4]Although these individuals are not language experts, since they have valuable experience in requirements verification, their feedback was considered a valid complement in this research.

6. A software prototype was written for a tool that is capable of examining a list of requirements applying equations 2 and 3 in section 4.1.

Section 5 briefly describes the capabilities of the prototype tool that was developed.

## 5 Automated Evaluation

This section provides a brief description of the software prototype. A more in depth description would be ideal; however, due to space limitations we will focus on two items only. First, an overview of the tool's architecture and technologies involved (section 5.1). Second, a description of the outputs this tool produces (section 5.2).

### 5.1 Building the Prototype

Our prototype tool receives the name of SRR-Director from *Software Requirements Reviewer Director*. This prototype was built using open source software and tools that are freely available for research. Our goal was to integrate several of these available resources into a single piece of software that helped us solving the problem we are studying.

Perl[5] was used as the main language for the software and Awk[6] was used as an independent tool to check some of the results while developing the tool. Input requirements normally exist in various formats such as MS Word[7], MS Excel[8], structured XML, or plain text files. We provide a tool that can be configured to read those inputs converting them into XML documents that follow a normalized structure which basically separates requirements identifiers from the actual text of the requirement.

The three main techniques used during automated inspection of the requirements were the following:

**Lexical Analysis**: this is a common and simple technique that is based on regular expressions. Perl's engine for regular expressions was particularly useful in this task. This type of analysis allows identification of key words or phrase structures that reveal specific types of weaknesses in requirements.

This technique helped identifying issues of all three types. For ambiguity it allowed to locate vague adverbs and non deterministic language constructs; for accuracy, we detected tolerance issues, non deterministic adverbs and general verbs. Finally, to check for verifiability this technique was used to capture negative requirements, infinite requirements, and wrong usage of the term *only*.

**Syntactic Analysis**: consists of parsing the requirements to transform language statements into their grammatical constituents which enables other specific analysis such as ambiguity analysis. This process was performed using a parser made available by Eugine Charniak and Brown University (Charniak et al., 2006). In this case, the CLAIR group at University of Michigan made available a Perl wrapper for the Charniak parser(CLAIR, 2009).

Studying the syntax tree produced by the parser, it was possible to identify accuracy issues such as requirements without explicit condition statements (or condition blocks). Also, studying the output of the parser along with lexical analysis of the requirement reveals cases of ambiguity when logical conditions are not stated clearly.

**Dictionaries**: two great resources were also incorporated in this research to support our analysis: WordNet (Miller, 1993) and VerbNet (Kipper, 2005). Both of this tools can also be accessed from Perl via wrappers and provide useful information about words and verbs that were used to ensure some conditions were valid while we perform the analysis of the requirements.

Dictionaries allow identification of human specific verbs and ambiguous verbs. In this case, the parser makes it possible to capture the main verb for a requirement, and further queries into dictionaries complete the task. VerbNet provides a mechanism to classify requirements according to their degree of ambiguity. This mechanism may be too stringent for flagging ambiguous verbs sometimes. There are verbs tagged as ambiguous in VerbNet, but they have a fairly well known and shared meaning in the domain of software engineering such as: *set, shutdown, turnoff, send, receive* among others.

SRR-Director runs from a command line and it is currently controlled using a number of arguments and switches. Even when this is still a prototype tool, our experiments show that the tool is very efficient capturing weaknesses in the requirements with a marginal error rate ($< 5\%$) for the rules included

[5] http://www.perl.org
[6] http://www.gnu.org/software/gawk/
[7] http://office.microsoft.com/word
[8] http://office.microsoft.com/excel

in the current version of the tool. More importantly, the tool is able to examine hundreds of requirements in a matter of minutes when the same work takes hours or even days for a human reviewer.

### 5.2 Using the Reports

In the current prototype version, the tool produces seven types of reports that provide information for three types of users:

**Quality engineers**: two reports show general information about the quality of the requirements that were analysed. Quality engineers are interested in the overall percentage of requirements compliance with the quality objectives, and they don't need details on the types of failures.

**Requirements engineers**: four reports are available for the largest audience of users who are actually interested in learning the details about the types of failures identified in the requirements. Not only are the engineers notified of the weaknesses but also they are provided with suggestions on how to fix the issues. The evaluation they receive is not only qualitative but also quantitative since they can see the score for individual requirements against each of the three properties being studied.

**Software engineers**: this is a miscellaneous report that provides performance information which may later help software engineers while tuning certain processes in the tool.

## 6 Experiments and Results

Experiments were performed using sample requirements from three distinct and real word applications in embedded systems. Test data was selected from a pool of reserved requirements that were not used during development of the tool.

Four groups of 20 requirements each were selected and given to three experienced professionals in the field of software verification. The subjects were asked to identify weaknesses in the requirements using their own criteria. They were asked to classify ill requirements as *inaccurate*, *ambiguous* or *non-verifiable* when applicable. The same groups were input to the prototype for evaluation, and results were compared.

As it was mentioned before, the tool recognizes all deficiencies described by a rule or *element* with a low error rate ($< 5\%$). We believe this is mostly due to the fact that –in this initial phase of the tool– rules are not complex, and can indeed be automated without using complex techniques.

One interesting result was that a high degree of discrepancies and disagreement between the subject reviewers was observed . On average, the three reviewers agreed only in $14\%$ of their evaluations, and only in $62\%$ of the cases there was agreement between at least two reviewers. These unexpected discrepancies certainly make it difficult to compare the tool's results with the reviewer's results to identify areas of agreement or disagreement.

A more in depth analysis of the results suggests that human beings may perform erratically when it comes to reviewing requirements that contain the types of errors we are looking for. Some of the weaknesses we want to uncover are rather subtle and, as we argued before (section 1.3), require a good level of language and technical knowledge as well as a detail oriented attitude. People are also affected by external factors such as fatigue that negatively affects the quality of their work.

## 7 Conclusions

The results of this research show that it is actually possible to automate the review process of software requirements identifying valuable sources of deficiencies that otherwise make requirements *inaccurate*, *ambiguous* or *non-verifiable*.

Besides, there are resources freely available for research that can be integrated into more specific tools to solve a variety of problems. Specialized dictionaries, stand alone tools, such as parsers, and a general purpose scripting language (Perl) were combined in order to create the tool prototype.

Finally, a simple but rather useful nomenclature to represent different scenarios that occur during requirements verification was proposed. This contribution allows us to provide a quantitative analysis of the requirements as opposed to traditional qualitative-only analyses.

## 8 Collaboration Opportunities

This section answers two specific questions to describe possible collaboration opportunities between investigators doing research on similar topics.

### 8.1 How can this work benefit other research projects?

This research was focused on three properties applicable to software requirements for aerospace systems. However, it would be ideal to apply similar techniques to examine other types of properties that are crucial in similarly critical application domains such as finance, transportation, medicine and communications.

In this work, inputs are text documents with natural language text in the form of software requirements. Those inputs are preprocessed and converted into simpler representations that basically consist of sentences. Those sentences at the end are the main input for the tool that performs the automated quality analysis.

Researchers wishing to learn more about this work are strongly encouraged to contact the author to share ideas on this topic and benefit from one another. We believe it is possible to reuse part of the approach to build similar tools to analyse requirements in languages other than English.

### 8.2 What are some resources and expertise the author lacks?

One of the main difficulties the author faced is the absence of collaboration between researchers interested in similar topics. This work has been produced mostly in isolation as part of academic research in a masters program.

Being able to share ideas with working groups either academic or industry sponsored would be a great channel to improve research scope and produce more significant results. For the nature of this research, a mixed team of linguists and software engineers would presumably improve the quality of the work.

On the one hand, linguists would provide valuable knowledge that would help identifying additional language structures that represent symptoms of weaknesses in requirements. On the other hand, software engineers would be closer to requirements engineers and could contribute with implementation details so that new rules are added to the system.

## References


Wilson, W. and Rosenberg, L. and Hyatt, L. 1997. *Automated Analysis of Requirement Specifications.* Nineteenth International Conference on Software Engineering (ICSE-97), Boston, MA.

Galin, D. 2004. *Software Quality Assurance From theory to implementation.* Pearson Education Ltd.

Leffingwell, D. and Widrig, D. 2003. *Managing Software Requirements*, 2nd Ed. Addison-Wesley.

RTCA/EUROCAE. 1992. *DO-178 Software Considerations for Airborne Systems and Equipment Certification.* RTCA, Inc., Washington, DC.

Drazen, M. and Berander, P. and Damm, L. and Eriksson, J. and Gorschek, T. and Henningsson, K. and Jonsson, P. and Kagstrom, S. and Martensson, F. and Ronkko, K. and Tomaszewski, P. . 2005. *Software quality attributes and trade-offs, Software Quality Models and Philosophies.* Blekinge Institute of Technology.

IEEE Standards Board. 1990. *IEEE Standard Glossary of Software Engineering Terminology*, Std 610.12-1990.

Berry, D. and Kamsties, E. and Krieger, M. . 2003. *From Contract Drafting to Software Specification: Linguistic Sources of Ambiguity.*

Miller, G. and Beckwith, R. and Fellbaum, C. and Gross, D. and Miller, K.. 1993. *Introduction to WordNet: An Online Lexical Database.* Cognitive Science Laboratory, Princeton University.

Kipper, K.. 2005. *VerbNet: A broad-coverage, comprehensive verb lexicon.* Computer and Information Science, University of Pennsylvania.

Lami, G. and Gnesi, S. and Fabbrini, F. and Fusani, M. and Trentanni, G. . 1997. *An Automatic Tool for the Analysis of Natural Language Requirements.* C.N.R. Information Science and Technology Institute, Pisa Italy.

McClosky, D. and Charniak, E. and Johnson, M.. 2006. *Reranking and Self-Training for Parser Adaptation.* 21st International Conference on Computational Linguistics.

CLAIR official website. 2009. *URL* `http://belobog.si.umich.edu/clair/clair/downloads.html`. Visited on March 12, 2009.

Fuchs, N. and Schwertel, U. and Schwitter, D.. 1998. *Attempto Controlled English Not Just Another Logic Specification Language.* Eighth International Workshop on Logic-based Program Synthesis and Transformation LOPSTR'98, Manchester, UK.

Firesmith, D.. 2003. *Specifying Good Requirements.* Journal of Object Technology, ETH Zurich.

# Recognition and extraction of definitional contexts in Spanish for sketching a lexical network

**César Aguilar**
Department of Linguistics
Autonomous University of Queretaro
Cerro de las Campanas, s/n, Queretaro, Mexico
CAguilar@iingen.unam.mx

**Olga Acosta**
Postgraduate School of Computer Science
UNAM
Ciudad Universitaria, Mexico City
OAcostaL@iingen.unam.mx

**Gerardo Sierra**
Language Engineering Group
Engineering Institute, UNAM
Ciudad Universitaria, Mexico City
GSierraM@iingen.unam.mx

## Abstract

In this paper we propose a method to exploit analytical definitions extracted from Spanish corpora, in order to build a lexical network based on the hyponymy/hyperonymy, part/whole and attribution relations. Our method considers the following steps: (a) the recognition and extraction of definitional contexts from specialized documents, (b) the identification of analytical definitions on these definitional contexts, using verbal predications, (c) the syntactic and probabilistic analysis of the association observed between verbal predication and analytical definitions, (d) the identification of the hyponymy/hyperonymy, part/whole and attribution relations based on the lexical information that lies between predications and definitions and other types of phrases, in particular prepositional phrases mapped by the preposition *de* (Eng. of/from).

## 1 Introduction

Nowadays, the possibility of searching and recognizing lexical relations in definitions occurring in specialized text corpora is an important task in computational lexicography and terminology.

In this sense, authors such as Vossen and Copestake (1993), as well as Wilks, Slator & Guthrie (1995) are pioneers in offering a relevant set of experiments and techniques about how to identify hyponymy/hypernymy relations from analytical definitions, taking into account the underlying association that exists between terms and genus terms.

Complementary to these first attempts for identifying such lexical relations, Riloff & Shepherd (2004) argue that while these efforts have been oriented to extract lexical relations from corpus of general language, it is necessary to focus on domain-specific corpora, in order to obtain a specialized knowledge that is required for in-depth understanding of the subject matter.

In line with the argument formuled by Riloff & Shepherd, Buiteelar, Cimiano & Magnini (2005) have proposed several methods for building ontologies from text corpora, priorizing the automatic recognition of syntactic patterns that codify hyponymy/hyperonymy relations.

Following all these authors, we sketch here a research project to design a lexical network, focused on classifying scientific and technical concepts extracted from Spanish text corpora. In particular, we obtain these concepts by extracting definitional contexts (DCs) with terms and definitions clearly formulated, according to the theoretical framework developed by Sierra, Alarcon & Aguilar (2006).

After extracted these DCs, we propose a method to identify lexical relations between terms inserted into the DCs. The method considers, on the one hand, a grammatical analysis for detecting syntactic patterns that represent term and genus term, bearing in mind their association through lexical relations such as hyponymy/hyperonymy, part/whole or attribution relations. On the other hand, we proposed a semi-automatic evaluation to determine the degree of accuracy respect to the results obtained by our method.

The issues that we will deal in this paper are organized as follows: (a) as a starting point, we expose briefly the theoretical framework to extract DCs from Spanish corpora. (b) According to this framework, we describe how analytical definitions



*Proceedings of the NAACL HLT 2010 Young Investigators Workshop on Computational Approaches to Languages of the Americas*, pages 109–116, Los Angeles, California, June 2010. 

linked to terms can be identified, considering the identification of verbal predications that function as connectors between such definitions and terms. (c) Thus, we offer a probabilistic evaluation for determining the degree of association between predications and analytical definitions. (d) After this evaluation, we sketch a method for exploiting this association between predications and definitions, in order to identify lexical relations, specifically hyponymy/hyperonymy, part/whole and attribution relations.

## 2 Theoretical framework: DC extraction

We situate our analysis within the framework of definitional contexts (or DCs) extraction. According to Sierra *et al.* (2008), a DC is a discursive structure that contains relevant information to define a term. DCs have at least two constituents: a term and a definition, and usually linguistic or metalinguistic forms, such as verbal phrases, typographical markers and/or pragmatic patterns. An example is:

(1) *La* ***cuchilla fusible*** [Term] *se define como* [Verbal Phrase] *un elemento de conexión y desconexión de circuitos eléctricos* [Definition]. (Engl. The fuse-switch disconnector is defined as an element of connection and disconnection of electric circuits).

In (1), the term *cuchilla flexible* is emphasized by the use of bold font, and it appears linked with the verbal predication *se define como*, and the definition *un elemento de conexión y desconexión de circuitos eléctricos.* Following to Sierra *et al.* (2008), we consider the term, the verbal phrase and the definition as the three main units constituting the syntactic structure of a DC.

This kind of syntactic structure introduces an analytical definition (in the Aristotle's sense), where the genus term is represented by a noun phrase (NP) *un elemento* and the differentia is represented by a prepositional phrase (PP) *de conexión y desconexión de circuitos eléctricos.*

In a detailed analysis on these syntactic structures, Aguilar (2009) explains that these structures are predicate phrases (PrP), according to the description proposed by Bowers (1993, 2001). A PrP is a phrase mapped by a functional head, and its grammatical behavior is similar to other functional phrases such as Inflexional Phrase (IP) or Complement Phrase (CP). A graphical tree representation of a PrP is:

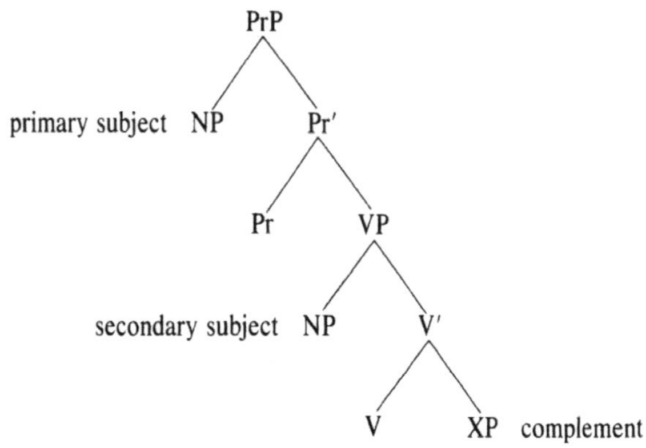


Figure 1: Tree representation for PrP, according to Bowers (1993: 596)

The Figure 1 describes the syntactic configuration of a PrP. We recognise a functional head with the feature $^{+/-}$ predicative (Pr). This head maps two subjects: a primary subject in the Specifier position of PrP (represented for a NP); and a secondary subject, in the Specifier position of verbal phrase or VP (often a NP). Finally, both subjects, the VP and the PrP are linked to one or several complements, which assume phrasal representations (e.g.: NP, IP, CP, and other types of phrases).

Based on this description about PrP, Sierra *et al.* (2008) and Aguilar (2009) observed that both primary and secondary predications have a close relation with analytical definitions expressed in specialized texts. Examples of this relation between PrP and analytical definitions are:

(2) [*Una computadora* [*es* [*un tipo de máquina electrónica que sirve para hacer operaciones* $_{PrP}$] $_{VP}$] $_{IP}$] (Eng. [A computer [is [a kind of electronic machine used to make operations $_{PrP}$] $_{VP}$] $_{IP}$]).

(3) [*Turing* [define una computadora [como un mecanismo electrónico que procesa conjuntos de datos $_{PrP}$] $_{VP}$] $_{IP}$] (Eng. [Turing [defines a computer [as a kind of electronic device that processes a set of data $_{PrP}$] $_{VP}$] $_{IP}$]).

We observe in (2) a canonical primary predication where the subject *una computadora* represents a term directly associated to predicate *es un tipo de máquina que...* This predicate introduces an analytical definition, conformed by a genus term *eletronic machine*, and the differentia *que sirve para hacer operaciones*. In (3), the predicate *como un mecanismo electrónico*... (Engl. *as a kind of electronic device*...) affects the secondary subject *una computadora* (Engl. *a computer*), in concordance with the explanation of Bowers (1993). Our analysis considers both types of predications as regular patterns that codify syntactically sequences of terms, verbal predications and definitions.

## 3 Searching analytical definitions in text corpora

We have adapted the predicative patterns deduced from our syntactic analysis, in order to search and find (semi-)automatically analytical definitions linked to these patterns. So, we conducted an experiment of identification of these definitions in two text corpora:

- Linguistic Corpus on Engineering (or CLI). The *CLI*, prepared by Medina and others (2004), is a collection of technical documents in different thematic areas of engineering, with an extension of 500,000 words, approximately.
- Corpus on Informatics for Spanish (or CIE). This corpus was built under the supervision of L'Homme and Drouin (2006). The *CIE* compiles several documents related to computer science and informatics. For our experiment we took a portion of *CIE*, which contains articles extracted from Wikipedia. This portion has an extension of 500,000 words.

Following to Aguilar *et al.* (2004) and *Sierra et al.* (2008), we selected a set of verbs that function as heads of predicative patterns in Spanish, taking into account the distinction between primary and secondary predications.

In the case of primary predication, the analytical definition is integrated in a sequence Term + Verbal Predication + Definition. This definition does not refer to possible author(s) of a definition. An example is:

(4) [El apartarrayos $_{\text{Term}}$] [es $_{\text{Verbal Predication}}$] [un dispositivo $_{\text{Genus Term}}$] [que protege las instalaciones contra sobretensiones de origen atmosférico $_{\text{Differentia}}$] (Engl. [The lightning conductor $_{\text{Term}}$] [is $_{\text{Verbal Predication}}$] [a device $_{\text{Genus Term}}$] [that protects electrical systems against surges of atmospheric origin $_{\text{Differentia}}$]).

Having in mind this sequence, we propose a grammatical description model for this relation:

Table 1: Construction patterns derived from the relation between primary predication and analytical definition

| Definition | Genus Term | Differentia |
|---|---|---|
| Analytical (Primary Predication) | NP = Noun + {AdjP/PP}* | CP = Relative Pronoun + IP |
| | | PP = Preposition + NP |
| | | AdjP = Adjective + NP |

The verbs that operate as head of these predications are: *referir* (to refer to), *representar* (to represent), *ser* (to be) and *significar* (to signify/to mean). In contrast, when a secondary predication introduces an analytical definition, this predication follows the sequence Author + Term + Verbal Predication + Definition, where the Author is equivalent to the primary subject, the Term assumes the position of secondary subject, and the definition is introduced after the Verbal Predication. In this case, the adverbial particle *como* (Eng. *as/like*), or the preposition *por* (Eng. *for/by*) indicates the place of the definition. An example is:

(5) [Carlos Godino $_{\text{Author}}$] [define $_{\text{Verbal Predication}}$] [la arquitectura naval $_{\text{Term}}$] [como la ciencia que se enfoca en la construcción de los buques $_{\text{Definition}}$] (Eng. [Carlos Godino $_{\text{Author}}$] [defines $_{\text{Verbal Predication}}$] [the naval architecture $_{\text{Term}}$] [as the science that focuses on the construction of ships $_{\text{Definition}}$])

Thus, the formal description of this sequence is:

Table 2: Construction patterns derived from the relation between secondary predication and analytical definition

| Definition | Adverb/ Preposition | Genus Term | Differentia |
|---|---|---|---|
| Analytical (Secondary Predication) | *Como* *Por* | NP = Noun + {AdjP /PP}* | CP = Relative Pronoun + IP |
| | | | PP = Preposition + NP |
| | | | AdjP = Adjective + NP |

The verbs linked to secondary predications are: *caracterizar + como/por* (Engl. to characterize + as/for), *comprender + como* (Engl. to comprehend

+ as), *concebir* + *como* (Engl. to conceive + as), *conocer* + *como* (Engl. to know + as), *considerar* + *como* (Engl. to consider + as), *definir* + *como* (Engl. to define + as), *describir* + *como* (Engl. to define + as), *entender* + *como* (Engl. to understand + as) , *identificar* + *como* (Engl. to identify + as) and *visualizar* + *como* (Engl. to visualize + as).

In order to recognize these sequences of predications and analytical definitions, we employed a system developed in Python by Rodríguez (2004). Broadly speaking, the input for this system is a set of previously delimited text fragments. The output is a XML table with a list of patterns, the verb used for searching these patterns, and the frequency of use in both corpora.

## 4 Results

Once we accomplished the process of searching and extracting of fragments with sequences of predication patterns of analytical definitions, we determined values of precision and recall for the CLI and CIE corpora based on the real number of analytical DCs in the corpus. This data was determined by a human expert through an exploration in the corpora mentioned above. In table 3 we showed DC candidates, as well as the real number of true DCs extracted from these candidates.

Thus, from CLI corpora we obtained a total of 1686 candidates. From these candidates, the human expert recognized a set of 111 true DCs to analytical definition linked to primary predication patterns. Our recall was 100% because we obtained all of the DCs with analytical definitions, but the precision achieved was very low (6.6%).

The main cause about this low precision is due to the verb *ser* (Eng. to be). The verb *ser* is highly productive in Spanish, however, much of the fragments found are not analytical definitions. In contrast, from secondary predication patterns, our recall was 100% and precision 9.4%. Thus, the CIE corpora showed measures of precision and recall higher than those of CLI corpora because most of documents were extracted from resources as Wikipedia. We suppose this factor is related with a definition scheme more canonical in scientific and technical documents.

Table 3: Sequence frequencies of predication patterns and analytical definitions

| **Analytical Definitions** | | **CLI** | **CIE** |
|---|---|---|---|
| **Primary Predication** | Candidates | 1686 | 494 |
| | DCs | 111 | 127 |
| | Recall | 100% | 100% |
| | Precision | 6.6% | 25.7% |
| **Secondary Predication** | Candidates | 701 | 61 |
| | DCs | 66 | 11 |
| | Recall | 100% | 100% |
| | Precision | 9.4% | 18.0% |

We derived a frequency distribution of the verbs with type of predication for CLI and CIE corpora. The table 4 shows the relative frequency of use of each verb explored. Most of these verbs do not have been considered in automatic extraction tasks of hyponymy-hyperonymy relations, e. g.: Hearst (1992) or Wilks, Slator & Guthrie (1995).

Table 4: Frequency distribution of verbal predicate, and its use in analytical definitions

| **Predication** | **Corpora** | |
|---|---|---|
| | **CLI** | **CIE** |
| **Primary** | | |
| Referir(a)/To refer | 0 | 0.02 |
| Representar/To represent | 0 | 0.04 |
| Significar/To signify | 0 | 0.03 |
| Ser/To be | 1 | 0.91 |
| **Secondary** | | |
| Caracterizar/To characterize | 0.12 | 0.18 |
| Concebir/To concibe | 0.09 | 0 |
| Conocer/To know | 0.17 | 0 |
| Considerar/To consider | 0.21 | 0.27 |
| Definir/To define | 0.27 | 0.27 |
| Describir/To describe | 0.03 | 0.09 |
| Entender/To understand | 0.06 | 0.18 |
| Identificar/To identify | 0.03 | 0 |
| Visualizar/To visualize | 0.02 | 0 |

Once established this distribution, we have analyzed the degree of assurance to find a good candidate for analytical definitions. We have applied a method of conditional probabilities for primary and secondary predications. Our conditional probabilities are formulated by the hypothesis that the probability (*P*) of co-occurrence of predications (*Pred*) linked to analytical definition (*AD*) is high. Thus, we apply the following formula of conditional probability:

$$P(AD|Pred) = \frac{P(AD \cap Pred)}{P(Pred)}$$

Taking into account the formula mentioned above, we obtained the following results:

Table 5: Conditional probabilities of co-occurrence between predications and analytical definitions

| Predication | | CLI | CIE |
|---|---|---|---|
| Primary | Analytical definitions | 93% | 100% |
| | Not-analytical definitions | 7% | 0% |
| Secondary | Analytical definitions | 95% | 100% |
| | Not-analytical definitions | 5% | 0% |

Therefore, we considered that the possibility to identify a good candidate of analytical definition is high, insofar as we took into account their relationship with primary and secondary predications.

In addition, Alarcón, Bach & Sierra (2007), propose a methodology for filtering true DCs from a set of candidates to DCs. An important advance provided for this work is the application of a filter phase that discards those syntactic patterns without true analytical definitions. For example, if we find a particle as *no* (Eng. not) or *tampoco* (Eng. either) in the first position before or after of a predication, there is a high probability these pattern do not introduce a good analytical definition. In Table 5 we showed some results in terms of precision and recall reported by authors only for analytical definition patterns.

Table 6: Precision & recall values

| Verbal pattern | Precision | Recall |
|---|---|---|
| Concebir(como)/To conceive(as) | 0.67 | 0.98 |
| Definir(como)/To define(as) | 0.84 | 0.99 |
| Entender(como)/To understand(as) | 0.34 | 0.94 |
| Identificar(como)/To identify(as) | 0.31 | 0.90 |
| Significar/To signify | 0.29 | 0.98 |

## 5 Sketching a method

In this section, we propose a method for recognizing lexical relations from the previous extraction of DCs. In particular, we assume that a good way to reach these relations is to improve the syntactic association observed between predications and analytical definitions inserted into these DCs.

This assumption is in line with the methodology proposed by Buitelaar, Cimiano & Magnini (2005) for building ontologies based on textual information obtained from corpora. These three authors conceive a chain of processes and sub-processes, represented with a layer cake scheme:

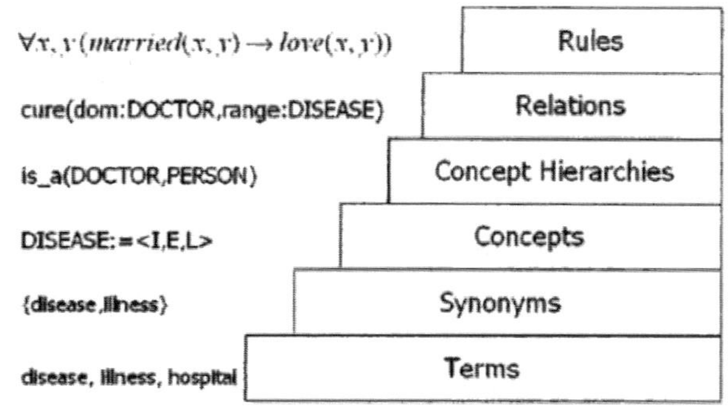


Figure 2: Ontology learning layer cake (according to Buitelaar, Cimiano & Magnani 2005)

Briefly, in this scheme Buitelaar, Cimiano & Magnini establish a sequence of 6 basic tasks for developing a possible ontology. Thus, the first task is the identification of a set of specific terms to a certain knowledge domain (in this case, a medical domain). After that, it is necessary to identify synonyms related to these terms (e.g., disease/illness). Given both sets of terms and synonyms, the following task is to determine concepts in a formal way. For delineating these concepts, in the next task are deduced lexical relations following lexical networks formulated by WordNet (Fellbaum 1998).

Once these lexical relations are established, the semantic relations are proposed, keeping this in mind, for example, first-order logic to represent predicate-arguments structures. The final process of this chain is to derive universal rules for building concepts, joining lexical and semantic relations deduced previously.

Thus, the recognition and extraction of concepts is a step towards the general goal proposed by Buitelaar, Cimiano & Magnini for building ontologies. For this particular phase, our proposal consists on identifying and extracting conceptual information through lexical-syntactic patterns as we mentioned above.

## 6 Towards the (semi-)automatic identification of lexical relations

In agreement with the methodology of Buitelaar, Cimiano & Magnini mentioned above, we propose to extract lexical relations from analytical definitions for covering the next step about hierarchical relations. Hiponymy/hypernymy and meronym/holonymy relations are considered as relations organizing a conceptual space in a hierarchical way (Winston, Chaffin & Herrmann 1987).

Additionally, our method provides a way to get more relations from a domain corpus through the application of a bootstrapping technique with the genus terms/wholes set as seed set.

- **Hyponymy/hyperonymy relations:** We consider works such as Hearst (1992), as well as Wilks, Slator & Guthrie (1995), because their methods allow combining linguistic and probabilistic criteria.
- **Part/whole relations:** In this case, we consider works such as Charniak & Berland (1999), as well as those results reported by Girju, Badulescu & Modolvan (2006). We propose a method exploiting the pattern with preposition *de*, due to its use frequency to link parts and wholes in Spanish. Table 6 shows examples about meronymy/holonymy relations using this pattern compared with other patterns worked in the literature.

Table 7: Number of hits returned by the search engine Google

| Part | Whole | X is part of Y | Y has X | X of the Y |
|---|---|---|---|---|
| Mouse | Computer | 27360 | 514 | 280400 |
| Keyboard | Computer | 60800 | 64730 | 1798000 |
| Screen | Computer | 58800 | 64100 | 556000 |

- **Attribution relations:** Attribution relations play an important role in disciplines involved with conceptual representation as artificial intelligence/knowledge representation, linguistics and psychology (Poesio & Almuhareb, 2005). So, we consider the work about the automatic extraction of attribution relations proposed by Poesio & Almuhareb (2004). They used an approach as that proposed by Charniak & Berland (1999) but to extract attribution relations using the pattern:

  "the * of the C [is|was]"

  Here, * represents a potential attribute for the concept C. In Spanish a common pattern to express attribution relations is the use of the preposition *de*, e.g.: *edad del paciente* (Eng. age of patient/patient's age), *altura del paciente* (Eng. height of the patient/ patient's height), and so on.

Summarizing, our methodology to extract lexical relations starts with the extraction of hyponymy-hypernymy relations from analytical DCs. For this phase we consider a lexical-syntactic approach due to the regularity of the definition schemes using predication patterns as those mentioned above.

Additionally, we propose a bootstrapping technique starting with the set of genus terms as a seedset to extract more lexical relations from a domain corpus. We use the preposition *de* to link genus term and other potential terms due to its importance to produce lexical relations of our interest.

For example, in a first phase exploring a domain corpus, a genus term as *dilatación* (Eng. dilation) links with a set of two elements {*vena*, *pupila*} (Eng. {vein, pupil}). In a next phase, the element *pupila* is linked to *ojo* (Eng. eye), and so on. Thus, on the one hand we have two relations IS-KIND-OF: *dilatación de la pupila* and *dilatación de la vena*. On the other hand, we have a meronymy-holonymy relation: *pupila-ojo*.

Integrating the three relations described above, we will implement a lexical network that allows organizing concepts related to terms. An example of this possible network is:

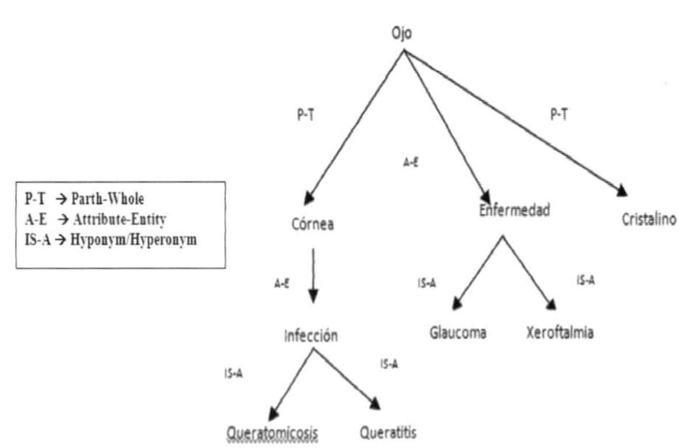


Figure 3: Example of a possible lexical network

In the figure, we can distinguish a set of sub-terms linked to the main term *Ojo* (Engl. Eye). These sub-terms operate as nodes, and the possible lexical relations are branches connected with the main term. Thus, based on a lexical Parth/whole relation, we can infer that *córnea* (Eng. cornea), is a constituent of eye. In contrast, the term *enfermedad* (Engl. *disease*) is an attribute of eye. Finally, the *glaucoma* is a type of disease that affects the eyes.

## 7 Work in progress and possible topics of collaborations

In this paper we proposed a method for recognizing lexical relations, taking into account the identification and extraction of analytical definitions situated into DCs in Spanish. This extraction considers verbal predications associated to these definitions. So, in order to explain this extraction, we have showed a formal syntactic analysis, based on the idea that these predications: (a) could be described in terms of predicative phrases, and (b), the association of predications and analytical definitions has a high frequency of use in specialized documents. For evaluating this frequency, we have exposed the results obtained for an experiment of extraction in two technical corpora.

Currently, we are situated in the phase to implement and evaluate a new experiment oriented to the detection of lexical relations between the term and the genus term formulated for analytical definitions. In particular, we are interested in discovering three types of relations: hyponym/hyperonymy, part-whole and attribution-entity.

We conclude suggesting some topics of collaborations for our potential colleges:

I. The construction of specialized texts corpora with good candidates of DCs, having in mind the basic features for identifying a DC.
II. The implementation of new linguistic and statistical methods for detecting and extracting lexical relations from text corpora.
III. The improvement of search systems, using these underlying lexical relations in electronic documents.
IV. Following to Wilks, Slator & Guthrie (1995), the design of lexical-semantic tags for recognizing and classifying concepts in taxonomies.

Similarly, according to Buitelaar, Cimiano & Magnini, we can use external lexical resources as Spanish WordNet and Spanish FrameNet (Subirats 2009) for determining and evaluating our lexical networks, in order to enrich the results that we could generate.

## Acknowledgments

This paper was made possible by the financial support of the Consejo Nacional de Ciencia y Tecnología, CONACYT, and DGAPA-UNAM. Also, we wish to thank the anonymous reviewers for theirs comments and suggestions.

## References

César Aguilar, Rodrigo Alarcón, Carlos Rodríguez and Gerardo Sierra. 2004. Reconocimiento y clasificación de patrones verbales definitorios en corpus especializados". En Cabre T., Estopà R. & Tebé C. (Eds.). *La terminología en el siglo XXI*, IULA-UPF, Barcelona, Spain: 259-269.

César Aguilar. 2009. *Análisis lingüístico de definiciones en contextos definitorios*. Ph. D. Thesis, Department of Linguistics, UNAM, Mexico.

Rodrigo Alarcón, Gerardo Sierra and Carme Bach. 2007. Developing a Definitional Knowledge Extraction System. *Conference Proceedings of Third Language & Technology Conference LTC'07*, Poznań, Poland.

John Bowers. 1993. The Syntax of Predication, *Linguistic Inquiry*, 24(4): 591-636.

John Bowers. 2001. Predication. In Baltin, M. & Collins, C. (eds.), *The Handbook of Contemporary Syntactic Theory*, Blackwell, Oxford, UK: 299-333.

Paul Buitelaar, Philipp Cimiano and Bruno Magnini. 2005. *Ontology learning from text.* IOS Press, Amsterdam, The Netherlands.

Eugene Charniak and Matthew Berland. 1999. Finding parts in very large corpora. *Proceedings of the 37th Annual Meeting of the Association for Computational Linguistics*: 57-64.

Christiane Fellbaum. 1998. *WordNet: An Electronic Lexical Database*, MIT Press, Cambridge, Mass.

Roxana Girju, Adriana Badulescu and Dan I. Moldovan. 2006. Automatic Discovery of Part–Whole Relations. *Computational Linguistics*, 32(1): 83-135.

Marti Hearst. 1992. Automatic Acquisition of Hyponyms from Large Text Corpora. *Proceedings of the Fourteenth International Conference on Computational Linguistics*, Nantes, France.

Marie-Claude L'Homme and Patrick Drouin. 2006. *Corpus de Informática para el español*, Groupe Éklectick, OLST-Université de Montréal, Montréal, Canada: http://www.olst.umontreal.ca/.

Alfonso Medina, Gerardo Sierra, Gabriel Garduño, Carlos Méndez and Roberto Saldaña. 2004. CLI: An Open Linguistic Corpus for Engineering. In De Ita, G. Fuentes, O. & Galindo, M. (Eds.) *Proceedings of IX Ibero-American Workshop on Artificial Intelligence*, Puebla, BUAP: 203-208.

Massimo Poesio and Abdulrahman Almuhareb. 2004. Feature-Based vs. property-based KR: An empirical perspective. In *Proceedings of International Conference on Formal Ontology in Information Systems FOIS 2004*, Torino, Italy.

Ellen Riloff and Jessica Shepherd. 1999. A corpus-based bootstrapping algorithm for Semi-Automated semantic lexicon construction. *Journal of Natural Language Engineering* . 5(2): 147-156.

Carlos Rodríguez. 2004. *Metalinguistic Information Extraction from specialized texts to enrich computational lexicons*. Ph. D. Thesis, Universidad Pompeu Fabra, Barcelona, Spain.

Gerardo Sierra, Rodrigo Alarcón and César Aguilar. 2006. Extracción automática de contextos definitorios en textos especializados. In Inchaurralde, C. & Ibarretxe, I. (Eds.). *Memorias del XXII Congreso de la Sociedad Española para el Procesamiento del Lenguaje Natural*, University of Zaragoza, Zaragoza, Spain: 351-352.

Gerardo Sierra, Rodrigo Alarcón, César Aguilar and Carme Bach. 2008. Definitional Verbal Patterns for Semantic Relation Extraction. In Auger A. & Barrière C. (Eds.), *Pattern-based Approaches to Semantic Relation Extraction. Special issue of Terminology*, 14(1): 74–98.

Carlos Subirats (2009). Spanish Framenet: A frame semantic analysis of the Spanish lexicon. In Boas H. (Ed.), *Multilingual FrameNets in Computational Lexicography. Methods and Applications*, Mouton de Gruyter, Berlin/New York: 135-162.

Yorick Wilks, Brian Slator and Louise Guthrie. 1996. *Electric Words*. MIT Press, Cambridge, Mass.

Morton E. Winston, Roger Chaffin and Douglas Herrmann. 1987. A taxonomy of part-whole relations. *Cognitive Science*, 11(4): 417 – 444.

# Computational Linguistics for helping Requirements Elicitation: a dream about Automated Software Development

**Carlos Mario Zapata J.**
Leader of the Computational Language Research Group, School of Systems, Mines Faculty, Universidad Nacional de Colombia
Cra. 80 No. 65-223, of. M8A-310
Medellín, Colombia, South America
cmzapata@unal.edu.co

## Abstract

Requirements elicitation is one of the first processes of software development and it is intended to be hand-made by means of analyst-stakeholder interviews. As a natural-language-based activity, requirements elicitation can take advantages of Computational Linguistics techniques, in order to achieve better results looking for automation in this field. In this paper we survey some of the work related to software development automation, guided by Computational Linguistics techniques, and performed by the Computational Language Research Group from the Universidad Nacional de Colombia. We aim the definition of future trans-national effort to be made in this research line.

## 1 Introduction

When stakeholders need to solve their information problems, they commonly search for the development of software applications (Pressman, 2005). At the beginning of this process, a set of analyst-stakeholder interviews take place, in order to capture the requirements belonging to the domain in which future software application must work. After that, in a hand-made process called "requirements elicitation", the analyst transforms the captured information into formal and semi-formal artifacts, mostly diagrams. At this stage, software application is specified by means of such diagrams (Leite, 1987).

Since interviews are the most used techniques for collecting software requirements, they experiment some of the most common problems of natural language (NL) communication: misunderstanding, ambiguity, and lack of clarity (Christel and Kang, 1992). However, as an NL-based process, requirements elicitation can use some of the Computational Linguistics (CL) and Natural Language Processing (NLP) techniques, as a way to solve such problems. The main goal of using CL and NLP techniques in this particular problem is related to the search for automation in the software development process.

This is the strategy we (the Computational Language Research Group—CLRG) choose to follow for clarifying requirements elicitation process and, therefore, for trying to automate the first phases of software development process. In this paper, we summarize some of the CLRG effort invested in helping requirements elicitation process with mostly CL techniques, but searching for strong NLP techniques, for instance, syntactical and discourse parsers, and named entity recognition systems, among others. We aim to show how we try to solve our problems in this field (recognizing the existence of too much effort from other groups in the world, but focusing on our own work), as a way to motivate the definition of trans-national projects searching for the same goals as us. Because our native language is Spanish, some of the examples we provide in this paper are encoded in this language.

The structure of this paper is the following: in section 2, we discuss our solutions to common problems of requirements elicitation process; in section 3 we propose some possible joint projects in this field of knowledge; finally, in section 4 we present conclusions and future work.



*Proceedings of the NAACL HLT 2010 Young Investigators Workshop on Computational Approaches to Languages of the Americas*, pages 117–124, Los Angeles, California, June 2010. 

## 2 Solutions to common problems of requirements elicitation process

Figure 1 gives us the overall software engineering process envisioned by this research. This is a kind of "big picture" about the way we are creating CL- and NLP-based tools for helping automated software development process. In the following subsections, we discuss a more detailed view of every tool.

### 2.1 Pre-conceptual schemas

The first gap we needed to bridge in this process was related to the knowledge representation of requirements. In this context, the UML (Unified Modeling Language, OMG, 2010) is the *de-facto* standard for representing requirements, but it is a language directed to technical readers, and stakeholders are not usually technical people. For this reason, we explored the possibilities to use a graphical language closer to the stakeholder discourse, and we created the pre-conceptual schemas (Zapata, 2007) by adapting some previous effort made by Sowa's Conceptual Graphs (Sowa, 1984). Figure 2 shows an example of the pre-conceptual schemas, manually created by an analyst during the software elicitation process of one software application.

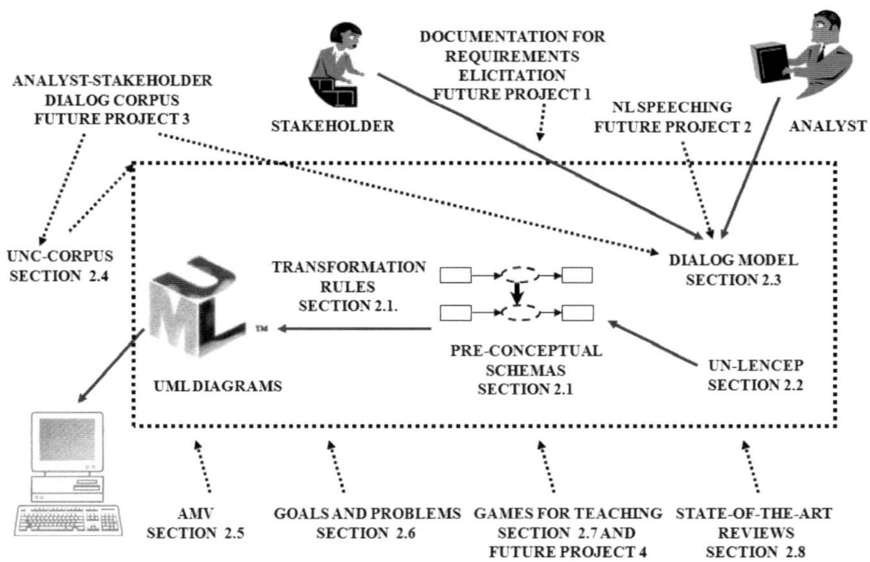


**Figure 1.** Overall view of CL- and NLP-tools for automated software development.

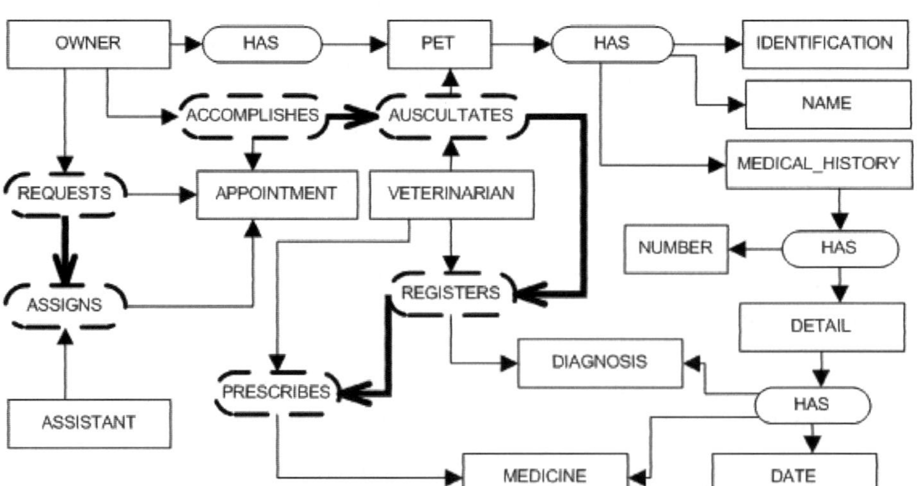


**Figure 2.** An example of Pre-conceptual Schemas (Zapata, 2007).

Pre-conceptual schemas have provided a new way to validate the stakeholder discourse, in order to clarify and understand what stakeholder has to say about the domain information related to the software application to-be-made.

### 2.2 UN-Lencep: Specifying pre-conceptual schemas

Pre-conceptual schemas gave us a new way to communicate with stakeholders in the requirements elicitation process, but their usage was limited to analysts. However, if we are interested in creating a pre-conceptual schema, we need the involvement of both kinds of actors in such action. In this case, we need to communicate each other in an NL-like way.

The solution to this problem came from two of the several techniques from Computational Linguistics: Information Extraction (IE) and Controlled Languages. In first place, we use a set of templates, in the same sense of IE templates, for matching in a stakeholder discourse the same features of a pre-conceptual schema. Then, we constrained the NL discourse, and we created UN-Lencep (*Universidad Nacional de Colombia—Lenguaje para la especificación de esquemas preconceptuales*, Zapata *et al.*, 2008). By combining both techniques, we had the possibilities to create a textual discourse in UN-Lencep. In the case of the pre-conceptual schema in figure 2, the UN-Lencep discourse could be something like this:

> *A pet belongs to an owner.*
> *The pet has identification, name, and medical history.*
> *The medical history has a name and one detail.*
> *The detail has a date, a diagnosis, and a medicine.*
> *When the owner requests an appointment, the assistant assigns an appointment.*
> *When the owner accomplishes the appointment, the veterinarian auscultates the pet.*
> *When the veterinarian auscultates the pet, the veterinarian registers the diagnosis.*
> *When the veterinarian registers the diagnosis, the veterinarian prescribes the medicine.*

Note that UN-Lencep phrases can be made by non-technical people, like stakeholders. The task of capturing requirements is now under the responsibilities of the analyst-stakeholder team, instead of the analyst alone. Again, the UN-Lencep discourse is manually created by the analyst with the help of the stakeholder. We have developed a tool called UNC-Diagrammer, for helping the software elicitation process in creating UN-Lencep discourses and pre-conceptual schemas. This tool has some minimal NLP processing, because UN-Lencep is a template-based controlled language.

### 2.3 Dialog model

UN-Lencep and pre-conceptual schemas provided the partial solution to our requirements capture problems. However, the fact that requirements elicitation was initiated by a set of stakeholder-analyst interviews reminded us the rest of the task. If we could discover a way to obtain the UN-Lencep discourse from something like an interview, we could link the beginning of the process to our partial solution.

The answer, again, came from previous experiences in Computational Linguistics. The work made on dialog models provided us an environment to prove our hypothesis about stakeholder-analyst interviews. We found some previous work on dialog models related to train reservations, and we employed it to discover the structure of dialog, as sets of tagged utterances and turnovers. With these ideas in mind, we propose a structure for requirements elicitation dialog (Zapata and Carmona, in press), as shown in figure 3. We are, also, exploring the close relationship between dialog models for requirements elicitation and ontologies (Zapata *et al.*, in press).

We are currently working on some projects for obtaining UN-Lencep discourses from a dialog with the structure provided by figure 3. Also, we are working in proving the utilities of such conversion in order to diminish software costs and development time in Latin-American software companies, and we select the COMPETISOFT model for promoting such improvement.

### 2.4 UNC-Corpus

Modeling is the center of requirements elicitation activities. We need models to understand the structure, the behavior, and the interaction among the concepts belonging to some domain. Traditionally, analysts make models by using their own knowledge and understanding of the world domain, in a subjective way. But, is it possible to simulate such activity? How can we represent the knowledge acquired about modeling by an analyst in creating models? The work in Corpus Linguistics provided us some useful ideas about these questions. A corpus is a collection of proved uses of a language. If we considered UML as a graphical modeling language (but, finally, *a language*), we could gather several "proved" uses of this language in the shape of computationally readable files. We employed these files to create UNC-Corpus (Zapata *et al.*, 2008), a UML-diagram corpus. Also, we used UNC-Corpus for "completing" diagrams, as analysts actually does, by reviewing the contents of the corpus as shown in figure 4.

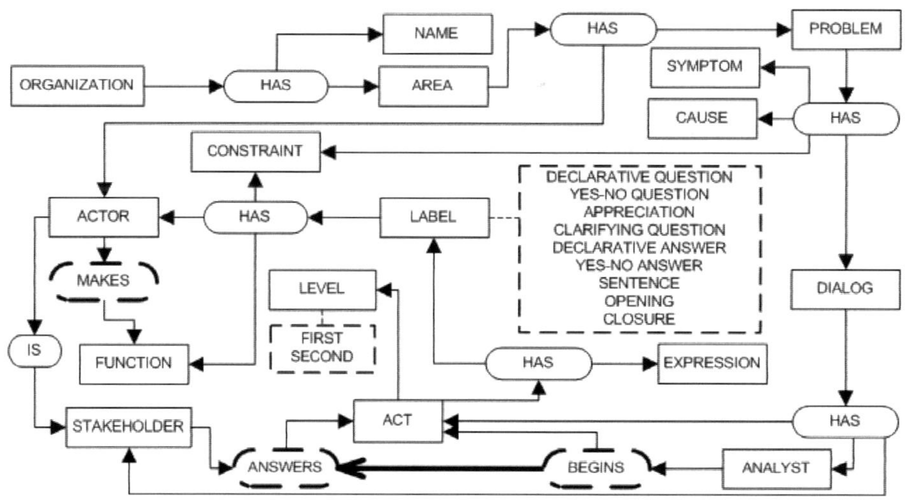


**Figure 3.** Requirements elicitation dialog model (Zapata and Carmona, in press).

### 2.5 AMV: a solution for conjugating and lemmatizing Spanish verbs

Spanish is one of the most difficult languages for tasks related to conjugate and lemmatize verbs. Our language has a complex structure when we need to use a verb.

CLRG have assumed these difficulties and, after exploring state of the art in Spanish conjugators, decided to create AMV (*Analizador Morfológico de Verbos*, Zapata y Mesa, 2009), an application that recognize the internal structure of the vast majority of Spanish verbs. AMV can be shown in figure 5.

### 2.6 Goals and problems

AMV gave us some insight about the structure of Spanish verbs, so we could discover some differences about these verbs. For example, we discovered state verbs, action verbs, and goal verbs. Goal verbs are slightly different from the other kinds of verbs, because they express activities with no duration, generally associated to states to be reached. Three kinds of goal verbs can be identified: improvement, maintenance, and achievement verbs. Goal verbs are not recognized by most of the people, and their usage tends to be misunderstood along the software development process.

CLRG devoted some effort to identify goal verbs from NL discourses, and then represent them into pre-conceptual schemas (Zapata *et al.*, 2007). For completing this task, we used previous work of Antón (1997) for gathering some verbs in the above mentioned categories, and then we employed a lexicon from Maryland University in order to discover the internal linguistic features of such verbs. With this information in hand, we increased the number of available verbs for expressing goals. After that, we define a new set of symbols to be used in pre-conceptual schemas for representing goal verbs and then translating them into goal diagrams (Lezcano, 2007). Figure 6 shows an example of pre-conceptual schemas including goal verbs.

We are currently exploring the relationships among goals and problems. In our theory, problems are seen either as negative goals or obstacles for a goal to be reached. So, we are trying to define a set of structures for representing goals and another set for representing problems. Also, we are defining some rules for obtaining goal expressions from problem sentences and *viceversa*. The first step of the process was the state-of-the-art review of such structures (Zapata and Vargas, 2009), and we are delivering a Master's Thesis with the structures and the heuristic rules for proving such relationship.

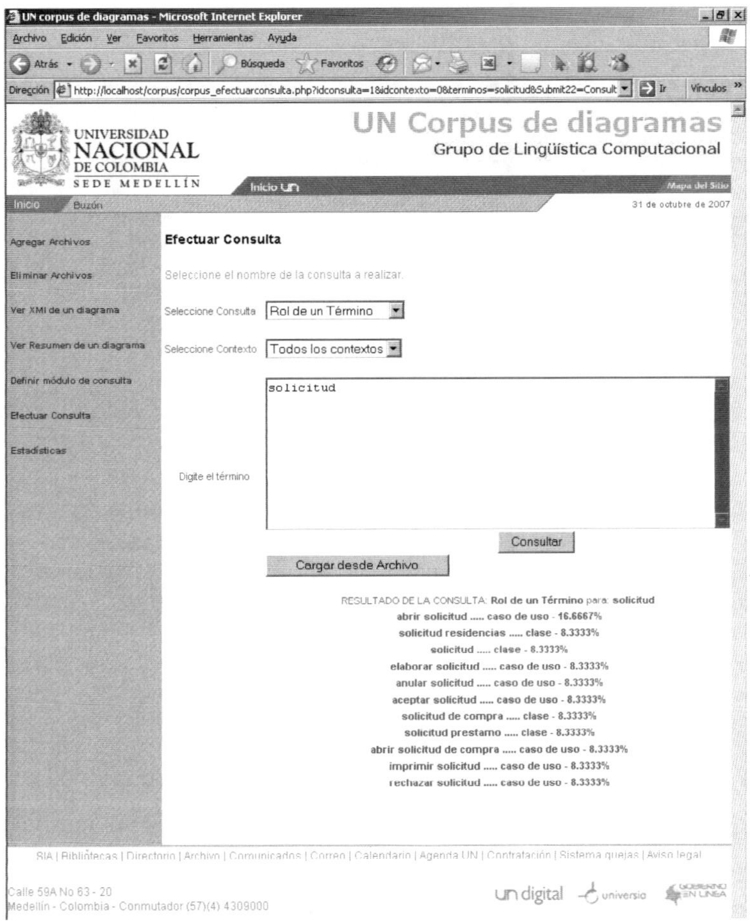


**Figure 4.** A snapshot of the use of UNC-Corpus (Zapata *et al.*, 2008).

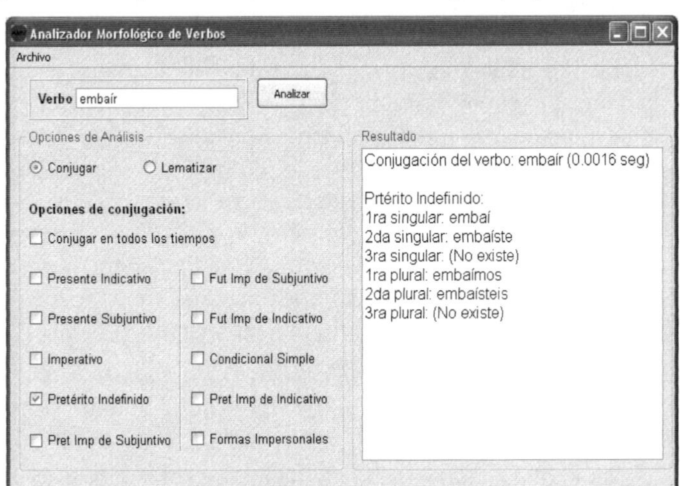


**Figure 5.** Snapshot of AMV (Zapata and Mesa, 2009).

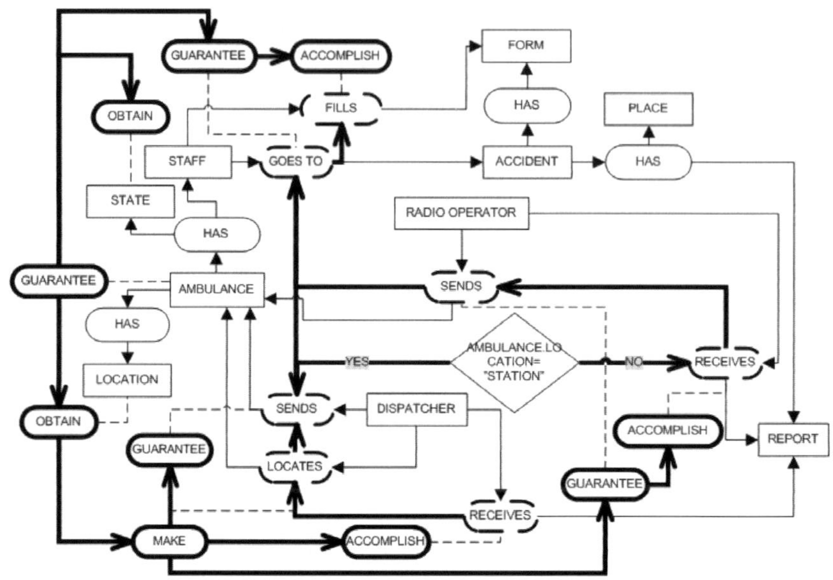


**Figure 6.** An example of pre-conceptual schemas including goal verbs (Zapata *et al.*, 2007)

### 2.7 Games for teaching

As a part of our research and teaching strategy, we use games to show and reinforce some concepts about our knowledge area. For example, we are currently developing an on-line game—called "Software Boulevard"—for understanding how software industries make their intangible products. In this game, we intend to simulate the real behavior of this kind of companies, but making the actors answer questions about software development process in several phases. Another example of our strategy is "Requirements elicitation dialog game" (Zapata and Giraldo, 2009), which is based on the importance of dialog inside the software development process. This game is like a word puzzle in which players must fill in the blanks a set of words previously acquired by answering questions related to software development. The blanks are located inside a simulated analyst-stakeholder interview and also as parts of a pre-conceptual schema. The main goal of the game is make conscious the players about the importance of good answers in requirements elicitation, in order to adequately "translate" the given information into diagrams that consistently reflect such information.

### 2.8 State-of-the-art Reviews

The definition of several projects requires the extensive search for papers and journals related to the topics we need to incorporate in the process. In addition to the mentioned review on goals and problems (Zapata and Vargas, 2009), we conducted some other state-of-the-art reviews on Controlled Languages (Zapata and Rosero, 2008), Dialog Models (Zapata and Mesa, 2009b), and the Wizard-of-Oz experiment (Zapata and Carmona, 2007). Also, we made a review on Interlinguas (Zapata and Benítez, 2009), and we are preparing some other reviews on Computational Dialog and Code Generation.

## 3 Joint projects on requirements elicitation and computational linguistics

Our final goal—and probably "dream"—is the automation of software development process from early stages related to speech discourses. We strongly believe this goal is so big enough to be reached by only one research group. We made now some part of the task, but we need help to complete it. For this reason, we want to create some transnational projects related to this field of knowledge to be executed by several research groups in Latin America, for example the Computation Research Centre from the Instituto Politécnico Nacional in Mexico, the Linguistic Engineering research group from the Universidad Nacional Autónoma de México, the Working Group 2.9 (Software Requirements Engineering) from IFIP (International Federation for Information Processing), and the Human-Computer Interaction Research Group from the Pontificia Universidad Católica de Valparaíso. We have contacts inside these research groups and we are willing to initiate joint research projects related to Computational Linguistics and Requirements Engineering.

The first project in which we are concerned is the use of technical documentation for requirements elicitation. In almost every organization in the world, technical documents define the way such organization must behave. If we were capable to understand the surrounding information in these documents, we could elicit many concepts to be validated in the analyst-stakeholder interviews, making too much work before the interviews take place. In this project, we need groups with expertise in analyzing and processing some kind of technical documents (for instance, technical reports, law sentences, instructions, and so on).

The second project we need to propose have natural language speeching as the main issue. The way a stakeholder-analyst interview is conducted suggests that some expressions are repeated once and again in the context of the dialog. These expressions are guidelines to gather important information about the domain. In this case, we need groups with larger experience in recording, retrieving, and analyzing speech dialogs.

A computational corpus of stakeholder-analyst interviews is the main product of the third project we want to execute. Corpus linguistics can offer many techniques for analyzing such corpus, in order to discover meta-information about the process of requirements elicitation by means of interviews. The common uses of expressions can lead to predictive information concerning one domain. Consequently, we need to gather as many recorded interviews as we can, and research groups with this kind of information.

Finally, games are needed for understanding and simulating the entire process of requirements elicitation as a result from stakeholder-analyst interviews, and this is the goal of the fourth project we need to propose. Our group has been using games in the shape of teaching strategies and we plan to keep using this strategy, because we think we are successful on it. Here, we need research groups with the intention to co-create and use games as teaching strategies. Also, we need people with some experience in evaluating the impact of games as teaching strategies.

The above mentioned projects have some CL- and NLP-based techniques as good offerings to find a solution. Also, for achieving the goals of every project, we need to interact with experts in software elicitation process. We hope this cross-functional and trans-national effort will give the necessary tools to make true the dream about automation in software development process.

## 4 Conclusions and future work

The Computational Language Research Group has been developing some projects for helping requirements elicitation process by means of Computational Linguistics, and we shown some of this work in this paper. We tried to summarize the most important of our projects concerning this issue, because our aim is to propose and develop trans-national projects in searching for automated software development.

The "big picture" of this work exhibits joint projects for making requirements elicitation closer to natural language dialog and speech. We look for a dream in which software development will be a simpler task, developed by common people by using natural language speeching interfaces.

Some work has still to be done:

- Eliciting requirements from technical documents belonging to an organization.
- Incorporating speech recognition to the requirements elicitation.
- Building a computational corpus of analyst-stakeholder interviews.
- Creating new games as teaching strategies for understanding the entire requirements elicitation process.

All of these projects are intended to be made by trans-national groups with some concern about software development process, computational linguistics, and natural language processing.

## Acknowledgment

This work is founded by the *Vicerrectoría de Investigación* from *Universidad Nacional de Colombia,* under the project: "Software Boulevard un juego de estrategia en Web para la enseñanza de competencias de gestión en Ingeniería de Software", Project number 9766.

## References

Annie Antón. 1997. *Goal Identification and Refinement in the Specification of Software-Based Information Systems*. PhD Thesis, Georgia Institute of Technology, Atlanta, USA.

Michael Christel and Kyo Kang. 1992. *Issues in Requirement elicitation.* Technical Report, CMU/SEI-92-TR-012, ESC-TR-92-012. Software Engineering Institute, Carnegie Mellon University, Pittsburg.

Julio Cesar Leite. 1987. *A survey on requirements analysis*. Department of Information and Computer Science, University of California, Irvine, Advanced Software Engineering Project Technical Report RT-P071.

Luis Lezcano. 2007. *Elaboración semiautomática del diagrama de objetivos.* M.Sc. Thesis, Universidad Nacional de Colombia, Sede Medellín.

Object Management Group (OMG). 2010. *UML Superstructure.* Available at: http://www.omg.org/uml.

Roger Pressman. 2005. *Software Engineering: a practitioner's approach, 6th ed.* McGraw Hill, New York.

John Sowa. 1984. *Conceptual Structures: Information Processing in Mind and Machine*. Addison-Wesley Publishing Co., Reading, MA.

Carlos Zapata. 2007. *Definición de un esquema preconceptual para la obtención automática de esquemas conceptuales de UML.* Ph.D. Thesis, Universidad Nacional de Colombia, sede Medellín.

Carlos Zapata and Servio Benítez. 2009. Interlingua: Análisis crítico de la literatura. *Revista Facultad de Ingeniería Universidad de Antioquia*, 47:117–128.

Carlos Zapata and Nicolás Carmona. In press. Un modelo de diálogo para la Educción de Requisitos de Software. *Dyna.*

Carlos Zapata and Nicolás Carmona. 2007. El experimento Mago de Oz y sus aplicaciones: Una mirada retrospectiva. *Dyna*, 74(151):125–135.

Carlos Zapata and Gloria Giraldo. 2009. El juego del diálogo de educción de requisitos de software. *Avances en Sistemas e Informática*, 6(1):105–114.

Carlos Zapata, Gloria Giraldo, and John Mesa. In press. Una propuesta de Metaontología para la Educción de Requisitos de Software. *Ingeniare.*

Carlos Zapata, Alexander Gelbukh, and Fernando Arango. 2006. UN-Lencep: Obtención Automática de Diagramas UML a partir de un Lenguaje Controlado. *Memorias del VII Encuentro Nacional de Computación ENC'06*, San Luis Potosí, México, 254–259.

Carlos Zapata, Juan Hernández, and Raúl Zuluaga. 2008. UNC-Corpus: corpus de diagramas UML para la solución de problemas de completitud en ingeniería de software. *Revista EAFIT*, 44(151):93–106.

Carlos Zapata, Luis Lezcano, and Paula Tamayo. 2007. Validación del método para la obtención automática del diagrama de objetivos desde esquemas preconceptuales. *Revista Escuela de Ingeniería de Antioquia*, (8):21–35.

Carlos Zapata and John Mesa. 2009. Una propuesta para el análisis morfológico de verbos del español. *Dyna*, 76(157):27–36.

Carlos Zapata and John Mesa. 2009b. Los Modelos de Diálogo y sus Aplicaciones en Sistemas de Diálogo Hombre-Máquina: Revisión de la literatura. *Dyna*, 76(160):305–315.

Carlos Zapata and Roberto Rosero. 2008. Revisión Crítica de la Literatura especializada en Lenguajes Controlados. *Avances en Sistemas e Informática*, 5(3):27–33.

Carlos Zapata and Fabio Vargas. 2009. Una revisión de la literatura en consistencia entre problemas y objetivos en Ingeniería de Software y Gerencia Organizacional. *Revista Escuela de Ingeniería de Antioquia*, 11:117–129.

# Text Generation for Brazilian Portuguese: the Surface Realization Task

**Eder Miranda de Novais** **Thiago Dias Tadeu** **Ivandré Paraboni**
University of São Paulo - School of Arts, Sciences and Humanities (USP-EACH)
Av. Arlindo Bettio, 1000, Ermelino Matarazzo
São Paulo, Brazil 03828-000
eder.novais@usp.br tdtadeu@gmail.com ivandre@usp.br

## Abstract

Despite the growing interest in NLP focused on the Brazilian Portuguese language in recent years, its obvious counterpart – Natural Language Generation (NLG) – remains in that case a little-explored research field. In this paper we describe preliminary results of a first project of this kind, addressing the issue of surface realization for Brazilian Portuguese. Our approach, which may be particularly suitable to simpler NLG applications in which a domain corpus of the most likely output sentences happens to be available, is in principle adaptable to many closely-related languages, and paves the way to further NLG research focused on Romance languages in general.

## 1 Introduction

Data-to-Text Natural Language Generation (NLG) systems produce text or speech from a given non-linguistic input. Systems of this kind usually follow a pipelined architecture (Reiter, 2007) comprising data interpretation, document planning, sentence planning and surface realization tasks. In this work we discuss the latter, that is, the task of producing surface word strings from a non-linguistic input specification.

Existing approaches to surface realization may vary greatly in their input requirements and, consequently, in the level of control over the output text. On the one hand, more sophisticated, grammar-based surface realization systems such as KPML (Bateman, 1997) allow maximum flexibility and productive coverage. These advantages, however, are only useful if the underlying application is capable of providing a detailed semantic specification as an input to the surface realization module in the first place.

As an alternative to surface realization grammars, NLG systems may also rely on *template-based* surface realization, that is, the use of predefined structures with a number of variable fields (or slots) to be filled in with values provided by the application. For a comparison between templates and other approaches to NLG, see for instance van Deemter et. al. (2005).

Adapting an existing application to a template-based realization system is usually much simpler than in a grammar-based approach. Yet, in order to take full advantage of template definitions and to obtain a degree of control over the output text that is comparable to what a grammar-based system would allow, it is still necessary to master the use of templates and their rules to fill in each slot adequately.

The problem of input specification to surface realization has been discussed at length in the literature in the field - see for example Langkilde (2000) – and we of course do not dispute that more sophisticated NLG systems will require a detailed input specification. However, given that the available semantics may not be provide in this level of detail, in this paper we discuss an alternative that



*Proceedings of the NAACL HLT 2010 Young Investigators Workshop on Computational Approaches to Languages of the Americas*, pages 125–131, Los Angeles, California, June 2010. 

may be suitable to simpler applications, namely, those cases in which it is known in advance what the most likely output sentence structures are, for example, because a corpus on that particular domain happens to be available. In these cases, we will argue that it may be possible to take advantage of the available knowledge to quickly deploy a surface realization component based on existing corpora.

The underlying assumption in our work is that there are simpler NLG applications for which it may be sufficient to select a sentence that *resembles* the desired output, and then modify some or all of its constituents as needed to achieve the desired output. For instance, an application that is not linguistically-oriented may produce its output results as natural language text by selecting a standard imperative sentence as in "Please reply to this message" and, leaving all other sentence constituents unchanged, specify that the action to be realized in the output is "delete", and that its patient object is "file". This will have the effect of producing the output sentence "Please delete this file".

In this introductory work we intend to outline our ongoing efforts to develop one such approach to surface realization for the Brazilian Portuguese language. In doing so, we shall focus on the general principles that guide our research, leaving much of the theoretical details to be discussed elsewhere. The present work has been developed within the context of a query-and-answer application under investigation, in which questions sent by undergraduate students enrolled in a particular course will be matched to existing entries in a large database of standard replies written by the professors in charge to the most frequently asked questions made by the students, and tailored to each particular context accordingly. Details of this particular application will not be dealt with in this paper either.

The reminder of this paper is structured as follows. Section 2 briefly discusses related work on surface realization; Section 3 provides an overview of our system's architecture; Sections 4 describes the extraction of syntactically-structured templates from a target corpus and Section 5 presents the current features of our template-based surface realization engine. Finally, Section 6 draws preliminary conclusions and describes ongoing work, and Section 7 hints at possible collaboration with the wider NLP research community in Latin America and elsewhere.

## 2 Related work

Mapping an application semantics to surface strings usually involves the use of surface realization grammars or similar resources, which can be either built manually (e.g., Bateman, 1997) or acquired automatically from a corpus (Ratnaparkhi, 2000; Zhong & Stent, 2005; DeVault et. al., 2008).

The surface realization task proper can be divided into two relatively independent procedures: a domain-dependant mapping from the application semantics onto linguistic structures (including, e.g., lexical choice), and a language-oriented task of linearization. As pointed out in Gatt & Reiter (2009), most of the existing systems tend to perform both tasks, but in some cases they focus on the latter, assuming that all lexical choices and other domain-dependent decisions have already been made. This is the case for example of SimpleNLG (Gatt & Reiter, 2009), a surface realization engine implemented as a Java library for sentence linearization.

Central to the development and use of a surface realization system is the kind of input specification that will be expected from the application. In order to take full advantage of grammar-based surface realization, it is usually necessary to provided detailed linguistic knowledge as an input. This is the case, for example, of a number of corpus-based approaches to grammar acquisition, which may take logical forms as an input (e.g., Smets et. al., 2003; Zhong & Stent, 2005; Marciniak & Strube, 2005). The Amalgam system, for instance (Smets et. al., 2003), takes as an input a graph conveying fixed content words (lemmas) and detailed linguistic information such as verb tense and mode, gender, number and definiteness of all its constituents, and additional semantic features (e.g., 'human', 'animated' etc.)

Detailed input specification as required in grammar-based surface realization is however often unavailable from the semantics of the application. As an alternative, template-based surface realization makes use of predefined structures (e.g., syntactically-structured sentence templates) with slots to be filled in with values provided by the application. A prominent example of template-based surface realization system is YAG (McRoy et. al., 2003), which may accept both feature structures and propositional semantics as an input. The following is an example of input feature structure in YAG, taken from McRoy et. al. (2003). In this example, the structure represents the fact that a discourse subject (George) performs an act (understand) on a particular object (a book), in which both subject and object happened to be realized as pronouns as "He understands it".

```
((template clause
 (process "understand")
 (agent   ((template noun-phrase)
           (np-type PROPER)
           (head "George")
             (gender MASCULINE)
             (pronominal YES)))
 (object ((template noun-phrase)
          (head "book")
          (pronominal YES))) )
```

**Input feature structure in YAG.**

The input requirements of a template-based surface realization system are obviously much simpler – and more likely to be available from the application – than a full set of linguistic instructions on how to generate the desired output. Still, in this work we would like to produce surface strings using even less knowledge, namely, by using sentence-level templates extracted from a domain corpus as a basis to generate original and modified versions of the corpus sentences.

We will refer to this as an example-based approach to surface realization[1], although this is not to be mistaken for example-based learning techniques to perform automatic grammar induction as in DeVault et. al., (2008), or other forms of grammar acquisition as in Zhong & Stent (2005). Our work is more related to Ratnaparkhi (2000) in the sense that we also use a large collection of generation templates for surface realization, but still distinct in that we intend to generate text from minimal input.

## 3 Project Overview

Template-based surface realization systems such as YAG (McRoy et. al., 2003) make use of a relatively small number of template definitions and some kind of descriptive language to provide fine-grained input sentence specification with flexibility and wide coverage. However, if a corpus on the application domain happens to be available, and assuming that the corpus sentences resemble those that we intend to generate, then it may be convenient (at least for applications that are not linguistically-motivated in the first place) to simply use the corpus sentences as examples, and allow an input specification that makes explicit only the changes that need to take place to convert the selected example into the desired output.

For example, in order to produce the sentence "He understands it" we may select an example such as "People will understand it" from the corpus, and then redefine its agent head type as a pronoun, and its action tense as present. The difference may not seem so dramatic if compared to, e.g., an input specification to YAG, but it will obviously grow as more complex sentence structures are considered.

If the selected example differs greatly from the target sentence, then a large number of modifications will have to take place, and in that case our example-based approach may not seem very useful. On the other hand, if the corpus is representative of the sentences that are likely to be generated, then little or no additional modifications will be required, in which case new sentences may be generated indeed from a minimally specified input. In either case, we notice that since the examples are represented directly in natural language in the corpus, new instances can be easily added to expand the system coverage.

In our present approach to the surface realization task, syntactically-structured templates are selected from a target corpus on the application domain and used as a basis to produce original and modified versions of the corpus sentences by a combination of canned text and basic dependency-tree operations. Each sentence in the target corpus makes a sentence template in which the agent, patient and action constituents may be modified or replaced by the application by combining lower-order templates (e.g., for NPs and VPs), and new sentences may be supported by adding the corresponding examples directly to the corpus.

Our current work can be divided into two main tasks: the extraction of syntactically-structured templates from corpora and the actual development of the surface realization engine. The following sections 4 and 5 discuss each of these tasks in turn.

[1] Perhaps 'select-and-modify' would be closer to our current purposes.

## 4 Template Extraction

Using a collection of emails sent to undergraduate students by their professors in reply to their most frequent questions regarding a particular project, we developed a database conveying 597 instances of surface realization templates for Brazilian Portuguese NLG as follows.

After sentence segmentation, the corpus was tagged and parsed using PALAVRAS (Bick, 2000). A number of critical parsing errors were removed, and thus we arrived at a set of 578 sentence-level templates represented in XML format.

In our example-based approach to surface realization we consider two kinds of structure: sentence and constituent templates. Sentence templates are high-level representations of the sample sentences taken from our target corpus, and they contain a number of variable fields (the constituents) to be filled in with application data (in most cases having an agent, action and patient fields.)

Everything else within the sentence is simply canned text as seen in the corpus, and cannot be modified by the application. In other words, if the application needs to generate a sentence that differs from the template in any constituent other than its NPs and VPs, it is necessary to define a new template by adding a new example to the corpus.

Sentence templates are highly redundant in the sense that many of them keep a similar syntactic structure in which only the surrounding text might change significantly. For example, many sentence templates in our domain represent a simple piece of advice in the form agent + action followed by some canned text, as in "You should enroll by Friday" and "All smokers are supposed to quit by the end of the month".

Although we could have defined a smaller (and more flexible) set of templates by generalizing over these structures, in practice this would increase the complexity of the required input (e.g., with the addition of a 'time' field to a common template to be shared by both examples above.) As mentioned in the previous section, we intend to keep input specification as simple as possible (i.e., in natural language format) by allowing the target sentences to be specified directly in the corpus.

The contents of the variable fields in a sentence template act as default values for the surface realization algorithm, and they may be changed individually (e.g., by setting a different tense or gender value for a particular field) or replaced by another constituent template entirely. We notice that default values are acquired automatically from corpora, i.e., they do not need to be hard-coded as in McRoy et. al., (2003).

Unlike sentence templates, constituent templates are not extracted from corpora. Instead, constituents are dependency-trees generated by a small set of grammar rules that covers the instances of VPs and NPs found in our corpus, including support to relative clauses and the most common forms of PP attachment. The choice for a grammar representation for the more fine-grained constituents was mainly motivated by the need to achieve wider coverage and to support linguistic variation beyond what the actual phrases found in the corpus would allow. In doing so we are able to fill in sentence templates with phrases of arbitrary complexity, as in the NP "You should enroll by the end of *the month in which you are expected to complete your current assignment*", and not simply using those NPs found in the target corpus.

The set of mappings from domain concepts to their dependency-trees (i.e., constituent templates) makes a dictionary of realizations in the application domain. As in related work in the field (e.g., Gatt & Reiter, 2009), we presently assume that the actual mappings are to be provided by the application.

Concept-to-strings mappings are usually handcrafted, but may also be acquired automatically from corpora, as in Bangalore & Rambow (2000). For testing purposes, we have extracted 1,548 instances of concept-to-string mappings from the target corpus, being 1,298 mappings from agent/patient entities to descriptions, pronouns and proper names, and 250 mappings from actions to VPs, even though many of them will not be of practical use from the point of view of our intended application.

## 5 Surface Realization

Using the template definitions from the previous section, we designed a simple corpus-based surface realization component for our ongoing project.

Our surface realization module is currently able to accept as an input a template id (to be taken as a sample structure with inherited default values for the output sentence) and, optionally, parameters representing the alternative semantics of its agent, patient and action constituents. Alternatively, it is also possible to specify a sentence from scratch (that is, without using any existing template as a basis) in a standard NP VP NP format. The latter choice was added to the system as we noticed that simpler sentence structures may be specified more conveniently in this way, as opposed to looking up an example in the corpus. In our project, this is the case of short reply sentences as in "Yes, of course", "Thank you" and others, in which there is hardly any point in selecting a template from the corpus and then commanding the required changes.

The underlying application selects a target template and provides a set of values to fill in the template variable fields. These input values overwrite the default values provided by the template (that is, those values that were inherited from the corpus data) and adjusted by basic agreement rules to reestablish grammaticality if necessary, as we will discuss later.

The currently supported variable fields for NPs are determiner type, gender, number, person, determiner lemma, pre and post modifiers, the NP head, an attached pp-list and relative clause (which may recursively convey NPs within themselves.) As for VPs, the variable fields are VP type (finite vs. infinite etc.), person, mode, verb type, verb tense and adverbial modifiers. Verbal gender and number are not specified directly but simply inherited from the subject's own data to avoid a possibly conflicting input specification.

The most obvious limitation to this kind of approach is the case in which there is a need to generate a sentence that does not resemble any example in the corpus at all. Yet again, we notice that this difficulty may be overcome by simply adding a natural language example directly to the corpus, a method that is arguably simpler than providing detailed instructions on how to select and combine template structures in a traditional template-based approach, and even simpler than providing a full sentence specification in grammar-based surface realization.

The following is a complete example of how the example-based approach is expected to work. In its simplest form, the application may select the required template to produce the desired output verbatim as in (a); with some extra knowledge available, the application may also change some of the values of the variable template fields as in (b); finally, with even more complete linguistic knowledge available, the original structure may be changed even further as in (c), in which case only the original sentence structure remained (besides the canned text component "on Friday").

| | **Input** | **Expected output** |
|---|---|---|
| (a) | template #17 | $[\text{You}]_{agent}$ $[\text{should deliver}]_{action}$ $[\text{your results}]_{patient}$ on Friday. |
| (b) | template #17,<br>patient=essay,<br>action=not_complete | $[\text{You}]_{agent}$ $[\text{did not complete}]_{action}$ $[\text{your essay}]_{patient}$ on Friday. |
| (c) | template #17,<br>agent=teacher,<br>determiner=possess,<br>action=give,<br>tense=future,<br>patient=talk,<br>determiner=indefinite | $[\text{Our teacher}]_{agent}$ $[\text{will give}]_{action}$ $[\text{a talk}]_{patient}$ on Friday. |

**Table 1. Examples of (semantic) input and expected (surface text) output.**

Depending on the changes in the constituent values requested by the application, a number of agreement rules may be invoked to re-establish fluency and grammaticality. In our work this is aided by a Brazilian Portuguese lexicon presented in Muniz et. al. (2005) and a thesaurus. For example, if a sentence template as (d) below is selected, and then the value of the agent head field is changed to represent a singular concept as in (e), agreement rules are required to modify the verb number as in (f).

(d) $[\text{All students}]_{agent}$ $[\text{have submitted}]_{action}$ $[\text{their papers}]_{patient}$

(e) $[\text{Your teacher}]_{agent}$ $[\text{\#have submitted}]_{action}$ $[\text{their papers}]_{patient}$

(f) $[\text{Your teacher}]_{agent}$ $[\text{has submitted}]_{action}$ $[\text{their papers}]_{patient}$

**Table 2. An original example (d) reused with a new agent head value (e) and agreement (f).**

More complex or fine-grained dependencies (e.g., the anaphoric reference 'their' in Table 2 above) are not currently implemented. One possible approach to this is a standard generate-and-select approach to NLG as in Langkilde (2000), Oh & Rudnicky (2000) and others. More specifically, we may over-generate all possible realization alternatives and then use a statistical language model to select the most likely output. In our work we intend to apply a similar approach also to handle the lexical choice task, i.e., by selecting the most likely wording for each concept based on a language model.

## 6 Discussion

In this paper we have described a simple approach to surface realization based on the reuse of syntactically-structured templates acquired from corpora. Although not nearly as flexible as a full NLG approach, our system may represent a straightforward solution to the problem of input specification, which in our case is simply based on natural language. Our corpus-based approach is able to generate single sentences from an input conveying various degrees of semantic knowledge, which may be suitable to a wide range of NLG applications that are able to support only less detailed input specification.

Much of the present work is however to be regarded as tentative. One major issue that is yet to be discussed is how far we can go with an example-based approach to surface realization without compromising the quality of the output text. For instance, it is not clear what it means for the NLG system if the application selects a sentence template that (in Portuguese) does not have a subject field (e.g., "Please send it now") and then attempts to specify a subject. A similar conflict arises, for example, if the application specifies an action that is semantically incompatible with the selected template, in which case the output sentence could become ungrammatical. In both cases, we believe that more research is still needed.

Being currently functional at a prototype level only, our system is undergoing a number of improvements. First, we are expanding the possible lexical choices by making use of a thesaurus, and then we intend to use a language model to handle synonymy.

Second, the mappings from semantic concepts to surface strings still need to be revised and adapted to the domain (questions and answers about students' undergraduate projects) in order to deploy a fully functional application.

Finally, template selection needs improvement to allow for a truly minimal input specification in an application-friendly fashion.

With these tasks accomplished, we will be able to attach a surface realization component to our ongoing Q&A project and generate context-sensitive replies to students' most frequent questions.

## 7 Final Remarks

In the context of the NAACL-HLT Young Investigators Workshop on Computational Approaches to Languages of the Americas, there are a number of ways in which our work could benefit from co-operation with researchers in Latin America, and also help the development of NLP research in these countries.

At the current stage, our work still relies heavily on a Portuguese parsed corpus and grammar, which may be seen being of limited interest outside the Brazilian NLP research community. However, given the close relation between Portuguese and other languages spoken in the region (e.g., Spanish and its variations), we believe that it would be a rewarding experience to adapt similar language resources (e.g., sentence templates, phrase grammars etc.) that have been developed elsewhere, and use these resources to deploy a multilingual NLG application to validate our current approach.

Beyond the usefulness to the research communities involved, we would expect that this kind of co-operation would be an effective means of sharing costs and spreading the interest in NLG research across the region, and a much-needed motivation for young researchers to join the field.

## Acknowledgments

The authors acknowledge support by FAPESP and CNPq. We are also thankful to the anonymous reviewers of the original submission, and to the organizers of the NAACL-HLT Young Investigators Workshop on Computational Approaches to Languages of the Americas for the travel award given for this presentation.

## References


Bangalore, S. and O. Rambow (2000) Corpus-based lexical choice in natural language generation. Proceedings of the 38th Meeting of the ACL, Hong Kong, pp. 464-471.

Bateman, J.A. (1997) Enabling technology for multilingual natural language generation: the KPML development environment. Natural Language Engineering, 3(1):15–55.

Bick, E. (2000) The parsing system PALAVRAS: automatic grammatical analysis of Portuguese in a constraint grammar framework. PhD Thesis, Aarhus University.

DeVault, David, David Traum and Ron Arstein (2008) Practical Grammar-Based NLG from Examples. Proceedings of the 5th International Natural Language Generation Conference (INLG-2008) Columbus, USA.

Gatt, Albert and Ehud Reiter (2009) SimpleNLG: A realization engine for practical applications. Proceedings of the European Natural Language Generation workshop (ENLG-2009.)

Langkilde, Irene (2000) Forest-based statistical sentence generation. Proceedings of the 6th Applied Natural Language Processing Conference and 1st Meeting of the North American Chapter of the Association of Computational Linguistics (ANLP-NAACL'00), pp. 170–177.

Marciniak, T. and M. Strube (2005) Using an Annotated Corpus As a Knowledge Source For Language Generation. Proceedings of the Corpus Linguistics'05 Workshop Using Corpora for NLG (UNNLG-2005), pp. 19-24.

McRoy, Susan, Songsak Channarukul and Syed S. Ali (2003) An augmented template-based approach to text realization. Natural Language Engineering 9 (4) pp. 381–420. Cambridge University Press.

Muniz, M. C., Laporte, E., Nunes, M.G.V (2005) UNITEX-PB, a set of flexible language resources for Brazilian Portuguese. Proceedings of the III Information and Language Technology Workshop (TIL-2005).

Oh, A. and A. Rudnicky (2000) Stochastic language generation for spoken dialogue systems. Proceedings of the ANLP-NAACL 2000 Workshop on Conversational Systems, pp. 27–32.

Ratnaparkhi, A. (2000) Trainable methods for surface natural language generation. Proceedings of ANLP-NAACL 2000, pp.194–201.

Reiter, E. (2007) An Architecture for Data-to-Text Systems. Proceedings of the European Natural Language Generation workshop (ENLG-2007), pp. 97-104.

Smets, M., M.Gamon, S.Corston-Oliver and E. Ringger (2003) French Amalgam: A machine-learned sentence realization system. Proceedings of the TALN-2003 Conference, Batz sur-Mer,

van Deemter, K., Emiel Krahmer and Mariët Theune (2005) Real versus template-based NLG: a false opposition? Computational Linguistics 31(1).

Zhong, Huayan and A. J. Stent (2005) Building Surface Realizers Automatically from Corpora. Proceedings of the Corpus Linguistics'05 Workshop Using Corpora for NLG, pp. 49-54.

# Dialogue Systems for Virtual Environments

**Luciana Benotti, Paula Estrella, Carlos Areces**
Grupo de Procesamiento de Lenguaje Natural (PLN)
Sección de Ciencias de la Computación
Facultad de Matemática, Astronomía y Física (FaMAF)
Universidad Nacional de Córdoba, Argentina

## Abstract

We present an on-going research project carried out at the Universidad Nacional de Córdoba in Argentina. This project investigates theoretical and practical research questions related to the development of a dialogue system situated in a virtual environment. We describe the PLN research group in which this project is being developed and, in particular, we spell out the areas of expertise of the authors. Moreover, we discuss relevant past, current and future collaborations of the research group.

## 1 Introduction

The goal of this project is to implement a dialogue system which automatically generates instructions in order to help a user to fulfill a given task in a 3D virtual environment. In this context, we will investigate fundamental issues about human-computer interaction. The expected results of the project can be classified in three areas: pragmatics of interaction; information representation and inference; and evaluation of dialogue systems. Once a working prototype is finished, we will adapt it to the specific task of language learning, using the system as a virtual language teacher. Our prototype will teach English to native Spanish speakers. Hence, it will need to understand and produce both languages.

Initially, we will investigate a model of unidirectional linguistic interaction (i.e., linguistic information flows only from the system to the user). In subsequent stages, the model will be extended to allow bidirectional language exchange. For example, the user may ask clarifications to the system or redefine the goal of the interaction.

The architecture of the envisioned dialogue system presents both theoretical and practical challenges. On the theoretical side, heuristics are needed in order to govern decisions such as what to say, when, and how (given the current context). In addition, the system should implement inference methods in order to figure out how to modify the current situation and reach the task goal. The complexity of the theoretical issues is reflected, in practice, in a system of multiple components: a natural language generator, a planner, a 3D interactive environment, to mention a few. Designing and implementing all these components from scratch would require a prohibitive effort. Instead we will adapt tools already implemented and freely available for prototyping this kind of systems, such as the platform *GIVE*[1], *Generating Instructions in Virtual Environments* (Byron et al., 2009).

The quality of each of the components of the system affects the perception users have of it. It is imperative to carry out extensive evaluation. We plan to adapt and apply different evaluation techniques and metrics from the area of Machine Translation to assess the performance of the system.

The plan of the paper is as follows. Section 2 describes the project in detail. Section 3 spells out the expected results as well as their foreseen impact in the Argentinean socio-economic landscape. Section 4 presents the PLN research group including its lines of research. Section 5 discuss past, current and future collaborations that are relevant to the project.

[1] `http://www.give-challenge.org`



*Proceedings of the NAACL HLT 2010 Young Investigators Workshop on Computational Approaches to Languages of the Americas*, pages 132–140, Los Angeles, California, June 2010. 

## 2 Description of the Project

This section first introduces the virtual environment in which our dialogue system will be situated, namely the GIVE platform, which is the basic architecture of our dialogue system. Then we explain in detail the tasks that our situated dialogue system will implement, and we spell out the evaluation challenges that such a system poses. We close the section discussing the application of our dialogue system for the task of second language learning.

### 2.1 The Virtual Environment

In the scenario proposed by GIVE (Byron et al., 2009), a human user carries out a "treasure hunt" in a 3D virtual environment and the task of the generation system is to provide real-time, natural language instructions that help the user find the hidden treasure.

In the GIVE setup, the instruction giving system must guide the user through interconnected rooms. The final goal is to get a trophy which is hidden in a safe. In order to achieve this goal, the system instructs the user to perform several subtasks such as deactivating alarms and opening the safe combination by pressing a sequence of buttons on the walls of the rooms.

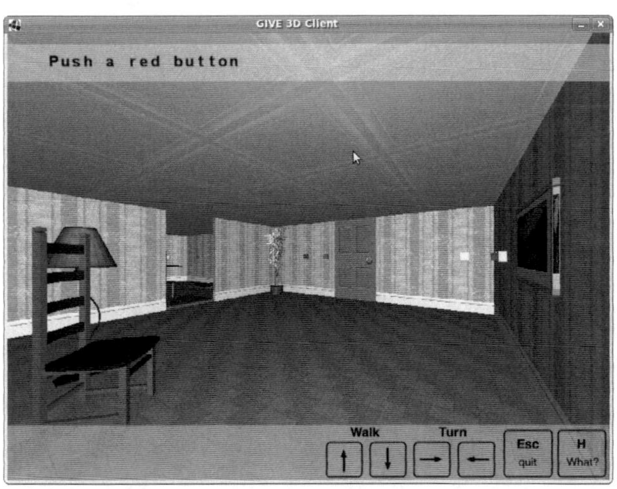


Figure 1: The user's view of the 3D world

Figure 1 shows a screen-shot of the user's view on the 3D world. On the top of the picture, the current instruction generated by the dialogue system is displayed. The picture shows a closed door and an open door that has an activated alarm (that looks like a red tile) in the doorway. There are five visible buttons in this room (two yellow, two red and one green) and the instruction giver is instructing the user to press a red button. Pressing a button can have different effects such as opening a door, moving an object, deactivating an alarm, etc.

The characteristics of the world, including the functions of the buttons, are described in the world specification by the world designers. The user can move freely around the world (using the direction keys as indicated in the bottom of the screen) but she can loose the game if she triggers an alarm. The user can also ask for help pressing 'H' if she did not manage to read or understand the last instruction.

For the correct definition of the interaction policies of our prototype we need a corpus that provides examples of typical interactions in the domain. GIVE provides tools for collecting such a corpus in the form of a Wizard of Oz platform that records all details of the interaction, thus allowing to easily obtain a corpus of interaction in virtual environments annotated automatically.

### 2.2 The Dialogue System Tasks

From the collected corpus we will begin the design, implementation and testing of our dialogue system. The main components that we will have to design and implement can be organized using the traditional four tasks that a dialogue system should address: (1) content planning, (2) generation of referring expressions, (3) management of the interaction context, and (4) interpretation of user responses.

*(1) Content Planning:* Given the envisioned setup we described before, the first task of the system is to obtain a plan to reach the desired goal, from the current state. The plan will contain physical actions to be performed in the virtual environment. The second step is to decide how to transmit this sequence of actions to the user. E.g, to decide how many actions to communicate per instruction, and how to aggregate them coherently. The result of the action aggregation process can be represented as a tree describing the task structure at different levels of abstraction. The third and final step is to decide how to navigate the tree of actions to verbalize the instructions (for example, post or preorder as explored in (Foster et al., 2009)). We will investigate different

aggregation policies (e.g., aggregating actions that manipulate similar objects) and innovative ways in which to navigate the task tree (e.g., moving to a lower level of abstraction in case of misunderstandings). Plan computation can be solved using classical planners (Kautz and Selman, 1999; Hoffmann and Nebel, 2001; Nau et al., 2004). However, while there are planners that work well when optimized for certain applications, none provides services such as the generation of alternative plans, or the generation of incomplete plans in case of the absence of plan. One of the goals of the project is to design and implement these extensions to classical planning algorithms. We will also study the theoretical behavior (e.g., complexity) of these new algorithms.

*(2) Generation of Referring Expressions:* Once content planning is complete, the next step is to generation adequate referring expressions. This task involves producing a phrase that describes a referable entity so that the user can identify it (e.g., "the vase on the table"). To be acceptable, these expressions should be "natural:" they should be at the same time sufficiently but not overly constrained, and they should not impose on the user a heavier cognitive load than necessary. For example, producing the expression "the vase that is not above the chair or sofa or under the table" would probably not be acceptable. Areces et al. (2008b) propose to use symbolic minimization of the model that represents the state of the world, in order to obtain a logical representation that describe each object uniquely. In our project we will implement this method and evaluate it within the dialogue system.

*(3) Management of the Interaction Context:* To manage the use of the interaction context we will use existing knowledge maintenance systems such as RACER[2] or Pellet[3], which support inference tasks such as definition, maintenance and querying of ontologies. These systems have been used as inference engines in numerous applications in the area and, in particular, in dialogue systems for text adventures (Benotti, 2009b). Once we have studied the behavior of these inference engines on the task, we will analyze its limitations and investigate the required extensions.

[2]`http://www.racer-systems.com`

[3]`http://clarkparsia.com/pellet`

*(4) Interpretation of User Responses:* The interpretation of user responses in the unidirectional system is relatively simple: it amounts to discretizing the continuous flow of user behavior in the 3D world into actions meaningful for the domain task. In a first stage, we will use the discretizer provided by GIVE. After evaluating it we can determine whether or not this module meets the requirements of our task and what are its limitations. In the bidirectional system, however, the interpretation of user responses is the task that will require more attention. To start with, the bidirectional system should be expanded with capabilities for processing statements coming from the user (namely, parsing, semantic construction, resolution of references, etc.). We will study, in particular, two types of user contributions: requests for clarification of the instruction given (what we call 'short-term repairs'), and for redefinition of goals (what we call 'long-term repairs'). We will implement short-term repairs using the approach described in (Purver, 2006). For long-term repairs we will use the guidelines of (Blaylock, 2005).

A sample interaction with the unidirectional system guiding the player in the identification of a particular blue button is as follows:

(1) System says: Push a blue button.
*The user focuses a blue button.*
System says: Not this one.
Look for another one.
*The user turns and focuses another blue button.*
System says: Yes this one!
*The user pushes the button.*

This interaction illustrates the tasks described above. To begin with, the verbalization of the instruction "Push a blue button" is making explicit one of the steps of the plan that needs to be performed in order to achieve the task goal. As we can see, the system implements in this case a referring strategy which does not uniquely identify the referent (the system generates "a blue button" when there is more than one blue button in the domain). But it is capable of producing further details about the referent if the user focus in the wrong object. Finally, this example makes evident that the interpretation of the user responses is crucial even in a linguistically unidirectional system. The user cannot make linguistic contributions but can change the context by performing physical acts, the correct interpretation of such acts is essential if the system is to react coherently.

### 2.3 Evaluation

To determine the quality of the obtained prototypes we propose to create a quality model following the ISO/IEC 9126 and 14528 standards for the evaluation of software products (ISO/IEC, 2001; ISO/IEC, 1999). These standards were successfully applied to the Machine Translation domain, resulting in the *FEMTI*[4], *Framework for the Evaluation of Machine Translation* (Estrella et al., 2005). FEMTI guides evaluators towards creating parameterized evaluation plans that include various aspects of the to-be-evaluated system and offer a relevant set of metrics. The identification of relevant metrics can be performed using various methods, e.g., based on previous experience (Hajdinjak and Mihelic, 2006; Litman and Pan, 2002), conducting surveys or requirement specifications (Lecoeuche et al., 1998), or collecting such data through Wizard of Oz experiments (Dahlbäck et al., 1998). After developing a quality model, several methodologies to assess various aspects of the system can be applied: automatic metrics, subjective metrics or metrics based on the task (to evaluate both the contribution of each component and the quality of the whole system).

The GIVE platform is used every year as a unified framework for evaluating generation systems. Systems have to generate natural language instructions and be able to participate in a real-time interaction situated in a 3D environment. The GIVE Challenge is one of the shared tasks endorsed by ACL's special interests groups in generation, dialogue and semantics. We plan to participate in the challenge, which will serve as an additional source of information about aspects of the system that need improvement. The evaluation metrics used in the Challenge (such as average reference identification time) are described in (Byron et al., 2009). In (Amoia et al., 2010) we extended such metrics in order to measure alingment between system and user. Once the prototype is evaluated and improved using the results of the challenge, we will investigate its use as a virtual language tutor as described in the next section.

[4] http://www.issco.unige.ch/femti/

### 2.4 An Application: A Virtual Tutor

The project outcome will be a system capable of giving natural language instructions situated in a virtual 3D environment. The technology and theoretical advances of the project could be used in various applications, but one of the most interesting characteristics we plan to investigate is that, a priori, by just changing the linguistic resources, the language of interaction with the system (input and output) can be changed as desired. After obtaining a first prototype of an instruction giving dialogue system, we will investigate its use for distance learning, adapting the system to operate as a foreign language tutor (Wik and Hjalmarsson, 2009).

A one-way system that generates instructions in English can be used to test the user understanding of a foreign language. The correct interpretation of the instructions can be evaluated from the proper execution of the instructions. The two-way system will allow the user to formulate clarifications (either in their native language or in the foreign language). The user may also redefine the objective to be achieved during the interaction, and thus select the type of vocabulary he wants to practice.

Virtual worlds (like Second Life) are being rapidly incorporated into education, both initial and superior (Doswell, 2005; Molka-Danielsen and Deutschmann, 2009). The use of a virtual tutor has certain advantages over a human tutor. Engwall (2004) mentioned the following. (1) Amount of practice: the chance to practice the new language is essential for learning, and a virtual tutor provides opportunities only limited by the technological resources. (2) Prestige: a student may feel embarrassed about making mistakes with a human tutor, and this might limit his willingness to speak in the foreign language. (3) Augmented Reality: a virtual tutor can provide additional material (e.g., examples in context, explanatory images, etc.) with less effort than a human tutor.

Such a virtual tutor can be used in distance learning. To develop distance learning systems, it is essential to model the user's learning progress. This requires a system aware of the evolution of the user, and that takes into account their achievements and their problems. The system must be able to interpret requirements, and generate appropriate responses, for non-experts uses whose knowledge evolves during the interaction. Moreover, the system must be able to properly represent both the information concerning the course material, and information about the evolution of the user. For example, the system must be able to diagnose what part of the course material should be reviewed from the wrong answers of the user. Finally, the system must be able to evaluate the user interaction in order to decide which learning objectives have been achieved. The theoretical and practical results of the project contribute to solving these difficult problems.

## 3 Impact of the Project

This project aims to achieve a balance between a system which is sufficiently generic to be applicable in different areas, and specific enough to benefit from the efficient use of existing techniques for knowledge management, planning and natural language processing. Designing and implementing such a system is a multidisciplinary effort leading to research in diverse scientific areas:

**Pragmatics** is an interdisciplinary field which integrates insights from linguistics (e.g., conversational implicatures (Grice, 1975)), sociology (e.g., conversational analysis (Schegloff, 1987)) and philosophy (e.g., theory of speech acts (Austin, 1962)). It aims to explore how the context (in which a conversation is situated) contributes to the meaning (of everything that is said during that conversation). The meaning conveyed during a conversation depends not only on linguistic information (entities in focus, grammatical and morphological rules, etc.) but also on extra-linguistic information (physical situation of conversation, previous experiences of speakers, etc.). As a result, the same sentence may mean different things in different contexts. The area of pragmatics studies the process by which a sentence is disambiguated using its context. A dialogue system needs to have pragmatic capabilities in order to interact in a natural way with its users. In particular, it must define what kind of contextual information should be represented; and what inference tasks on a sentence and context are necessary in order to interpret an utterance. In such a system it is important that sentences makes explicit the right amount of information: too much information will delay and bore the user, but if the information is not enough the user will not know how to perform the task and make mistakes.

One of the major contributions of the project in this area will be a virtual laboratory for pragmatic theories: a controlled environment for studying interaction set in a world where physical actions and language intermingle. The prototype will let us investigate the impact that different instruction giving policies (e.g., post order on the tree structure of the task) have on successful achievement of the goal. Similar studies have been done before (e.g., (Foster et al., 2009)) but they usually assume a predetermined task. Since our prototype allows for the specification of the virtual world, the available actions, and the goal, we will be able to determine when the impact associated to a particular policy is dependent on the task or not. We will also investigate short and long term repairs. Repairs are usually caused by conversational implicatures (Benotti, 2009a). Modeling these implicatures in a generic dialogue system is difficult because they are too open ended. However, since the present prototype provides a situated interaction, restricted to the virtual world, it will be possible to test the relationship between implicatures, the type of repairs they give rise to, and the inference tasks needed to predict them.

**Inference** can be understood as any operation that transforms implicit information in explicit information. This definition is general enough to cover tasks ranging from logical inference (i.e., deduction in a formal language) to inference tasks common in AI (e.g., planning and non-monotonic inference), as well as statistical operations (e.g. obtaining estimators on a data set). A dialogue system has to continually perform inference operations. E.g., inference is needed to interpret information received from the user, incorporate it to the system's data repository, and then decide what should be conveyed back to the user. The very problem of deciding what kind of logical representation and what type of inference to use in a given situation is complex (propositional logic vs. first-order logic, validity vs. model checking, logical inference vs. statistical inference). Independently of which type of inference is used, they are usually computationally expensive. The challenge here is to find the appropriate balance between the expressivity of the representation formalism and the cost of the required inference methods.

The main contribution of the project in this area is in the design, development and study of planning algorithms. A typical planning system takes three inputs –initial state, possible actions and expected goal– and returns a sequence of actions (a plan) that when sequentially applied to the initial state, ends in a state that satisfies the goal. Different methods to obtain a plan have been studied (forward chaining, backward chaining, coding in terms of propositional satisfiability, etc.), and they are currently implemented in systems that can solve many planning tasks efficiently. However, most of these systems make assumptions that simplify the problem (deterministic atomic time, complete information, absence of a background theory, etc.). And most of them return a single plan. We will investigate algorithms that eliminate some of these simplifications (in particular, we will study planning with incomplete information and based on a background theory). We will also provide extended planning services: alternative plans, minimal plans, conditional plans, incomplete plans, affordability of a given state, etc.

**Evaluation** of natural language generation systems is one of the most difficult tasks in the area of NLP. A given concept can be expressed in many different ways, all of them correct. Hence, it is not possible to determining the quality of a generated sentence simply by, for example, comparing the result with a gold standard. The problem of absence of gold standards is shared with another area of the NLP, namely Machine Translation, for which various evaluation methodologies, both direct and indirect, have been proposed. Direct methods applies a metric to the text generated by the system, while indirect methods evaluates the performance of the system through the use of the generated text to perform some task. But none of these methods is a standard and generally accepted methodology, which has been proven to be effective in all cases. Since what is being evaluated in this project is a system that interacts via the generation of natural language instructions, we can determine its performance through quantitative metrics (e.g., average task completion time), qualitative metrics (e.g., general user satisfaction) and metrics based on the context (e.g., how well the system addressed the user needs in particular situations). We will study the portability of evaluation techniques from the domain of machine translation and multimodal human-computer interaction to the evaluation of the system proposed in this project.

One of the main contributions of our project at this respect is the integration of assessment techniques from different areas into a methodology for evaluating dialog systems for virtual environments, aiming to estimate their usability and effectiveness. This methodology could be used both to determine whether a system is suitable for a task type and user, and to compare the performance of different systems of the same type. Another contribution will be the study and application of software evaluation standards to the developed systems, creating a standardized quality model and proposing a set of appropriate metrics to assess each of the aspects of the model. Finally, the annotated corpus of human-human interaction, together with the corpus of human-machine interaction collected during the project will be made public. Such corpora will serve, for example, to design more general platforms for evaluating dialog systems, going beyond the aspects evaluated by existing platforms like GIVE.

**Impact in the Argentinean Landscape:** Natural language processing, and in particular the field of dialogue systems is a rapidly growing area in developed countries. The automatic processing of natural language has become a strategic capability for companies and the wider community. However, this area is extremely underdeveloped in Argentina. This can be attributed to several factors. (a) The relative youth of the area of NLP, which implies a relative dearth of trained professionals throughout the world. (b) The underdevelopment of the area of research in Artificial Intelligence and Formal Linguistics in Argentina, for historical reasons and lack of industry demand. (c) Poor interaction between the few researchers in NLP that are in the region.

NLP is a strategic research area for Argentina which can achieve academic excellence and industry relevance. We believe in supporting the development of this area by promoting the following. (a) Training of human resources through doctoral programs and courses taught in Argentina by internationally renowned professionals. (b) Incorporation of trained human resources to contribute to the growth and diversification of the critical mass in the area. (c) Improving interaction between various groups and individual researchers in NLP, through the organization of workshops, courses, visits, co-tutoring, coordinated specialization programs, etc.

The particular topics investigated in the framework of this project are of relevance in the current Argentinean landscape for at least two reasons. On the one hand, the project integrates and develops various key aspects of the area of computational linguistics (syntax, semantics, pragmatics, representation, inference, evaluation); an area which, as we mentioned, is today almost nonexistent in Argentina. This project will be a step towards reversing this situation. On the other hand, the ultimate goal of the project is to investigate the use of the developed platform for distance education (specifically, as a tool for language learning). Distance education is a valuable resource to overcome the problem of centralization of educational resources in the country.

## 4 Introducing the Research Group

The PLN[5] research group, in which the describe scientific project will be carried out, was funded in 2005. Te group is developing an important role in human resource training, delivering courses to undergraduate and postgraduate student at the Universidad de Córdoba and other universities. It also works in the development of various research projects and integration with other groups in the region, both within Argentina and with neighboring countries (Chile, Brazil and Uruguay).

The current project pools together many of the key areas of expertise of the members of the group. To begin with, some members of the group specialize in computational logic, particularly in the theoretical and applied study of languages for knowledge representation (e.g., modal, hybrid and description logics). They have also developed automated theorem provers for these languages[6]. In relation with the study of knowledge representation, they have also investigated and developed algorithms for generating referring expressions (Areces et al., 2008b).

The second line of research of the PLN group that is relevant for this project is context-based evaluation. Members of the group have proposed an evaluation model for machine translation systems which relates the context of use to potentially important quality characteristics (Estrella et al., 2008; Estrella et al., 2009). This model is general enough to be applied to other systems that produce natural language like the ones proposed in this paper. Thanks to the background on machine translation systems the team has experience evaluating and comparing natural language output produced in different languages (Spanish and English in particular), which will be relevant for the development of the language tutor described in Section 2.4. Finally, the team has experience developing and evaluating multimodal corpora like those described in Section 2 (Estrella and Popescu-Belis, 2008).

The third line of research that is relevant for this project is pragmatics. In this area the team has implemented a conversational agent which is able to infer and negotiate conversational implicatures using inference tasks such as classical planning and planning under incomplete information (Benotti, 2009b). We have also investigated how to infer conversational implicatures triggered by comparative utterances (Benotti and Traum, 2009). Recently we have done corpus-based work, which shows what kinds of implicatures are inferred and negotiated by human dialogue participants during a task situated in a 3D virtual environment (Benotti, 2009a).

Other lines of research in the PLN group are not directly related to the project at this stage, but might become relevant in the future. They include grammar induction, text mining, statistical syntactic analysis and ontology population from raw text.

## 5 Ongoing and Future Collaborations

The members of the PLN in general and the authors of this paper in particular have several collaborations with national and international research groups in computational linguistics and related fields that are relevant for this project.

At the international level, we have ongoing collaboration with the TIM/ISSCO[7] *Multilingual Information Processing Department* at the University of Geneva, with the Idiap Research Institute[8] and

[5] `http://www.cs.famaf.unc.edu.ar/~pln`
[6] `http://www.glyc.dc.uba.ar/intohylo/`
[7] `http://www.issco.unige.ch/en`
[8] `http://www.idiap.ch`

with some members of the PAI[9], *Pervasive Artificial Intelligence* group of the University of Fribourg. These collaborations include the evaluation of NLP systems and the development of multilingual and multimodal human language technology systems.

Members of the group have a long standing collaboration with the TALARIS[10] group of the *Laboratoire Lorrain de Recherche en Informatique et ses Applications (LORIA)*. The main research topic at TALARIS is computational linguistics with strong emphasis on semantics and inference. In the framework of this collaboration we are participating in the 2010 edition of the GIVE Challenge. In the process of designing the systems that will participate in the challenge we jointly investigated the use of different referring strategies in situated instruction giving (Amoia et al., 2010).

We have also collaborated with the Virtual Humans group of the Institute for Creative Technologies[11] from the University of Southern California. In particular we computationally modeled the inference of conversational implicatures triggered by comparative utterances (Benotti and Traum, 2009). The Institute for Creative Technologies offers Internship programs every year that we plan to use in order to strengthen our collaboration.

All these collaborations are directly related to the main theme of the project described in this article. The PLN group has also research collaborations with other international research teams in the framework of other scientific programs. For example, the PLN group has being part of a recently finished international project MICROBIO[12] on ontology population from raw text. The project was funded by the Stic-Amsud[13] program, a scientific-technological cooperation program integrated by France, Argentine, Brazil, Chile, Paraguay, Peru and Uruguay. The expertise obtained during this project might be useful in the future when trying to extend our GIVE ontologies to new domains. Similarly, the team maintain scientific relations with the University of Texas at Austin (mainly with Dr. J. Moore in projects related to the development of the ACL2[14] prover); and with the Research team Symbiose[15] of the Institut de Recherche en Informatique et Systémes Aléatoires (working on the use of linguistic techniques for the modelisation of genomic sequences).

At the national level, the group has intensively collaborated with GLyC[16], *Grupo de Lógica, Lenguaje y Computabilidad* on knowledge representation and inference (see, e.g. (Areces and Gorín, 2005; Areces et al., 2008a)). GLyC is part of the Computer Science Department of the Universidad de Buenos Aires. During 2010, teams PLN and GLyC will join forces and collaborate in the organization of ELiC[17], the *First School in Computational Linguistics* in Argentina, which will take place in July at the Universidad de Buenos Aires. ELiC 2010 will be co-located with the ECI[18], Escuela de Ciencias Informáticas which has a long standing reputation as a high-quality winter school in Computer Science in Argentina, and is being organized yearly since 1987. With ELiC we aim at creating, for the first time, a space to introduce the field of computational linguistics to graduate students in Argentina. Thanks to the support of the North American Chapter of the Association for Computational Linguistics (NAACL) and of the Universidad de Buenos Aires, ELiC is offering student travel grants and fee waivers to encourage participation.

The PLN group is also contacting other groups working in computational linguistics in Argentina like the research group in Artificial Intelligence from the Universidad Nacional del Comahue[19]. Taking advantage of previous co-participation in different project we plan to organize exchange programs in the framework of a research network.

Finally, the PLN group is planning to organize a workshop on Computational Linguistics as a satellite event of IBERAMIA 2010[20], the Ibero-American Conference on Artificial Intelligence, that will be organized by the Universidad del Sur, in the city of Bahía Blanca, Argentina.

[9] `http://diuf.unifr.ch/pai/wiki`

[10] `http://talaris.loria.fr`

[11] `http://ict.usc.edu/projects/virtual_humans`

[12] `http://www.microbioamsud.net`

[13] `http://www.sticamsud.org`

[14] `http://www.cs.utexas.edu/users/moore/acl2`

[15] `http://www.irisa.fr/symbiose`

[16] `http://www.glyc.dc.uba.ar`

[17] `http://www.glyc.dc.uba.ar/elic2010`

[18] `http://www.dc.uba.ar/events/eci/2009/eci2009`

[19] `http://www.uncoma.edu.ar/`

[20] `http://cs.uns.edu.ar/iberamia2010`

## References


M. Amoia, A. Denis, L. Benotti, and C. Gardent. 2010. Evaluating referring strategies in situated instruction giving. *Topics in Cognitive Science*. Submitted.

C. Areces and D. Gorín. 2005. Ordered resolution with selection for $H(@)$. In F. Baader and A. Voronkov, editors, *Proc. of LPAR 2004*, volume 3452 of *LNCS*, pages 125–141. Springer.

C. Areces, D. Figueira, S. Figueira, and S. Mera. 2008a. Expressive power and decidability for memory logics. In *Logic, Language, Information and Computation*, volume 5110 of *LNCSs*, pages 56–68. Springer.

C. Areces, A. Koller, and K. Striegnitz. 2008b. Referring expressions as formulas of description logic. In *Proc. of INLG-08*.

J. Austin. 1962. *How to do Things with Words*. Oxford University Press.

L. Benotti and D. Traum. 2009. A computational account of comparative implicatures for a spoken dialogue agent. In *Proc. of IWCS-8*.

L. Benotti. 2009a. Clarification potential of instructions. In *SIGDIAL-09*.

L. Benotti. 2009b. Frolog: An accommodating text-adventure game. In *Proc. of EACL-09*.

N. Blaylock. 2005. *Towards tractable agent-based dialogue*. Ph.D. thesis, University of Rochester, Department of Computer Science.

D. Byron, A. Koller, K. Striegnitz, J. Cassell, R. Dale, J. Moore, and J. Oberlander. 2009. Report on the 1st GIVE challenge. In *Proc. of ENLG*, pages 165–173.

N. Dahlbäck, A. Jönsson, and L. Ahrenberg. 1998. Wizard of Oz studies—why and how. In *Readings in intelligent user interfaces*, pages 610–619. Morgan Kaufmann Publishers Inc.

J. Doswell. 2005. It's virtually pedagogical: pedagogical agents in mixed reality learning environments. In *Proc. of SIGGRAPH-05*, page 25. ACM.

O. Engwall, P. Wik, J. Beskow, and G. Granström. 2004. Design strategies for a virtual language tutor. In S. Kim and D. Young, editors, *Proc. of ICSLP-04*, volume 3, pages 1693–1696.

P. Estrella and A. Popescu-Belis. 2008. Multi-eval: an evaluation framework for multimodal dialogue annotations. Poster at the Joint IM2 and ASSI.

P. Estrella, A. Popescu-Belis, and N. Underwood. 2005. Finding the system that suits you best: Towards the normalization of MT evaluation. In *Proc. of ASLIB-05*, pages 23–34.

P. Estrella, A. Popescu-Belis, and M. King. 2008. Improving contextual quality models for MT evaluation based on evaluators' feedback. In *Proc. of LREC-08*.

P. Estrella, A. Popescu-Belis, and M. King. 2009. The femti guidelines for contextual mt evaluation: principles and tools. In W. Daelemans and V. Hoste, editors, *Evaluation of Translation Technology*. Linguistica Antverpiensia.

M. Foster, M. Giuliani, A. Isard, C. Matheson, J. Oberlander, and A. Knoll. 2009. Evaluating description and reference strategies in a cooperative human-robot dialogue system. In *Proc. of IJCAI-09*.

P. Grice. 1975. Logic and conversation. In P. Cole and J. Morgan, editors, *Syntax and Semantics: Vol. 3: Speech Acts*, pages 41–58. Academic Press.

M. Hajdinjak and F. Mihelic. 2006. The paradise evaluation framework: Issues and findings. *Computational Linguistics*, 32(2):263–272.

J. Hoffmann and B. Nebel. 2001. The FF planning system: Fast plan generation through heuristic search. *JAIR*, 14:253–302.

ISO/IEC. 1999. *14598-1:1999 (E) – Information Technology – Software Product Evaluation – Part 1: General Overview*.

ISO/IEC. 2001. *9126-1:2001 (E) – Software Engineering – Product Quality – Part 1:Quality Model*.

H. Kautz and B. Selman. 1999. Unifying SAT-based and graph-based planning. In *Proc of the IJCAI*, pages 318–325.

R. Lecoeuche, C. Mellish, and D. Robertson. 1998. A framework for requirements elicitation through mixed-initiative dialogue. In *Proc. ICRE-98*. IEEE.

D. Litman and S. Pan. 2002. Designing and evaluating an adaptive spoken dialogue system. *User Modeling and User-Adapted Interaction*, 12(2-3):111–137.

J. Molka-Danielsen and M. Deutschmann, editors. 2009. *Learning and Teaching in the Virtual World of Second Life*. Tapir Academic Press.

D. Nau, M. Ghallab, and P. Traverso. 2004. *Automated Planning: Theory & Practice*. Morgan Kaufmann Publishers Inc.

M. Purver. 2006. CLARIE: Handling clarification requests in a dialogue system. *Research on Language and Computation*, 4(2-3):259–288.

E. Schegloff. 1987. Some sources of misunderstanding in talk-in-interaction. *Linguistics*, 8:201–218.

P. Wik and A. Hjalmarsson. 2009. Embodied conversational agents in computer assisted language learning. *Speech Commun.*, 51(10):1024–1037.

# Author Index